The Architecture of Light

How architects have spoken about and worked with light since electricity has become an alternative light source in buildings is the subject of this book. Not only does the book argue that natural light remains a fundamentally important source of orientation in architecture, but it underlines how and why the art of daylighting imposes creative discipline on design.

Examining a series of twentieth-century projects whose architects have a particular interest in light and window design, the book gives careful attention to the way in which words and practice in natural light are interconnected. In the process a number of key influences are revealed including the significance of Le Corbusier's written and built oeuvre for subsequent thinking. The book underlines how ambitions for light have been arrived at not only through reference to relevant precedents but an approach to context that sees light as a critical aspect of place.

A willingness to treat natural light seriously has prompted imaginative and resonant design approaches for a wide range of building types and contexts. In demonstrating such thinking, this sourcebook looks at climates of light as diverse as those of northern Europe and central Chile, eastern Australia and northern Portugal. Its overall argument is that a sensitive approach to daylighting not only remains a complex yet ultimately rewarding endeavour but a fundamental if under-appreciated aspect of the 'practical art' of architecture.

Mary Ann Steane is an architect and a lecturer at the University of Cambridge. Her research on the use of natural light marries an understanding of lighting design principles with a broader cultural perspective. She examines how architects handle the relationship between light, material and the occupation of space, looking closely at the way in which these factors affect perception of and attunement to the visual environment.

The Architecture of Light

Recent approaches to designing
with natural light

Mary Ann Steane

Routledge
Taylor & Francis Group

LONDON AND NEW YORK

First published 2011
by Routledge
2 Park Square, Milton Park, Abingdon, Oxon, OX14 4RN

Simultaneously published in the USA and Canada
by Routledge
711 Third Avenue, New York, NY 10017

Routledge is an imprint of the Taylor & Francis Group, an informa business

Typeset in Univers by
Pindar NZ, Auckland, NZ
Printed and bound in Great Britain by
TJ International Ltd, Padstow, Cornwall

British Library Cataloguing in Publication Data
Steane, Mary Ann.
The architecture of light : recent approaches to designing with natural light /
Mary Ann Steane.
          p. cm.
     Includes bibliographical references and index.
     1. Light in architecture. 2. Lighting, Architectural and decorative. I. Title.
II. Title: Recent approaches to designing with natural light.
     NA2794.S74 2011
     729'.28–dc22   2010041747

Library of Congress Cataloging-in-Publication Data
A catalog record has been requested for this book

ISBN13: 978-0-415-39478-9 (hbk)
ISBN13: 978-0-415-39479-6 (pbk)

Contents

Illustration credits

The authors and publishers gratefully acknowledge the following for their permission to reproduce material in this book. Every effort has been made to contact and acknowledge copyright owners. The publishers would be grateful to hear from any copyright holder who is not acknowledged here and will undertake to rectify any errors or omissions in future printings or editions of the book.

Archivo Histórico José Vial PUCV   2.7, 2.8, 5.1, 5.2, 5.3, 5.8, 5.9, 5.10, 5.11, 5.12, 5.14, 5.17, 5.18, 5.23
Archive of the Benedictine Monastery of Las Condes   2.5, 2.6
Kate Baker   5.13
Mike Baker/Anne Dye   4.1, 4.8, 4.9, 4.10, 4.11, 4.12, 4.13, 4.15
José Baltanas and FLC/ADAGP, Paris and DACS, London   1.2, 1.3
Max Beckenbauer   1.1, 1.8, 1.10, 1.12, 1.19, 3.6, 4.6, 4.7, 4.21, 4.22, 5.4, 6.9, 6.10. 6.11, 8.3, 10.1, 10.2
Noah Carl   10.6, 10.18
Bettmann/Corbis and FLC/ADAGP, Paris and DACS, London   1.14
James Bichard   6.6, 6.19
Reiner Blunck   6.7, 6.13, 6.14, 6.15, 6.16, 6.17, 6.18, 6.20
Simon Blunden   3.5
Bitter Bredt   8.5, 8.6, 8.15, 8.18, 8.20
Holger Ellgaard   4.5
FLC/ADAGP, Paris and DACS, London   1.4, 1.11, 1.13, 1.16, 1.18, 1.20, 1.21
National Gallery of Ireland   7.3
Dennis Gilbert   7.16, 7.17, 7.18, 7.19, 7.21
P. Gross and E. Vial   2.2, 2.3, 2.10
Max Gwiazda   8.4, 8.8, 8.10, 8.12
Wade Johanson   6.4
Hamburg Kunsthalle   4.4
Dean Hawkes   3.1
Sarah Honeyball   7.12, 7.13, 7.20, 7.22, 7.23
Soane Museum   9.2
Jeffery Howe   0.1
Niall MLaughlin Architects   9.5, 9.6, 9.7, 9.8, 9.9, 9.10, 9.11, 9.12, 9.13
George Middleton-Baker   8.17, 8.19, 8.21

Tomas Mikulas, École Athenaeum, Lausanne and FLC/ADAGP, Paris and
    DACS, London   1.5, 1.6
Michele Nastesi   8.11, 8.13,
Fernando Perez   2.18
O'Donnell and Tuomey Architects   7.5, 7.7, 7.8, 7.9, 7.10, 7.14
Gabriel Poole   6.12
Gunter Schneider   8.1
Patrick and Maura Shaffrey (*Irish Countryside Buildings*, O'Brien Press Ltd.,
    Dublin)   7.9
Lisa Shell Architects   9.3, 9.17, 9.18, 9.16, 9.19, 9.20, 9.21, 9.22, 9.25
David Steane   7.11
Wren Strabuchi   2.4
Studio Daniel Libeskind and Udo Hesse   8.2, 8.9, 8.14
Tate, London, 2010   10.3, 10.5
Alan Worn   3.19

Acknowledgements

I wish to acknowledge the help that a large number of people have given me during the course of this project. First of all I would like to express my thanks to the University of Cambridge Centre of Latin American Studies who awarded me a grant to cover the costs of a study trip to Chile in 2006 to look at buildings in and around Santiago and Valparaiso, and to the AHRC, who funded a research project entitled 'Designing with Light in Libraries' that enabled trips to Finland to carry out detailed photographic studies of the public library at Seinajoki. I am also indebted to my publisher Georgina Johnson for her patience and guidance in bringing this project to a conclusion.

Many individuals have also gone to great lengths to help me access buildings and to contact architects, and sometimes even to translate the interviews I held to discuss the ideas about light represented by a particular project. In this regard I am particularly grateful to Wren Strabuchi and Fernando Perez of the School of Architecture at the Catholic University of Santiago and to David Jolly, Miguel Eyquem and Alberto Cruz of the School of Art and Design at the Catholic University of Valparaiso, both for their generous hospitality during my time in Chile, and rapid response to subsequent queries. Luis Urbano who organized the 2008 study trip to look at contemporary architecture near Porto which introduced me to the work of Alvaro Siza, including his library at Viana do Castelo, is another colleague whose thoughtful reactions to conversation about light I have built on subsequently.

I would like to thank all the living architects whose work is discussed here. Sadly, I have not had the opportunity to meet all of them in person, though several have proved to be excellent email correspondents, Gabriel Poole in particular. Among those I have met, I owe a particular debt to Sheila O'Donnell and John Tuomey who not only showed me round their Multi-Denominational School in Dublin but arranged for me to visit other projects of theirs further afield; Brother Martin Correa who twice welcomed me to the Benedictine Monastery at Las Condes, Santiago; Lisa Shell, who moved out so I could experience her house by myself for a night; Niall McLaughlin, whose perceptive comments at student reviews, and during an interview carried out by one of my students stimulated my initial ideas for the book; and Tarla MacGabhann, whose enthusiastic response to the text of my chapter on the Jewish Museum in Berlin was a welcome confirmation that others might be interested in the subject of the book.

A number of individuals have helped me with images. Sound

judgement and no little skill has been exercised by Max Beckenbauer in the production of a number of the drawings; Max Gwiazda and Kate Baker took photographs especially for the book, and I am also grateful to Reiner Blunck for sending me some of his wonderful shots of Gabriel Poole's work at very short notice. Staff at Tate Images, The Soane Museum, The National Gallery of Ireland, Hamburg Kunsthalle, DACS, the Fondation Le Corbusier, the Art Gallery of Ballarat, Victoria, Australia and a number of the practices whose work I have discussed have also helped ensure the book is suitably illustrated.

Educators are in a privileged position when it comes to finding people with whom to discuss their ideas and I should like to express particular thanks to a number of the students I have been fortunate to work with during the past decade. They may not have realized it, but it was the thoughtful exchanges in which they participated that prompted either directly or indirectly several of the themes presented here. Chief among this group are Oriel Prizeman, Maria Konstadoglou, Ed Shinton, Philip Veall, Lynne Sandlands, Sarah Honeyball, Siobhan Kelly, Alan Worn and Andy Mackintosh. My co-author James Bichard has also proved a willing correspondent and I am very grateful to him for the time he has put in to review a text of which he was the original author, that has subsequently been reworked for the book.

Finally, I would like to acknowledge all those colleagues among the permanent and visiting teaching staff at Cambridge whose contributions have proved invaluable to my ongoing engagement with the principles and aspirations of environmental thinking in architecture, Dean Hawkes and Koen Steemers in particular. Last but not least, I want to end this expression of thanks by saying how fortunate I have been to enjoy stimulating conversation with Peter Carl for thirty years concerning architecture – ephemeral or permanent, light-filled or shadow-bound – and its ordering principles. He has been a major influence on all that I do and I dedicate this book to him.

Introduction

Daylighting in the era of electricity

There is only one day left, always starting over: it is given to us at dawn and taken away from us at dusk.[1]

A sensible man shows off his estate to his future mother-in-law at twilight.[2]

Arguably 'lighting' as an architectural topic is now largely determined by the terminology and assumptions of artificial lighting, and therefore by all the science and technology that has built up around it that is decreeing the weight now given to the predictability and control of light in buildings. On the one hand, electricity has enabled the working day to be 24/7, and cities to be safe, to handle traffic, as well as to be neon-fantasies of capitalist buying and selling; on the other hand, we have grown accustomed to viewing the satellite night view of the planet as marked with a luminous cancer of consumption that threatens human life itself. Its introduction may have resulted in elevating task-lighting to the quantifiable standards set out in current building codes,[3] but too frequently it is only possible to meet such standards with artificial sources and so lights are left on whether needed or not, leading to spaces baked in uniform lux, or where task-lighting is unnecessary, their counterform, lighting-specialist effects of colour and intensity. The latter date from the electricity pavilion of the 1893 Chicago World Fair, but have subsequently led to Albert Speer's 1935 encircling of the vast Nuremberg parade grounds with 130 anti-aircraft searchlights to create his 'cathedral of light',[4] contemporary 'light-shows', as well as unctuous corporate lobbies and florid monument lighting. Most critically of all it is the advent of electric light (with the support of air conditioning) that has enabled deep-plan buildings and the need for laws to decide what corner of sky office workers should be able to glimpse from their desks.

It cannot be emphasized enough that artificial light is only apparently effortless, its instant push-button availability coming to represent what technological culture is expected to deliver more broadly: a milieu of ease and efficiency in which all the effort is hidden and vitality is either downgraded as an ambition, completely ironed out or planned ahead with meticulous precision. In this regard the very term 'daylighting' used to describe the art of bringing natural light into buildings is arguably a tautology derived from privileging quantifiable/technological light.

0.1
All-consuming electric light.
The Electricity Building at
the 1893 Chicago World's
Fair designed by the Kansas
City practice of Van Brunt
and Howe.

What this undoubtedly too brief compilation of the impacts of electric lighting on architectural design underlines is that its defects largely concern sustainability and mental health (Sick Building Syndrome), but it is also worth stressing that its main implication is the need for a more careful use, not elimination, of artificial lighting, in conjunction with better planning of buildings and towns and more emphasis on the imaginative use of natural light in buildings.

As a subject 'light' touches on one of the most archaic and important symbolic structures in being human. Eyes have evolved because there was (day) light. The sustained power of the metaphor of sight in philosophy and theology arises because seeing/light is the principal medium of involvement with people and things. We still use 'see' to mean 'understand', and 'understand' carries all the implications of position, orientation, intent, foreground/background (importance/context), nuance, etc. that are the substance of visual perception. This archaism is still an element of natural light, as it remains authoritative with regard to how any material appears, i.e. a material announces itself properly only in daylight (even plastic, let alone natural materials); and accordingly daylight seems to carry with it this primordial materiality as well as its own character. Because the source of natural light is the sun, and sometimes the moon, the archaism is an aspect of the claim upon us of the cosmic conditions of existence. Because the sun is also responsible for fecundity, temporality, illumination – as well as for deserts, aridity, and, in its relative absence, for polar ice and snow – it is deeply implicated in the flourishing and limits of life, and has therefore been prominent in symbolic and metaphoric representations of being, order, justice, authority, truth, etc.

There is no question that, since the advent of Renaissance perspective, it has been possible to summarize all of this in 'shading' – the fall of light across surfaces, or of shadow across the foreground of an image to create a 'theatre' – and for 'shading' to become as procedural as it is in the drawings of the École des Beaux-Arts or contemporary rendering software. The consequence of this is that the light once reserved for saints is now to be found in advertising imagery. Therefore, even if one recognizes in movies, advertisements, architectural renderings, etc. an appeal through light to what is generally termed 'the' sacred, the absence of a shared symbolic culture typically means that such uses solicit scepticism or embarrassment. During a conversation concerning light's role in his own design process, Niall McLaughlin, one of the architects whose work is discussed in this book, drew attention to this uncertainty when he noted:

> I was once taunted by an art historian who said that artists who are excessively interested in light have got no moral sense. I think the implication was that light is pure epiphany, it's pure oblivion, it's the eternal, it's the unquestionable … an escape into epiphany from day-to-day problems.[5]

One can see this problem developing in nineteenth-century Northern European romantic painting (Caspar David Friedrich, Hans Gude). What art historians call 'Realism', as if it were a pre-photographic technique, is in fact a restatement of the problem, not the means of solving it – a question, not an answer. Through obsessive empirical research that might pass for adoration of things and people, these works attempt to discover the meaning of reality, being particularly concerned to embed within subtle effects of light (inevitably natural, and most often transitory) subject matter that may or may not be symbolic in a traditional sense (e.g. houses, boats, animals, trees, water, horizons). This condition of latent or potential symbolism still characterizes our present ambiguities or confusion regarding the subject of meaning – and makes natural light – and its use in buildings – a challenging subject to frame.

Like being, one is always inside architecture (even if outdoors), and it is something impossible to objectify completely. As a result, the structure of light within architecture always carries the latent symbolic possibilities inherent in 'I understand' – i.e. the mediation between individual history and the ultimate conditions. It is present as a possibility or challenge even in unsuccessful architecture. It is not something one can make over to theories of 'correctness' (in Aristotelian terms, it cannot be taught, and certainly iconography was exposed as empty signs, too easily confused with 'branding', in post-modern representation). It can only be done well or less well; but doing it well seems to involve a remarkably rich and yet precise imagination, rooted in a species of tact or generosity, a capacity to see the meaning in human situations. (Naturally lit office buildings, malls, department stores or airports seem presently to offer little in this regard however, partly because they are the kinds of public buildings where the artificial lighting is always left on – and the human situations are heavily qualified by the demands and assumptions of consumer culture.) As to the link between the impact of electricity and the meaning of 'light', the claims of sustainability – the acknowledgement that we are all responsible for the one world of which we are all part – reasserts the claim of the ultimate conditions.

Given this situation, it seems worth exploring in more detail how architects now understand and interpret natural light. Is the ease with which they can orchestrate electric light – anywhere they want, as much as they like – transforming how they think about natural light? In an era when the conspicuous consumption of artificial light symbolizes technological development can they still assess the daylight available and respond imaginatively to it?

Given the significance of light to discussions of modernity, how contemporary architects work with natural light, and what they have to say about it, has been given surprisingly little attention in recent years. *Experiencing Architecture*[6] by Steen Eiler Rasmussen was first published at the end of the 1950s in the decade when electricity was becoming cheap enough to displace daylight in the developed world. While it remains a compelling introductory text to the range of experiential issues that architects weigh up as they refine their ideas, and sensitive as it is to the modelling power of natural light – and the ways in which it can generate subtle spatial transformation – it has only one chapter devoted to daylight. For several generations of Western architecture students, *In Praise of Shadows*[7] by Jun'ichirō Tanizaki (originally published in 1933, but first translated into English in 1977) was one of a handful of texts to expand on this issue. Raising consciousness of the way in which modernist aesthetics has allowed the Western obsession with progress to be portrayed as an ongoing search for clarity to which whiteness and the forensic glare of strong light seem indispensable, the author suggests that the quieter, more reticent forms of oriental art continue to reflect an appreciation of shadow and the potential subtlety of more subdued light. Marietta Millett's 1996 *Light Reflecting Architecture* is an equally valid and more detailed appraisal of how and why the exploitation of natural light has been pursued by architects in relation to issues of inhabitation and climate, structure and form. It offers an intelligent commentary on a wide range of historic and contemporary daylighting strategies in and around buildings, but remains a broad overview. On the other hand, in his 2009 *The Architecture of Natural Light*[8] Henry Plummer is looking more closely at how modernist and contemporary architects across the globe are continuing to produce an architecture stripped to its essentials so it can more effectively display the passage of natural light. He however chooses to establish a series of shared themes in light, touching on the different philosophies that have led designers to adopt particular lighting approaches, rather than exploring the arguments in light that specific works present.

Taking the premise that only by looking closely at individual projects is it possible to convey how architects' ideas about natural light are being translated into resonant design decisions, the aim of this book is to redress this imbalance by giving careful attention to how light has been framed as an issue in a series of twentieth-century buildings. The intention is to explore why daylighting remains an important if underappreciated skill for architects and why deploying natural light tellingly is a complex but ultimately rewarding endeavour. In the process a number of key influences on ambitions for natural light are investigated including the significance of Le Corbusier's written and built *oeuvre* to subsequent thinking, and the range of precedents, natural and man-made – now acting as sources of inspiration for daylight. Beyond illustrating the unexpectedly creative task that reworking the light of an existing building – or an existing locale – can represent, the idea that nuanced approaches to daylighting reflect a concern for the lessons of the past, as they reveal a change of outlook concerning architecture's role, is a recurring theme.

It should be said that even some of the designers whose work is discussed have queried the book's title, wondering whether the goal is either to cover all recent approaches to daylight or to comment on the potential benefits of innovative window design. In fact the intention behind the title is to underline that natural light not only remains a potential source of order in architecture, but that daylighting strategies necessarily impose a creative discipline on design. Thus architects cannot make the most of daylight without considering the quality and quantity of the particular light they have to work with. They cannot use it well without relating their choice of colours or material to decisions about enclosure and the arrangement of spaces in section and plan. They cannot construct an intelligent thesis for a project without considering how access to view – and access to the right quality and amount of daylight – will provide resonant settings for inhabitation. And lest these restrictions be thought unhelpful, the book goes out of its way to demonstrate how a willingness to work within such limits can catalyse genuinely inventive, genuinely cogent design syntheses for a wide range of building types in locations as far apart as Northern Europe and Central Chile. In the process it argues that the architecture of daylight, well understood, continues to foster buildings in league with their environment, buildings that give due consideration to the role they play in a particular way of life, buildings that simultaneously allow their occupants to discover and acknowledge their place in the world.

What has determined the choice of projects and architects the book discusses? In this study the aim has been to examine a series of works constructed over the last ninety years, i.e. the period during which electricity has become a readily available alternative light source, at first in the developed world, and later in urban areas everywhere. It looks at examples from the Old World and the New, the North and the South, deliberately choosing projects that allow it to consider the impact of climatic variation on daylight, and architects who have made light, or the business of making windows, a central concern. It should be stressed that it is therefore by no means exhaustive. There are many other designers whose work might have illustrated its themes equally well. In this regard the intention of the book is to show both how words and practice in natural light are interconnected and the degree to which geography and history shape the experiential narrative that a building can stage, rather than to establish a definitive new canon of expertise.

It starts by looking at two projects by Le Corbusier, arguably the most important twentieth-century architect in terms of his global influence on design theory and its implementation. The first, the house he designed for his parents on the shores of Lake Léman in the 1920s, and the second from the 1950s, the chapel at Ronchamp, are the two buildings whose design processes he chose to record in detail via the heavily edited design diaries he termed 'carnets de recherche patiente'. The thinking on light that these analytical documents portray through a combination of words, diagrams and black and white photographs, and the way it evolved over this period, represent an important point of departure for this study. As several of the subsequent case studies illustrate, Le Corbusier's potent, if complex and contradictory, characterization of natural light continues to affect how architects think and work with daylight today.

After this the book largely follows a historical timeline, but in doing so deliberately explores how thinking about natural light is fostering different preoccupations and different responses that depend among other issues, on the climate, the character of the site, and the purpose of the building. Two subsequent chapters that discuss three projects from the 1960s investigate on the one hand how and why traditional assumptions about light were rejected in the Chilean monastery church of the Holy Trinity, Las Condes, Santiago; and on the other, how the history of light in a particular place (Venice) inspired and qualified a specific design response by Carlo Scarpa. The legacy in light – and the careful thinking on the place of reading – that a pair of libraries completed in Finland in the middle years of the twentieth century by Alvar Aalto represents for the contemporary Portuguese architect Alvaro Siza is the main focus of the following chapter. Chapter 5 then evaluates the architecture of the Open City, a settlement on the Chilean coast built by the staff of the Catholic University of Valparaiso School of Design. Begun in the 1970s, this unusual project has it roots in post-war discussions in Chile about the need to see architecture and architectural education in Latin America with a new post-colonialist eye, and the analysis concentrates on the dialectic in light and landscape that this design laboratory is continuing to reveal.

The second half of the book looks in turn at a series of more recent projects from the 1990s and the first decade of the twenty-first century. Here some of the arguments for natural light that are currently being aired are investigated. Whereas Gabriel Poole's lightweight house designs demonstrate the potential impact on ideas about dwelling – and wider questions of cultural identity – of his positive embrace of Australian light and landscape, a discussion of Daniel Libeskind's Jewish Museum, Berlin, explains how this project's interpretation of light touches on what a deeply vulnerable act building can be in contemporary culture. Light's role in establishing a cohesive working community is explored next in an assessment of the impact of O'Donnell and Tuomey's treatment of architecture as archaeology at their primary school in Ranelagh, Dublin. The final two chapters look at three recent refurbishment projects in London. The first two, by Lisa Shell and Niall McLaughlin, are small projects, and this appraisal reviews their approaches to reworking the city and the neighbourhood as they rework light in the slow, room-scale evolution that constitutes a new urban ecology. In contrast, the discussion of Herzog and De Meuron's idea that Tate Modern, their colonization and overhaul of the Bankside Power Station, is 'fuelled by light' argues that the sombre daylit turbine hall at its heart – rather than its bright white galleries or its new 'beam of light' (though these are both integral to its structuring of light) – is its most telling contribution to contemporary public life in the UK capital.

Perhaps no further words are needed to explain why presenting a series of buildings as a collection of theses in daylighting is a valid objective, and why exploring the links between philosophy and practice in natural light is a goal worth pursuing. As will become obvious, there are many possible responses to this issue, and as the different projects outlined here show, while a fascination with light may indeed sometimes betray an escape into epiphany, it can also indicate a careful engagement with what is measured, robust and tellingly down-to-earth. As long ago as 1959 Louis Kahn felt the need to explain why architects should always be looking to exploit natural light when he said to a building committee,

> All spaces need natural light. That is because the moods which are created by the time of day and seasons of the year are constantly helping you in evoking what a space can be if it has natural light and can't be if it doesn't. Artificial light is a single tiny static moment in light and can never equal the nuances of mood created by the time of day and the wonder of the seasons.[9]

Framing the significance of this insight even more boldly in 1971, he scrawled underneath a sketch entitled 'Architecture comes from the making of a room', 'A room is not a room without natural light.'[10] It remains the task of this book to elaborate the depth and complexity of narratives that resonant interpretations of 'ordinary' daylight have represented over the last century, in a world where the 'static moment' of artificial light too easily keeps the shadows at bay. With this in mind, it seems appropriate to end this preamble by stating that in order to dispel ambiguity, counter the suppositions referred to at the outset, and give daylight the primacy it deserves, the reader should assume that unless appropriately qualified, when the term 'light' is used, it is natural light that is meant.

Notes

1　Jean-Paul Sartre, *Le Diable et le bon Dieu*, Acte 3, tableau 10, scène 2, p 247. Gallimard, Paris,1962. First published Gallimard, 1951.

2　Chilean adage.

3　CIBSE is the UK standard setter and authority on building services engineering, publishing guidance and codes on lighting that are internationally recognized as authoritative and set the criteria for best practice in the profession.

4　Speer insisted that as many events as possible be held at night, to give greater prominence to his lighting effects.

5　Niall McLaughlin, personal interview, December 2004.

6　S.E. Rasmussen, *Experiencing Architecture*, MIT Press, Cambridge, Mass., 1964.

7　J. Tanizaki, *In Praise of Shadows*, trans. T.J. Harper and E.G. Seidensticker, Vintage, 2001.

8　H. Plummer, *The Architecture of Natural Light*, The Monacelli Press, 2009.

9　See Jean France, 'Louis Kahn's First Unitarian Church', October 2001, available online at http://www.rochesterunitarian.org/Building_desc.html (accessed 26 November 2010).

10　Louis I. Kahn, *Drawings for City/2 Exhibition: Architecture Comes from the Making of a Room*, charcoal, 864×864mm, 1971 (Philadelphia Museum of Art).

Chapter 1

Speaking of light, speaking with light

Le Corbusier's 'carnets de recherche patiente', *Une Petite Maison*[1] and *La Chapelle de Ronchamp*[2]

> As you can imagine, I use light freely; light for me is the fundamental basis of architecture. I compose with light.[3]

It is not easy to summarize Le Corbusier's architecture of light. Despite the fact that several of his most famous assertions about architecture concern light, he rarely discusses the topic in detail and his own photographs of his buildings are almost always in black and white. Moreover, through the course of his long career his ideas about light changed, even if its orchestration remained a central concern. This evolution was quite radical. His buildings move from a very general luminosity keyed to the tonalities of purist painting (the early houses like Villa Savoye, Villa La Roche-Jeanneret, the Atelier Ozenfant) to an approach in his late work where all the key spaces are dark (Ronchamp, La Tourette, Chandigarh), as the colours of his paintings became ever more vivid and the materiality of the buildings more attuned to the earth. In other words, while physical and spatial lightness were celebrated initially as a sign of health and modernity, his later pursuit of *l'espace indicible* prompted a bolder exploration of how shadow structures luminosity. This spectrum of design approaches and therefore of 'compositions in light' is well represented by the differences between the lighting strategies of the Villa du Lac Léman (1925, also known as La Petite Maison) and the chapel at Ronchamp (1950–1954). Fortunately, these are also projects whose design history was examined at length by Le Corbusier himself. His publication in the mid-1950s of extended photographic essays on both buildings, his 'carnets de recherche patiente' (just before and just after the 1955 publication in which the mythic themes of his late work are set out, *Le Poème de L'Angle Droit*[4]), suggest that in his mind each of these projects had a comparable significance. As documents that present the detailed analysis of his own design process in the form of an oblique yet grounded manifesto of his architectural philosophy, they would seem to provide a useful vehicle for examining his evolving arguments in light.

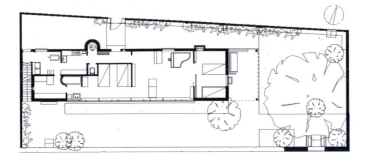

1.1
Site plan of La Petite
Maison after drawings by
Le Corbusier.

In the first two decades of the twentieth century the introduction of framing systems in reinforced concrete and steel meant that the use of thin, non-load-bearing external walls for masonry buildings became a possibility for European architects, even in small-scale urban projects. Not only did this dramatically change the potential appearance of a wall but also the very idea of a window. Windows no longer had to be holes in substantial walls whose size was constrained by constructional issues. Openings lost their depth and the relationship of interior and exterior was thrown into question. When whole walls could be made of glass, how an exterior view might be framed and how much light it was sensible to admit became subjects for discussion rather than assumptions based on long experience. And just as significantly the major ordering role that fenestration had previously played in masonry buildings no longer had relevance. Le Corbusier's initial reaction to this freedom of choice was to develop a vocabulary of different window shapes and sizes for different room types that reflected contemporary assumptions about what levels of illumination were appropriate in different areas.[5] While internal spaces like closets or bathrooms were frequently given roof-lights, small rectangular or square windows were used for spaces like corridors or staircases in which light levels did not need to be high. Where a greater amount of light was required, as in 'front of house' reception spaces like living rooms and galleries, and the grand domestic workspaces of Le Corbusier's laboratory-like kitchens, long horizontal windows, the famous *fenêtres en longueur*, stretched the entire width of a room. And where the highest levels of illumination were expected, *pans-de-verre*, walls entirely of glass (supplemented on occasion by additional roof-lights) were used to light entrance halls, offices and studios. Employing this vocabulary meant not only that his facades could be read but that a greater range of illumination levels and spatial moods became possible. As Le Corbusier optimistically declared, the windows of the new architecture would succeed in chasing nineteenth-century dirt and shadows away by giving access to the 'essential joys' of light, space and greenery.

In Le Corbusier's early distillation of the design principles of modernism two different perspectives on light emerge. The first of these, which

1.2
The soft light in the
main living room of
La Petite Maison.

concentrates on architecture as an illuminated object viewed statically at a distance, was epitomized in his messianic statement 'Architecture is the learned game, correct and magnificent, of forms assembled in light'[6]. Though less easily summarized, the second has an equally important place in his thinking: light's impact on the way buildings are encountered sequentially, as a series of visual (and ultimately tactile) experiences. The following collection of statements, first published in *Précisions* in 1930 give the best sense of this alternative outlook:

> To create architecture *is to put in order.*
> Put what in order? ... Functions and objects. To occupy space with buildings and roads. To create containers to shelter people and useful transportation to get to them. To act on our minds by the cleverness of the solutions, on our senses by the forms proposed and by the distances we are obliged to walk. To move by the play of perceptions to which we are sensitive, and which we cannot avoid. Spaces, dimensions and forms, interior spaces and interior forms, interior pathways and exterior forms and exterior spaces – quantities, weights, distances, atmospheres, it is with these we act. Such are the events involved.[7]

> ... Then by the opening of windows (the holes made by the windows are one of the essential elements of the reading of an architectural work), by the opening of windows an important play of secondary surfaces is begun, releasing rhythms, dimensions, tempos of architecture ... inside the house and outside.[8]

Consider then the capital importance of the point where you open a

1.3
View of Lake Léman from
the main window of La
Petite Maison.

window; study the way that light is received by the walls of a room. Here, in truth, an important game of architecture is played, on this the decisive architectural impressions depend.[9]

The first perspective makes light integral to the 'viewing' of building, implying that architecture can be visualized as a set of stable heroic forms in the universal illumination provided by a Beaux-Arts rendering of strong sunlight. The second reveals a much more practical, engaged position, and suggests instead that how light is handled is key to the architect's role as choreographer of events which decide the 'distances and atmospheres', the 'rhythms, dimensions and tempos' of everyday life. Here it is the significance of the dynamic play of real light to the unfolding of a building as a lived *promenade architecturale* that is given prominence. Light is something to be structured rather than accepted as a given. As an evocation of design thinking (the exploration of relationships in light) rather than an assertion about ideal form, it is perhaps sensible to consider his subsequent declaration, 'As you can imagine, I use light freely; light for me is the fundamental basis of architecture. I compose with light',[10] as a bridge between the two positions.

Une Petite Maison

First published in 1954, *Une Petite Maison* outlines the history of the small house Le Corbusier constructed for his parents on the northern shore of Lake Léman between 1920 and 1925. The embeddedness of the house in its site, both locally and with respect to the wider topography, and its measured orchestration of daily and seasonal life are the key themes of the book, and themes to which the lighting strategy is intimately linked.

1.4
Le Corbusier's sketch of
the view down the living
room towards the garden
from pp. 72–73 of *Une
Petite Maison*.

The windows of La Petite Maison

A tightly dimensioned rectangle 4m × 15m, the plan of the house is centred on
a long horizontal window, 'the primary actor of the house',[11] which commands
a view southwards over Lake Léman towards a range of Alpine peaks. As Le
Corbusier explains, it is this window that both orders the spatial field of the *plan
libre* and keys it to the landscape and its glittering light: 'One single window
11 metres long unites and lights all the elements, making the majesty of the
magnificent site enter into the house: the lake with its movement, the Alps with
their miraculous light.'[12] For him this window marries the house to the landscape
because it structures the view: throwing into prominence the landscape's major
horizontal, the line where lake and mountain meet. In working out its section
and choosing its dimensions he points out that the framing of the view, the mod-
eration of natural light and aspects of the building's theatre of occupation have
been considered together (reference is made to the rhythm of the mullions, sill
and lintel height, the size of the opening lights, the inclusion and careful placement of a curtain rod and an exterior roller-shutter). The important role it plays
in structuring daily life is given further emphasis in the only double-page spread
of the entire book, an image which focuses on its provision of side-light for the
main dining table[13] (*Une Petite Maison*, pp. 32–33) and in two of the drawings
with which the book ends. The first of these locates the dining table in front of
the view (*Une Petite Maison*, pp. 70–71, the view south across the living room),
while the second, which focuses more strongly on the distribution of light and
shadow, locates the public reception spaces of the living room and the guest
room in front of the lake and its light (the view east down the living room, *Une
Petite Maison*, pp. 72–73). In a sense, what Le Corbusier seems to be argu-
ing throughout is that the house is the space of this window, or perhaps more
precisely, the careful layering and sequencing of space and light it determines.

    Of course the project does have other windows, both in the house

1.5
Roof-light over laundry room
visible from main entrance.

and the garden, and the book makes clear that their place in the scheme of things also matters. A range of rectangular openings, they may be divided into five groups as follows:[14] an upper clerestory window and a glazed door in the house's short eastern facade; a series of windows in the northern and western facades that share the same sill and lintel heights as the main *fenêtre en longueur*; a group of three small lower-level openings to the *cave*; a number of roof-lights of more or less prominence in the diminutive landscape that is the building's planted roof terrace; and the 'windows' in the garden walls. Of these groups, only the third is not given an explicit role in the argument.[15]

The first of these other windows to receive comment is the clerestory of the guest room. Located above the main soffit beside a raised section of sloping ceiling, the lantern it creates is the only disruption of the section's orthogonal geometry. Pointedly, it is the 'awakening' it achieves in capturing morning sunlight that is emphasized. Below it stands the glazed door that links the garden room and the living space of the house. While not singled out in the text, the fact that in the promenade described by the photographs the reader enters and leaves through this 'back' door, suggests its pivotal significance to Le Corbusier. The drawing of the house's end wall (the view from the garden room, *Une Petite Maison*, p. 67) depicts it as part of an extended threshold that structures the transition between interior and exterior, one element of a small theatrical setting[16] whose use as an alfresco dining space is confirmed in the photographs entitled 'The door onto the garden, three steps, shelter' (Fig. 1.8).[17]

As it turns out, the apparently insignificant windows to the *cave* structure one of the book's most enigmatic and critical images. Entitled 'Architecture', this photograph depicts a corner of the garden (*Une Petite Maison*, p. 38 [Fig. 1.7]). On a sunlit gravelled surface a rustic bench is aligned with the white wall of the house, a wall in which two low horizontal openings are visible. The top surface of the bench leads the eye towards a shadowy stair that climbs upwards in the space between the corner of the house and an ivy-covered wall. It is an

1.6
Light from clerestory lantern
window in the guest room.

image that can be read in two ways. First, as a visual statement comparable to
that about the significance of the curtain pole, Le Corbusier is reiterating that
architecture locates the theatre of everyday life, giving it an appropriate human
scale (dining, conversing, or in this case, sunbathing). Secondly, the role light
plays in the composition is important. The view is on the diagonal, a *veduta per
angolo* towards a corner of the house that juxtaposes a lit wall with a shadowy
stair, and, by implication, the brightness of the terrace with the darkness of the
cave. As a summation of the project it states the house as a structured route,
a sequencing of settings, between the enclosure and shadowy coolth of the
womb-like *cave* and the extensive light, space and greenery of the roof terrace.
While it is possible that for Le Corbusier the image asserts that the introduction
of light into darkness is an archetypal architectural act, it is also possible to read
it as one of his abstract compositions[18] of darks and lights, figures and grounds,
orbiting about the rustic bench, as the only identifiable – because of the sitting
and the logs – locale in the composition – and hence 'architecture'. Like the free-
standing window and table in the garden room, it is a small model of the house.

    A diagram captioned 'The plan is located' explains the purpose of the
garden 'windows' (*Une Petite Maison*, p. 9). In this image a sketch of the lake/
mountain horizon is counter-posed to a site plan to demonstrate the views that
marry the project to its site via openings or breaks in its boundary wall. In addition
to the view from the main window already discussed, it shows that two views
are available from the garden room, and one from the front door (Fig. 1.1). As
a diagram which by implication relates territories of light, views and passages
of movement (the circuit of the sun, degrees of enclosure and the theatre of
events) it *locates* the house and its sunny front terrace (their staging of a view
to the lake and a view to the garden) adjacent to a narrow darker garden room
next to the street (the staging of an entrance for guests and a run for the dog
between views of the feet of passers-by). It also *locates* it between a garden
room of leaf-filtered sunlight (that coordinates settings for dining with a view to

1.7
Sketch of the photograph on
p. 38 of *Une Petite Maison* of
a rustic bench in front of the
windows to the basement
cave entitled 'Architecture'.

the lake and the passage/threshold between house and garden) and a shaded stair (that stages descent to the *cave* and ascent to the roof). And of course at another level it also seeks to *locate* the dwelling (house/garden) within the ultimate enclosure of the landscape.

The light of La Petite Maison

What Le Corbusier does choose to say about light more overtly in *Une Petite Maison* is interesting. As ever, the idea that the sun is a source of orientation is given particular prominence. In a Corbusian world the sun is always out, a building typically an orchestration of one (or several) routes from darker enclosed space to a distant sun-filled view. This project is no exception, representing as it does perhaps the most compressed example of such thinking. The house is understood as an unfolding of routes from darkness to light: the *cave* to the roof, the entrance hall to the living space, the front gate to the lakeside terrace.[19] When justifying his approach from a more technical standpoint, the text also focuses on the building's solar response, as when Le Corbusier demonstrates his awareness of the impact of solar geometry on the house's view across the lake:

> Glare? The sun is in front from east to west, only reaching (even now) the zenith at the summer solstice. Its angle of incidence means it will never affect the little house. It reaches (and dazzles) the inhabitants of the hillsides, those at heights of fifty to one hundred metres.[20]

This solar emphasis is further strengthened by the famous diagram which introduces the project. Entitled 'A circuit', this sketch-plan presents the building as a dwelling within a walled enclosure, over which the sun arrives from the south, in a powerful statement of the parallel significance (and potential reciprocity) of the daily passage of the sun around the building and the routes which give rhythm to its daily life (*Une Petite Maison*, p. 6).

As a light-filled, light-weight building dominated by the luminosity of

1.8
Section through the garden
room of La Petite Maison
illustrating 'The door onto
the garden, three steps,
shelter' beneath the lantern
window, after drawings by
Le Corbusier.

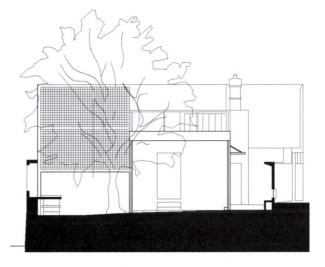

its main space, the house is typical of Le Corbusier's early work. This is because its plan's layering of space is keyed to light and orchestrated through colour. In this case the plan is divided by its zigzagging spine into two differently oriented territories placed back to back. To the south are sunny spaces lit by the *fenêtre en longueur*: the bathroom, the bedroom and the living space. To the north a series of more heavily partitioned (and thus less transparent) windows give steadier light to the laundry room, the kitchen and the entrance hall. (Here roof-lights also provide top-light, and some sunlight in spring and summer, above the laundry sink and an internal WC.) As is also typical of this period, the use of a Purist colour palette intensifies the way in which the free-flowing space of the *plan libre* is ordered and differentiated through light. The darkest areas for example are the more enclosed spaces to the east and west ends of the building. Given deep blue walls and small apertures (a use of dramatic chiaroscuro), their intense shadow frames the long, much calmer, lighter and light-filled space behind the main window (predominantly white, with areas of mid-tone turquoise or peach, and a brighter accent of burnt umber). In contrast whiteness, shallowness and a location beside this window make the bathroom the lightest area of all, while next to it, the peach-coloured inner walls of the main bedroom locate the 'warmest' space at the centre of the dwelling. The end result is that on walking through the *partie de réception* between the guest bedroom and the closet, the house is encountered as a rhythmic sequence of alternating lighter and darker spaces.[21]

As a project on a lakeside site, the house illustrates how a major theme in Le Corbusier's thinking, the poetics of water and light, is expressed in his early work. Here water is not the opposite of light (as he suggested in *Le Poème de l'Angle Droit*), but its ponderous equivalent in material terms. If one takes a section through the site east-west through the garden door looking south, it is evident that the two windows command the proposition. As the windows are openings in their walls, so is the house in its site, and so is the lake in its landscape. It is possible that this explains why the bath is given such prominence in the scheme, uniquely in his architecture. It and the boiler (both warm water)

have the only curved walls, and the brightly lit bath is the lake.[22] Both windows are depicted with archaic water jugs sitting on their ledges. Similarly, as the forms of the house sit on the land, so do the objects on tables (like the sailing boats on the lake). Moreover, the project's early attunement to the primitive[23] includes the roof, where the glass is set in the grass like little ponds (Le Corbusier would do this again on the terrace of Poissy). The character of the site as an abstract landscape is most evident, however, in the little image entitled 'la petite villa …' in the description of the project in the *Oeuvre Complète* (vol. 1, p. 75 [Fig. 1.9]). The way the trees, hills and the wall to the lake weave through the white architecture, and the way this image is paired with 'le jardin' below – the most obviously painterly rendering of dwelling (and a view redrawn by Le Corbusier at the end of *Une Petite Maison*) – all suggest that one is meant to think in terms of a *concetto* where the use of architectural 'windows' intimates a direct involvement with 'nature'. The way 'le jardin' is established by its two columns (and note the curtains) points to a conception of dwelling in this in-between condition where metaphors are allowed to flourish.

Une Petite Maison begins with a diagram of the region of Lake Léman, a written evocation of the landscape of ancient terraced vineyards which surround the lake, and an introduction to the building's clients, Le Corbusier's father, a nature lover, and his mother, a musician (*Une Petite Maison*, pp. 4–5). It ends with a series of drawings of the completed project (*Une Petite Maison*, pp. 63–77). Six of these drawings, dated 1945, are views drawn on site that 'confirm the architectural facts implied in this simple enterprise of 1923'. They are all drawings of the project in sunlight. The last, from 1951, is a portrait of his mother in front of the building and the view it commands across the lake (Fig. 1.11). This final drawing, a reworking of the book's introductory diagram, 'The site was discovered', is captioned, 'At ninety one years, Marie Charlotte Amélie Jeanneret-Perret reigns over the sun, the moon, the mountains, the lake, and the hearth, surrounded by the affectionate admiration of her children'. The message Le Corbusier is conveying via this careful structuring of his narrative is that the house is both another set of walls layered into the site, and a *domus*, the physical manifestation of a family's way of life centred on the hearth and enclosed by the landscape. What he emphasizes in the process is the response to the daily rhythms of the light that makes this possible.

1.9
Left: Plant foliage weaves through the white architecture so that its windows can intimate a direct involvement with nature.
Right: A composition of columns and curtains conveys the idea that dwelling is an in-between condition where metaphors flourish. Sketches of the photographs entitled 'la petite villa' and 'le jardin' in Le Corbusier's presentation of the project in the first volume of his *Oeuvre Complète*.

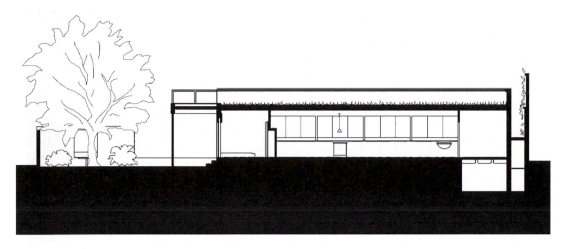

1.10
Site section through
La Petite Maison looking
south, after drawings by
Le Corbusier.

La Chapelle de Ronchamp

Le Corbusier's *La Chapelle de Ronchamp*, concerning the Marian pilgrimage church of Notre-Dame-du-Haut was published in 1957, three years after the building was completed and the publication of *Une Petite Maison*. It narrates its story somewhat differently. Here the concern with light is made more explicit, and the encounter with the architecture given greater priority in what is a more highly structured but considerably more oblique presentation of the project's *concetto*. In this case two photographic essays, several emblematic drawings, a dedication and a statement on light introduce the building (chapters 1 and 2), and only after that is the project's design history presented in a more straightforward final chapter. In other ways, however, the books are similar. As before, the reader is taken on an extended journey through and around the building. As before, the significance of the building's relationship to the site is given repeated emphasis throughout. The book – and by implication the building – begins and ends with the landscape. Whereas, by the time of the late drawings, *Une Petite Maison* is dedicated to his mother, the chapel is dedicated to Mary.

The windows of La Chapelle de Ronchamp

Both photographic essays introduce the building through its windows. The first of these (pp. 12–23) starts with a group of the prominently framed openings strewn with descriptions of Mary that face north. Three pages are devoted to the way these openings break the unmitigated darkness of the wall in which they are set. Only after this is the more dramatic impact of the apertures in the chapel's south wall revealed. Here, a six-page sequence conveys the purpose and scale of the building and its cave-like chiaroscuro through a description of this 'wall of light'. The first two of these images show how light and Marian symbols are captured within its depth for the pilgrims who pray beside it; the middle two, the worlds of light and shadow that individual windows compose (compositions of colour, light, shadow, surface texture, word, Marian symbol); the fifth, a split photograph looking down the nave during a crowded service, how the calm sweeping surfaces of the roof and back wall act as a foil for the dramatic modelling of the

1.11
The Corbusian light symbolism of dwelling: landscape and the rhythms of light and human life. Le Corbusier's sketch of his mother beside the house on pp. 76–77 of *Une Petite Maison*.

southern wall; and the sixth, the lighting of the main altar in relation to it. Only at this point, in the next pair of photographs is the building's exterior is shown for the first time. Images of the large congregation attending an open-air service on a major pilgrimage day indicate the location of the glazed niche in the eastern facade which holds the chapel's votive statue of the Virgin.

At the start of the second chapter Le Corbusier makes one of his most prominent assertions about light and its structuring role in architecture:

> The key is light
> and light illuminates shapes
> and shapes have an emotional power.
>
> By the play of proportions
> by the play of relationships
> unexpected, amazing.
>
> But also by the intellectual play
> of purpose:
> their authentic origin,
> their capacity to endure,
> structure,
> astuteness, boldness, even temerity, the play
> of those vital abstractions which are the essential qualities
> the components of architecture.[24]

The much longer photographic essay which then follows also starts inside the building before moving outside (pp. 29–85). This time, however, the initial focus is less on the individual windows and more on the fields of light they determine. The south wall, the south-west tower, the dark swooping surfaces of the roof and the curved west/north wall are each shown in turn. Two images that mark the

1.12
Ground plan of Notre-Dame-du-Haut after the drawing on p. 102 of *The Chapel at Ronchamp*.

half-way point of the journey are then included. In a return to the location pictured at the start, the first describes the corner – and the window – where the sacristy and the north wall meet, taken from the choir balcony. On this window Le Corbusier has painted a small black sun, whose significance is discussed below (Fig. 1.17). The second is the only image of the entire book that looks down the nave towards the main altar. The essay then continues by describing an extended and more obvious *promenade architecturale* – a complete circuit of the outside of the chapel and the hilltop site. It is a walk which ends where it begins, at the building's south-east pointing prow and the view it commands of the landscape.

At first glance the explicit aim of the final chapter is the detailed documentation of the building's innovatory construction. In fact its characterization of the roof and south wall as primary elements in the play of light and structure provides an opportunity to recast the architect's role. Via a provocative discussion[25] that moves between means and ends, between references to 'the shell of a crab' that 'will become the roof of the chapel', 'walls which are absurdly but practically thick', 'a horizontal crack of light ten cm wide that will amaze', and the comment, 'I defy the visitor to give, offhand, the dimensions of the different parts of the building', the architect is portrayed as an alchemist-like generator of an unexpected and indecipherable synthesis of light and matter, *l'espace indicible*. (In the dedication[26] Le Corbusier speaks of mathematics in respect of *l'espace indicible*. In *Le Livre de Ronchamp*[27] he speaks of 'word addressed to site' and therefore the fusion of language and earth as the meaning of *l'espace indicible* (literally 'unsayable space', but more usefully translated as 'space beyond words').[28]

1.13
Heightened chiaroscuro. The
windows in the dark north
wall behind the choir gallery
at Ronchamp.

The light of Ronchamp: Encounter, inhabitation and solar geometry

The interior of the chapel is very dark. Although it has many windows, most of them let in little light because they are either very deep or very small.[29] It is not easy to see at first. The spatial order and material character of the interior only emerge from the shadows, after the eyes have had time to adjust. In other words the measure of the space can only be taken in gradually. Although most of the wall surfaces are white, it slowly emerges that two areas are strongly coloured: the east end of the north wall, which is violet, and the north-east chapel which is red.

On entry[30] the visitor is faced by the south wall. In the context of a cave-like interior, most of whose wall surfaces are un-punctured, this element immediately draws – and occupies – the eye. Its many small apertures (bright sources of direct light) and textured surfaces help to compose a rich tapestry of light and colour. As a seemingly weighty, yet light-filled screen, it has a complex luminance pattern which is the result of the varied scale and geometry of the widely splayed embrasures that hold and give presence to the light.[31] It constantly changes in appearance, especially around midday. Close by and aligned with it, the chapel's only seating is a small fixed bank of pews. On sitting there, one is reoriented towards the field of light presented by the chapel's south-eastern corner. From here one no longer views the south wall but remains in the orbit of its light. Contained within the intimate, humanly scaled horizon of its

1.14
Blinding light and *l'espace indicible*. A woman at prayer in front of the south wall at Ronchamp.

lowest bank of windows one is made more aware of how these individual worlds of light write Marian symbols across the landscape (Fig. 1.15).[32]

The view now presented is towards the bright niche that contains the chapel's cult image. Located just to the south of the altar, and above the processional cross, this deep square window plays an important visual role in the daily – and annual – life of the building. Exceptionally bright during morning services when the sunlight pouring in ensures the figure it contains is consumed and dissolved by light,[33] it is the light from this niche that orients the ceremony and the space. Moreover, as the nave's largest unbaffled aperture and therefore a strong source of glare, it helps ensure the visitor's uncertain perception of form continues even after adaptation.[34] In overcast conditions, or later in the day, it remains a visual focus for pilgrims, though of a quieter kind (its inner surfaces are strongly coloured shades of bright red, yellow and green[35]). Perhaps more unexpectedly, as Carl[36] has shown, Le Corbusier's attentiveness to solar geometry means that the sunlight entering this window (the chapel's most obvious fecundation of darkness through light) is able to evoke the very moment of Mary's conception. Thus around 8 September, the day on which her nativity is celebrated, and the major pilgrimage day at Ronchamp, sunlight passing through this aperture projects Mary's shadow onto the nave floor beside the communion rail. When this shadow crosses the altar rail at around 10 am it briefly inscribes a cross within a square onto the chapel's centre line.[37]

1.15
Sketch of the window in
the south wall depicting
the traditional Marian
symbol of the moon, after
the photograph on p. 18 of
The Chapel at Ronchamp.

Ronchamp's fields of light

The marriage of light and form that Ronchamp represents is very different to
that of La Petite Maison. It is a less straightforward relationship, as much about
what is hidden as what is revealed, and one more concerned with issues of
inhabitation and orientation than view, even if the view on entry is still critical,
and other aspects of viewing still important. Through the three light towers, the
doorways (all of which create entry-points for light) and a carefully considered,
if apparently almost random distribution of apertures across the north, east and
south walls, Le Corbusier orchestrates fields of light and shadow that reorient
and anchor the chapel's unusual spatial geometry. As the drawings indicate, there
is barely a straight line at Ronchamp, barely an assumption about the geometry
of religious space that hasn't been questioned by Le Corbusier. Most of the
walls curve. The customary apse is convex. The floor slopes towards the altar.
The roof drops towards the centre of the building. Yet the structuring of space
through light is immediately apparent. A geometrically complex and more rectilinear corner articulated with southern light (the building's south eastern corner,
i.e. the south wall, the east door, Mary's niche, the pews) is set against the much
calmer curvilinear spaces at the back of the chapel that are lit from above via
the light towers. (This basic diagonal division is displayed in the earliest sketch-
plans of the chapel[38] and asserted by the narrow slot of light below the roof.[39])
A corner that exploits direct light is counter-posed to one that exploits indirect
light. In the dark interior this has a particular impact on how visitors encounter
the architecture. In the south-eastern corner direct light intensifies the darkness
as it pierces it, and here, because direct light sources are in view, form is more

1.16
The curvilinear back wall
of Ronchamp.

indistinct and the light almost palpable. Conversely, the diffuse top-light of the
secondary chapels at the back of the space erodes the darkness progressively,
producing a gentle overall gradation from light to shadow accentuated by the
heavily textured wall surface. Here, the indirect lighting of wall surfaces from
above means the form and spatial enclosure are more stable, the light more
elusive. Elsewhere strong colour intensifies darkness: candlelight is prominent
in the dim interior of the red chapel,[40] the violet of the north-east wall makes it
almost invisible.

Le Corbusier's evolving understanding of light

One typically moves in Le Corbusier's early projects from disorienting darkness
to space flooded with sunlight and given extensive views. In this project on the
other hand, as in his other late work (all of whose agonic settings – political or
religious – are caves), a superimposed dialectic of light and shadow, orientation
and disorientation, help to create *l'espace indicible*. In this work Le Corbusier
creates a world of shadow configured about the mutual play of fragments and
light that gives the architectural encounter an even more powerful initiatory
character (in this case a descent through darkness to blinding light). So, whereas
the Purist light compositions of his early work seek balanced harmony through
a measured layering and sequencing of space and light (light structures spatial
layering, compositions in light demonstrate spatial order), in his post-war projects
it is the restructuring of spatial fields through a more aggressive contrapuntal
orchestration of light and shadow that matters (fields of space are restructured as
fields of light, fields of light determine spatial order). This can be taken as a sign

1.17

Above: Sketch of the north wall window with its tiny black sun after the photograph on p. 39 of *The Chapel at Ronchamp*. This is the final image of the interior promenade through the chapel at the start of the book.

Below: Sketch of introductory image of a black sun on a ground of light, against which the word RONCHAMP is silhouetted on p. 11 of *The Chapel at Ronchamp*.

1.18
Ronchamp's south-east corner. View looking east down the nave towards the altar. The square window above the cross is the aedicule with the votive statue of Mary.

of his growing awareness of the architect's role in controlling visual perception, in deciding not only on the rhythms of spatial compression and extension, but their temporal equivalents, not only on what should and should not be seen, but how long this might take.

On the course of this journey Le Corbusier's windows change dramatically. Having rethought the window at the start of his career, he reinvents it again as his constructional preferences and material vocabulary evolve. First of all they are given three-dimensional depth (the windows in the north and south walls, Mary's niche). Secondly, as one aspect of his increasingly assured manipulation of curvilinear and rectilinear form, they become gaps or fissures between elements that qualify the perception of form and weight (the crack of light below the roof, the light slots beside the processional door). Thirdly, he realizes that depending on their distribution, they can transform walls into screens of differing depths, weights and opacities (the south wall, the brises-soleil of the light towers [Figs. 1.16, 1.18]). Although roof-lights and *fenêtres en longueur* are still deployed on occasion, large wall areas entirely of glass, *pans-de-verre*, are used more sparingly. Whereas darkness, by implication, had once been something Le Corbusier could not have too little of, its role in the structuring of luminosity becomes increasingly evident as he seeks more actively to ground his architecture, to employ more highly textured surfaces and stronger colour, and to qualify, redirect or filter light.

Corbusian light symbolism

As noted earlier, that 'light is the key' to Ronchamp, is stated quite explicitly by Le Corbusier. How he uses light is, however, barely discussed. It is only via three of

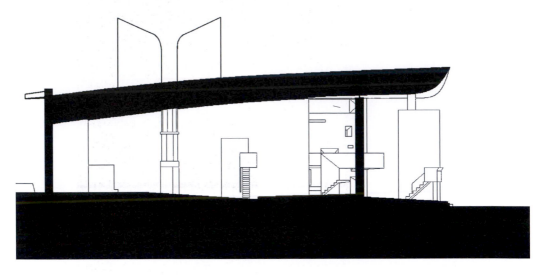

1.19
'Inside face to face with
yourself / Outside, 10,000
pilgrims in front of the
altar'. West-east section of
Notre-Dame-du-Haut after
the drawing on p. 122 of *The
Chapel at Ronchamp*.

the cryptic statements, which frame the visual argument presented in *La Chapelle de Ronchamp*, that the implicitly symbolic content of his new understanding of light emerges. The first of these is the sketch of the main processional door that proportions the entire book (both the door and the book are square [Fig. 1.21]). This is centred on a square compartmented window that is also a key (p. 10). The second is the enigmatic image on the opposite page of a black sun on a ground of light, against which the word RONCHAMP is silhouetted (p. 11 [Fig. 1.17]). The third is the caption scrawled beside the plans: 'Inside face to face with yourself/ Outside, 10,000 pilgrims in front of the altar' (pp. 102–103). As an image which can be read as a summary of the chapel with its inclined cloud, the first seems to underline the significance of a square window to the building's complex geometry. Presumably this is Mary's niche, or more precisely its once-a-year split projection in sunlight on the dark floor of the nave. The second emphasizes the reciprocity of sunlight and shadow in the violent but potent chiaroscuro created within the interior of both Mary's niche and the building (and is also an oblique reference to the nineteenth plate of *Splendor Solis*, a famous sixteenth-century alchemical treatise, in which a black sun is shown rising above a dark landscape, eclipsing the true sun beyond it, in order to illustrate Dissolution, the first operation of the art of alchemy). Finally the project is summarized in occupational terms as the juxtaposition of two back-to-back sanctuaries: an extensive public gathering place enclosed by the horizon, open to the sky but structured by shadow; and an intense world of darkness fecundated by light and conducive to private prayer. Though neither light nor landscape are mentioned, the comparison evokes the role light plays in structuring the daily and seasonal rhythms of life, and states the architecture's mutually defining coincidence of shadow and light, radical interiority and radical exteriority. Between these two sanctuaries, and participating of course in both, stands Mary herself, Notre-Dame-du-Haut, who as 'the woman clothed with the sun', the moon and the morning

1.20
Light and solar geometry.
The shadow cast by the
statue of the Virgin on the
floor of Ronchamp at mid-
morning in early autumn.

star is the guiding light in a dark landscape,[41] and thus both the window and
the building.

If the dialectics of matter and either mathematics or language lie at
the heart of *l'espace indicible*, this was manifest in Le Corbusier's architecture as
a dialectics of matter and light. More generally, the late works show a dialectics
of light and earth, where raw concrete (*beton brut*) sustains primordial qualities.
Often qualified by harsh colour contrasts, this earthly, henge-like architecture
also sustains a more subtle luminosity than the Purist works, with their regular
invocation of a Mediterranean life in the sun, even in northern cities. At the same
time, Le Corbusier's fascination with opposites allowed his settings to compose
themselves from randomly disposed fragments that also obeyed precise geometric relations, inspired by an experience on the Brittany foreshore recounted
in *Une Maison – Un Palais*.[42]

One can see premonitions of the later work already in the early
1920s, such as at La Petite Maison; and a turn towards more primitivist themes
is evident in architecture generally during the 1930s and certainly after World
War II. The dialectics of light and raw matter itself first appears in the stage sets
of Adolphe Appia at the beginning of the century; and it is easy to see that it has
its source in the turn to *poésie* in German Romanticism at the beginning of the
previous century. The romantic classic interpretation of this preference for a more
archaic or primordial architecture was reserved for the totalitarian regimes; but

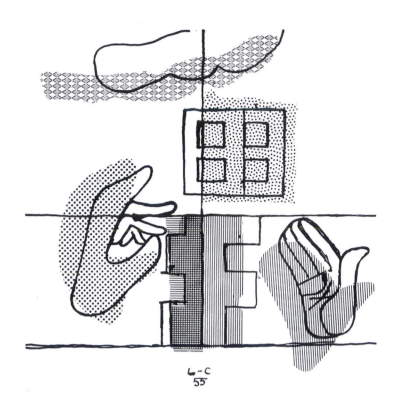

1.21
The projection of Mary's aedicule on the centre line of the nave floor as an archetypal window. Le Corbusier's drawing of the processional door from p. 10 of *The Chapel at Ronchamp*.

the persistence of the theme itself even into computer-generated, translucent earth forms in recent architectural speculation suggests that Le Corbusier's work must be seen as part of this more broad phenomenon.

The character and meaning of light itself changes under these circumstances. The subtle luminosity of his interiors enables the porous surface of raw concrete to appear to absorb the light, and therefore, in the shadowy context, to be a source of light, an effect enhanced by the fragments of harsh colours applied to the surfaces. The earth is made to embody luminosity. The recourse to rhythmic dispositions of apparently crude forms further orients the register of perception to primordial earth (most notably at La Tourette). Similarly the inclination to develop architectural settings as landscapes qualified by cubist frontalities and fragments includes the very earth in one's experience of orientation. Indeed, one may read the trajectory of *Le Poème de l'Angle Droit* as a movement from earth and water to thought in the culminating *signe* of the right angle. In such contexts, cast light or even the sun become representational and not simply illumination for tasks.

By way of understanding the phenomenon, one might adduce the earlier turn to earth-like settings, when, during sixteenth-century mannerism, the grotto and the grotesque appeared. The parallels between the sophistication of mannerist culture and that of modernism have been drawn frequently enough since Pevsner and Rowe in the early 1950s. This suggests that the turn to the primitive corresponds to a desire to anchor or, as the philosophers have it, to 'ground' the ambiguities and complexities, which otherwise might dissolve into fragmentary relativism. However, there is also always to such settings an allusion to death or at least to tragedy (which becomes simply bleak when mishandled, as in so many housing blocks of the 1960s). The forms are tough and confident but the spaces are melancholy, slightly anxious.

Le Corbusier's transformation of this into dignity in the interior of Ronchamp (while the exterior seems to be arbitrary sculpture) may simply test-ify to his talent and judgement; but the almost universal approval it has enjoyed may be taken to indicate what is sought in such settings. Le Corbusier's own comparison with the Parthenon suggests an element of nostalgia for an archi-tecture – and therefore a culture – which is more profound than a commodity or branding exercise (even if Le Corbusier indulged equal fascination for the milieu of movement, transformation, the mass culture of the motor car and traffic). The challenge of finding in modernist capitalism a culture equal in richness to those of the past remains a recurring motif, alongside the equally frequent calls for revolution. However, there is little interest presently in the sort of symbolism and mysticism of Le Corbusier's patient research, as if all human phenomena could be reduced to immanent concepts. Perhaps this last glimmer of transcendence, Le Corbusier's recall of ancient understandings of light as mediation with the universal (most-common-to-all) conditions of being human, is cast as tragedy because it has become so.

Notes

1   Le Corbusier, *Une Petite Maison*, Éditions d'architecture, Artemis, Zurich, 1954. Page numbers quoted here refer to the 3rd edition, 1981.

2   Le Corbusier, *La Chapelle de Ronchamp*, Verlag Gerd Hatje, 1957, trans. J. Cullen as *The Chapel at Ronchamp*, Architectural Press, London, 1957. Page numbers quoted here refer to English translation.

3   Le Corbusier, *Précisions sur un état present de l'architecture et de l'urbanisme*, Crès et Cie, Paris 1930, trans. E.S. Aujame as *Precisions on the Present State of Architecture and City Planning*, MIT Press,1991, p. 132. Page numbers quoted here refer to English translation.

4   Le Corbusier, *Le Poème de L'Angle Droit*, Éditions Verve, Paris, 1955.

5   H. Sobin, 'De la science à la poésie: L'utilisation de la lumière naturelle dans l'oeuvre de Le Corbusier', in *Le Corbusier et la nature*, Éditions de la Villette, Paris, 2004, pp. 75–83, pp. 76–77.

6   Le Corbusier, *Vers une Architecture*, Paris, G. Cres, 1924, p. 16.

7   Le Corbusier, *Précisions*, p. 70.

8   Le Corbusier, *Précisions*, pp. 72–73.

9   Le Corbusier, *Précisions*, p. 73.

10 Le Corbusier, *Précisions*, p. 132.

11 Le Corbusier, *Une Petite Maison*, pp. 30–31.

12 Le Corbusier, *Précisions*, p. 130.

13 While dining and bathing are side-lit, hand-washing and sleeping are front-lit: the wash-basin of the main bathroom and all the beds are oriented so that one washes before the view and wakes to the light.

14 A later extension to the house, added a room at first-floor level above the garden space outside the kitchen. A second guest bedroom (for Le Corbusier and his brother Alfred) illuminated by a row of windows, it includes a raised platform which provides another side-lit setting for a table. Though the addition appears in the photographs of *Une Petite Maison* its relationship to the rest of the project is not discussed. In fact the window looks south across the tableau of the roofscape and is framed by the free-standing wall at the very west of the

site. The light falls on the triangular housing for the stair, metaphorically bringing the mountain into the room. The effect is to create a sort of continuous landscape, perhaps like a 'dream'.

15 In Le Corbusier's hasty diagram of the plan in *Précisions* (p.129), the individual windows to the kitchen and laundry spaces of the north-west corner of the plan are actually drawn as a second *fenêtre en longueur*, a move which underlines the way in which the plan may be read as a nesting of southerly and northerly oriented space, set out yin-yang fashion to either side of the central zigzagging spine wall.

16 It is possible that Le Corbusier's drawing of the view down the living space towards this glazed door describes a sequence of light and dark *en filade* spaces that composes a staged view into which one may walk, at right angles to the view of the landscape horizon. It also shows how the end wall is also a backdrop when seen from the interior, the guest room a stage-like space with its 'wings' to either side, framing a deep perspective through the glazed door onto the garden.

17 Le Corbusier, *Une Petite Maison*, p. 28.

18 Le Corbusier first introduces primitivist themes as an argument in his *Une Maison – Un Palais* (Éditions Connivances, Paris, 1928, FLC, 1989), although the Maisons Loicheur have rubble walls (and there are decidedly primitivist elements in Pessac [1925] not to mention the rubble wall that frames the free-standing window of the garden room in La Petite Maison [1923], a date which conforms to the change in his painting).

19 As Le Corbusier declares, the plan ensures that the sudden disclosure of a view to a light-filled landscape punctuates the circuit of the building from gate to roof that is described in the photographic promenade: 'Unexpectedly the wall stops and the spectacle springs into view: light, space, this water and these mountains … Here it is! The trick is played!' (*Une Petite Maison*, p. 27).

20 Le Corbusier, *Une Petite Maison*, p. 11.

21 It is worth noting that this is the walk through the perspective whose unexpected length is cited by Le Corbusier in his original presentation of the building in the *Oeuvre Complète* (OC, vol. 1, pp. 74–75).

22 Le Corbusier begins his *Poème de L'Angle Droit* with a drawing of himself in a bath, rendered as an archipelago, and so one must imagine that the bath has an iconographic value beyond sanitation.

23 It seems possible that the roof gardens of these early houses were meant to make caves of the houses themselves, thus anticipating the more overtly primitivist later buildings, and particularly something like La Tourette.

24 Le Corbusier, *The Chapel at Ronchamp*, p. 27.

25 Le Corbusier, *Une Petite Maison*, pp. 89–122.

26 Le Corbusier, *Une Petite Maison*, p. 25.

27 Le Corbusier, *Le Livre de Ronchamp*, Les Cahiers Forces Vives/Editec, Paris, 1961, p. 18.

28 See P. Carl, 'The godless temple, "organon of the infinite"', in *The Journal of Architecture*, vol. 10, no. 1, February 2005, pp. 63–90, p. 66.

29 As Pauly notes, it was Canon Ledeur who can be considered responsible for the scattered star-like openings that puncture the wall surrounding Mary's niche. According to Ledeur, Le Corbusier knew of his wish to see Mary's statue crowned with stars like the Woman of the Apocalypse, 'the woman clothed with the sun' with whom she is traditionally identified. On seeing the holes left by the scaffolding beams during a site visit following the removal of the formwork from the east wall, Le Corbusier suddenly exclaimed, 'You have your stars! There they are!' (D. Pauly, *Ronchamp. Lecture d'une architecture*, Association des Publications près les Universitès de Strasbourg, Éditions Ophrys, Paris, 1987, pp. 58–59).

30 Again, it should be noted that at Ronchamp we are dealing with a landscape proposition. Here the first layer of facade is the hostel, on the way up the hill, which is the same length as the chapel.

31 The intermediate zones of luminance created by the internal embrasures attenuate the contrast between glazing and adjoining surfaces. The combination of these embrasures and

the deep overhang of the roof means that very little direct sunlight enters the interior. See 'Mastery of Daylight in an Emblem of Modern Architecture', in N. Baker, A. Fanchiotti and K. Steemers, eds, *Daylighting in Architecture: A European Reference Book*, James & James for the Commission of the European Communities, London, 1993, pp. 55–58.

32 This intention is cited by Le Corbusier in his presentation of the building in the *Oeuvre Complète* (OC, vol. 6, p. 36.)

33 H. Plummer, *Poetics of Light*, Architecture and Urbanism, Japan, extra edition December 1987, p. 157.

34 As Millet explains, 'The contrast between the daylight and the dim interior is great enough that the edges of the splayed openings of the south wall are veiled in *sfumato*, the tones from light to dark blurring so as to conceal the exact form. The light decomposes the edges … The chiaroscuro effects are mostly played at the low end of the scale, with a few bright counterpoints, such as the window behind the altar that admits daylight unabated maintaining the high end of the scale so that perceptions of form in light are made relative to that bright light' (M. Millet, *Light Revealing Architecture*, Van Nostrand Reinhold, New York, 1996, p. 58).

35 Pauly, *Ronchamp*, p. 127.

36 P. Carl, 'Ornamentation and Time, A Prolegomena', in *AA Files 23*, 1992, pp. 49–64.

37 On the inside this centre line is indicated in the flooring. It marks the axis which connects the main altar to the east with the major waterspout from the roof to the west.

38 It is these plans that are used to introduce the third chapter of *La Chapelle de Ronchamp*.

39 The way in which the book structures its story obliquely states this diagonal axis in light: images of the locations that mark each of its ends: the confessionals in the west wall (*The Chapel at Ronchamp*, p. 8) and the door in the east wall (*The Chapel at Ronchamp*, p. 41) bracket the two promenades through the interior (*The Chapel at Ronchamp*, pp. 13–40).

40 See Baker *et al.*, eds, *Daylighting in Architecture*, p. 57.

41 Le Corbusier's understanding of Marian spirituality was reinforced in a whole series of interviews with the man who had originally offered him the commission for the project, Canon Ledeur of Besançon (Pauly, *Ronchamp*, p. 54). A letter to Le Corbusier from Ledeur focused on the way the Virgin is traditionally symbolized in terms of light and of colour: 'star of the sea', 'morning star', 'bright like the sun', 'mystic rose', 'tower of ivory', 'house of gold', 'beautiful as the moon' (letter of 25 April, 1955, Archives Fondation Le Corbusier, as quoted in Pauly, *Ronchamp*, p. 96). It is certainly also likely that Le Corbusier knew of the most important litany to the Virgin, the Litany of Loreto, which addresses Mary as both 'spiritual vessel' and 'gate of heaven'.

42 'Let's admit the truth of La Palisse: the eye only measures what it sees. It doesn't see chaos, or rather it sees badly in chaos, in fog. And without hesitation it is drawn to things which have an aspect. All of a sudden, we are stopped, sized, measuring, appreciating: a geometric phenomenon develops before our eyes: rocks upright like menhirs, undoubted horizontal of the sea, meander of the beach. And by the magic of rapports, here we are in the land of dreams' (Le Corbusier, *Une Maison – Un Palais*, pp. 22–23).

Chapter 2

Desert tent

Light and geometry in the church of the Benedictine Monastery of the Holy Trinity, Las Condes, Santiago de Chile

> Much importance was given to light, which is the real vivifying soul of the whole. Light, which leads upon entrance, from the door to the altar by means of changes of intensity and colouring. Light which comes from above as in nature, and indirectly, transforming the rough walls into fountains of light ...[1]

After taking in breathtaking views across the landscape from the tree-lined road that leads to the building, and a brief ascent through a darker entrance corridor, visitors experience the church of the Monastery of the Holy Trinity of Las Condes as a serene cave of light. Here light animates an airy predominantly white space of almost total enclosure. Contrasts in light and shadow are generally not pronounced and the ambient light is cool and relatively even.[2] Yet as the sun moves round the building, the sparks of sunshine that come and go – and the subtle variation in appearance of the roughly textured surfaces qualify the otherwise timeless stillness of the space.

In the 1920s, it was the Liturgical Movement[3] which argued that church services had become a 'distant spectacle', contributing to the decline in attendance at communion. Rejecting nineteenth-century preoccupations with style or aesthetics, they urged that attention should be focused upon 'the gathering round the altar', and pointed to the simple, more austere buildings of the early Church as sources for a radical renewal of church design. In the decades that followed, church layout was completely rethought, in particular the placement and significance of the altar in relation to the clergy, choirs and laity. Ritual was recast as 'drama', in which all participants were expected to play their roles within a more or less complicated box that bore little relation to a traditional church interior. As a result by the early 1960s, the liturgical setting had acquired the character of a bare stage. Centred on an altar accented by light from the side or above, the attributes of ascetic modernism can be recognized here, a movement which had developed in the same period. While neither functionalist

unbuilt chapel   cell-block   initial refectory
                                                                                and chapel

2.1
Section across the Las
Condes Monastery site
looking east, 1953. After
the drawing of the project
in P. Gross and E. Vial,
*El Monasterio Benedictino
de Las Condes* (1988),
pp. 64–65.

planning nor the individualist aesthetics of modernism communicate easily with the traditional ethos of the Catholic *ecclesia*, the question of the spiritual orientation of modernism was always acute, particularly after the two World Wars and in the face of post-war consumerism and scientific rationalism. In this respect it appears that that the Church and otherwise wholly secular architects and artists were moving towards each other, and religious commissions became critical opportunities to confront the deeper questions of the culture. Yet the difficulty of recovering or discovering anew the spiritual resources in the new context can be measured by the great number of naively 'expressionist' or actually kitsch modern churches. It is therefore valuable to look closely at one of the acknowledged masterpieces of the genre, the church of the Benedictine Monastery of Las Condes, on the edge of Santiago, Chile. Ironically, and despite the long and profound history of light symbolism in church design, light is barely mentioned in the 1947 directives for church design[4] and there is no entry devoted to light in the otherwise exhaustive *Catholic Encyclopaedia* (although mentioned frequently elsewhere in this work). In declaring light to lie at the heart of their design, it is therefore clear that the architects of this building, Father Gabriel Guarda and Brother Martin Correa, were obliged to assemble their interpretation from a mixture of sources, both secular and sacred.

Completed in 1964, their monastery church represents an unusual approach to these issues. On the one hand its double-cube plan centred on the altar is clearly influenced by the wish to redraw the liturgical stage;[5] on the other the significance of natural light to its interior is immediately evident to anyone entering the building. Here, what appears in plan to be a space determined by the geometry of cubes is encountered on the interior as an austerely empty room whose floor extends beneath tent-like walls suffused with, or rent by, light. Here, in the creation of a deceptively complex yet airy space of enormous calm, heavy walls and ceilings are made weightless by light, heavy surfaces tremble with light. The questions which seem worth asking about the design strategy implemented here concern both its precedents and its performance as a setting for worship. What range of ambitions have inspired its 'architecture of light' and how was the form developed? How does it support or hinder the celebration of the liturgy? In what way is this setting in tune with or compromised by the spatial geometry?

In this chapter a concentration on the interplay between an unprecedented spatiality, a specific ambition for light quality and the role played by

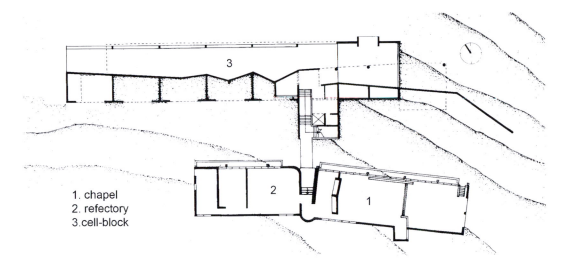

1. chapel
2. refectory
3. cell-block

2.2
Plan of the initial Las Condes
Monastery buildings, 1953.

the visual environment in both guiding movement and influencing perception allows the dilemmas raised by the design's marriage of concerns for geometry, nakedness and light to be examined in detail. The building presents a unique opportunity in a modern – and modernist – context to ground a discussion of the role played by light in the reinvention of liturgical space, examining the impact on design thinking of 'lived light', the extended experience of life and light in a particular place.[6] This is because the church was authored by two of the monks from this community who were intimately familiar with the site and the institution's own 'history of light' following completion of its first buildings in 1956. A discussion of the monastery's progressive evolution that investigates the sources of inspiration for the lighting strategy and the tools employed to evolve and refine the design therefore prefaces a detailed discussion of its primary intentions and the way in which they are expressed – or negated – by light. As this is a church where two separated worlds meet, that of the monks and that of the lay congregation, particular attention is given to the way in which the light and liturgy of the church is encountered by the two different groups.

Searching for light: Initial sources of inspiration

Scattered across the middle slopes of the Los Piques hill below the bleak emptiness of the high Andean Cordillera, and commanding long views over the leafy suburbs of the neighbouring valley, the architecture of the Las Condes Monastery seems consistent, but has in fact evolved slowly over time. Following a private competition in 1953, a small team headed by the architect and teacher Jaime Bellalta and his wife, Esmee Cromie, were awarded the commission. Yet a lack of money meant that only two buildings of their cloister-centred scheme were built. A second phase in 1960 saw a team from the Institute of Architecture of the Catholic University of Valparaiso[7] taking on the project. Their design, which turned its back on the initial proposals in a complete reworking of the relationship between monastery buildings and hill-slope, was not pursued further, although it did prompt a change of heart about where the monastery's main portal should stand and thus how it would be encountered by the public. Two years later in

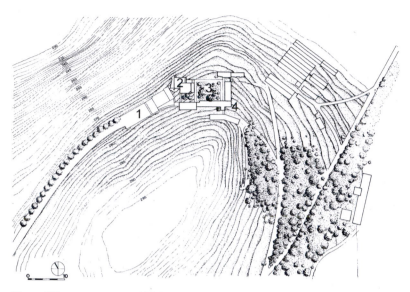

2.3
Plan of the Las Condes
Monastery site, 1988.

Plan of the monastery, 1988

1. esplanade
2. church
3. cloister garden
4. cell-block

1961, after protracted negotiations, Guarda and Correa, who had completed architectural training at the Santiago School of Architecture before entering the Benedictine Order, agreed to accept the commission for the church that would stand adjacent to the new gate. This building was completed three years later. During the following forty years this core has been expanded in a series of separate building projects with the addition of a library, an entrance building and hostels for male and female guests that have gradually allowed the cloister first envisaged as the heart of the monastery to re-emerge at the centre of a U-shaped complex of buildings.

Though Bellalta and his team played no further part in the monastery's development after 1956 it was their initial response to the brief and the site, and the ideas for light represented by their unbuilt project for a new larger chapel that offered Guarda and Correa some primary points of departure. The spare forms and primitive materiality of these first buildings were an important influence on physical form and spatial vocabulary while at the same time offering lessons on the role light plays in animating and conversely, grounding architecture. Of the two completed Bellalta buildings, the first was a single-storey block containing a provisional chapel and refectory, and the second immediately below and parallel to it, a linear volume, comprising a two-storey cell-block housing the monks' living quarters above a wide cloister walk (Figs. 2.2, 2.5, 2.6, 2.7). Beyond the large glazed volume of the cell-block stair, simple apertures in these side-lit buildings took a variety of forms: small openings cut into walls, full-height openings, half-height openings, and pockets of indirectly lit space. Their careful deployment in

2.4
The Las Condes Monastery
against the backdrop of the
Andes, 2008.

relation to interior vertical or horizontal surfaces gave a range of examples of how a sensitive balance of light and space could be achieved with very limited means. The unbuilt chapel project in particular, with its offset external walls, illustrated an unusual method of creating drama with indirect light.

In response to questions concerning what sparked the initial dialogue about design strategy between Guarda and himself, Correa confirms:

> The influence of light was everywhere in the first buildings ... The key was indirect light that we had seen in another part of the monastery, in the first church, which was also the first building. A wall of indirect light and a project with a displaced wall that we also saw. They indicated that indirect light should become a major idea. The light as important as the white.[8]

Emphasizing the significance of the light they had encountered together, he expands on this as follows:

> The provisional chapel had a low window from the floor up to about a metre high. It was strange. We were interested in the play of shadows, sun and light it produced. For us it was a new way of finding light. One that helped to engender a new emphasis, a new interest in light ... so that light became implicit in the project.[9]

These early buildings provided inspiration in other ways too. Though not the result of opposing views, initial discussions on design strategy between Guarda and Correa were slow and difficult, but the shared experience of living within Bellalta's architecture emerged gradually as a point of contact, and one with important effects. The first of these was the interest in the spatial implications

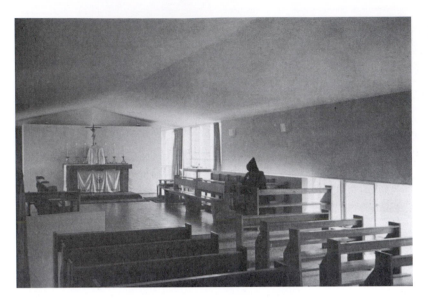

2.5
The interior of the initial
chapel looking west.

of indirect light already noted, but more importantly their knowledge of these buildings demonstrated that light had to be discovered not assumed. Finally, in qualifying their sensibility to light in the landscape, these first white buildings raised their awareness of the immediate visual context and the impact of the strong Chilean light in such an environment, a heightened consciousness that further spurred their search for an orienting light in their own project.[10]

Alongside this practical experience, the influence on their thinking of a contemporary theoretical text by Alberto Cruz, one of Chile's most important post-war architectural thinkers and teachers also deserves mention. Familiar to Guarda and Correa,[11] *Project for a Chapel on the Estate of Los Pajaritos* (Fig. 2.8)[12] is a detailed explanation of the ideas behind an unbuilt project defined by Cruz as, 'A cube of light … with the softest most delicate penumbra …'.[13] In this text, light, conceived as source of inspiration, end and means, is central to an argument that seeks to identify design principles for a pilgrimage chapel. As Cruz points out, the design process became a search to recreate a particular quality of light:

> I was studying my cube of light. Immobilized light that by its inter-reflections cast an enveloping homogeneity. Light without color. I thought of high and hidden windows that prevented a dual focus of light and opaque cloths of wall, and that evenly illuminated the walls. White walls for the inter-reflections of homogeneity without colour.[14]

> It had to be a large luminous space: so that the walls, the ceiling would expand, so that no limit would be approached in order that we would not feel compromised in any dimension. In no dimension distinct from the rest. Therefore a cube.[15]

In this description the significance for light distribution of the interplay between

2.6
Views of Bellalta's cell block.
Left: Internal corridor. Right:
Cloister walk.

spatial geometry, window location and surface colour, informs a discussion of the use of indirect light within a simple, white, almost-cubic space. Issues of visual perception are also given emphasis,[16] as is the idea that ambitions for light must be considered *specifically in relation to* the human acts and events they illuminate. Finally it is worth adding that this argument about light is framed by an extended analysis of the role such a chapel should play in the immediate physical and cultural landscape.

What is worth noting here is that the conversation is quite abstract. Correa and Cruz talk about light the way sculptors, artists or stage designers would. It is not immediately connected to traditional themes regarding the Christian interpretation of light. There is the landscape, there are planes and there are a range of effects of light. It may perhaps be assumed that a certain scale attached to these considerations, though it is not always mentioned. We find ourselves in a spiritual universe with its roots in the stage sets of Appia and the design philosophy of the Bauhaus– with perhaps the Impressionists and Symbolists more in the background – an immersive milieu of light itself, associated with a kind of implicit mysticism.

The light among the trees, imagining and modelling the light of a double cube

Like Cruz, Correa speaks of an encounter with a specific situation of light as a critical design catalyst:

> Anyway, searching for the soul of our church, I found myself one day in the middle of a pine-wood. Falling through the highest branches the brilliant sunlight was transformed into more subtly graded light … It was a space cleared of trunks, silent, secluded, welcoming, transcendent. It was a thrilling, enchanted space, in that despite the character of its enclosure, it created a 'religious atmosphere'.[17]

This was an epiphany that had two important consequences. First, the idea of recreating 'forest light' focused ambitions for the character of light and space that Guarda and Correa were looking to generate. Secondly, it suggested that the

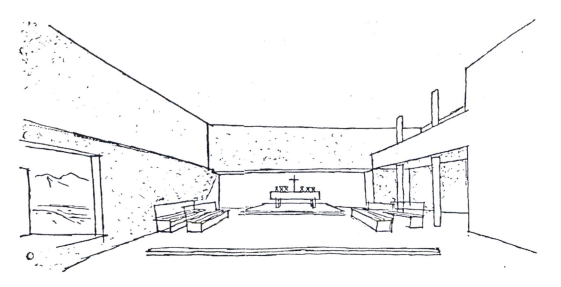

2.7
Sketch of Bellalta's proposed
unbuilt chapel project
drawn by the team from
the Valparaiso Architecture
School in connection with
their unbuilt scheme for the
monastery.

introduction of light from above might give a primary orientation to the space. As a result, lighting intentions informed and qualified even initial discussions about the form and plan of the church.

A series of design-concept diagrams by Correa illustrate how this process began to work. First of all the plan is explained: two adjacent squares are initially shifted and then laid over one another, the diagonal axis of the resulting plan form giving a greater length to a divided yet unified space. The altar is then located where the two squares overlap so that it is visible from all sides. Below this a simple section *taken on the diagonal* illustrates that this results in a room divided into three spaces (for monks, altar and laity) whose section focuses attention on a central altar. A further pair of three-dimensional studies begin to illustrate how light from above is used to make the monk's space brighter than the nave, and thus a source of orientation for the whole design.

From this point onwards attention was switched to plans and the construction of a white card model large enough to be placed over the head and thus to permit experimentation with the form 'that would realise the best possibilities for the light'.[18] What is interesting about this attempt to manage light is that science was not used, only perception and judgement, 'research' consisting of a model testing process that allowed the combined effects of light and geometry on walls and ceilings to be assessed from an eye-height perspective. What is relevant here is that the model was not divorced from its context. During the design phase the model was stored next to the ceiling in Correa's own cell, a narrow room on the second floor of Bellalta's cell block, and taken outside into the light in order to assess the impact of alternative design strategies.[19] As designer and client, an analytical observer and a committed occupant, Correa was in a position to live out imaginatively the implications of the building as he refined its design. As he explains, his thoughts on the relationship between the light of the project and the life of the monastery were subsumed in the procedure of making and remaking the model, a task which preoccupied him even when his mind was expected to be on other things:

2.8
Longitudinal section of Cruz's
Los Pajaritos Chapel project.

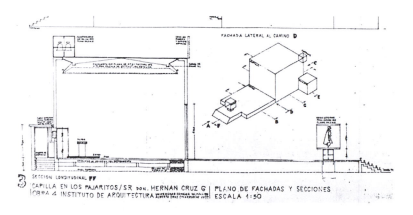

One was in this life. What was critical was the type of life, its rhythms, the moments of going to church … Many times when one is praying one's head is somewhere else – in this situation my head was in the building.[20]

The organization of the final design

In the final design the two major linked volumes of the nave and chancel described above have been surrounded with a series of subsidiary volumes: an entry passage or narthex, for the public, a Chapel of the Holy Sacrament, a sacristy and entry passage for the monks, a space for confession (Figs. 2.9, 2.11). Careful window design means that where light enters is generally disguised, though one large window in the chancel and five much narrower openings elsewhere add relatively small brighter sources of direct light within a set of spaces whose light is predominantly indirect. (The large vertical and horizontal openings which admit light onto the back walls of the nave from deep pockets let into the roof, or via narrow shallower gaps between wall-planes, are hidden from view). Constructed entirely from *in situ* reinforced concrete, the church is built across rather than along the slope of the site, an arrangement that ensures its diagonal axis is oriented north–south, the nave partially hanging over the slope to the north, the chancel partially cut into the ground to the south. Given the absence of other constraints, the fact that orientation to the movement of the sun takes precedence over the traditional liturgical orientation to the east is quite bold and telling (in the Southern Hemisphere the sun is in the north of course). It means that the northern 'front' walls of the chancel are exposed to sunlight. It also means that the lower volume of the nave is not in the shadow of the chancel, which gives it an exposure to light from sun, sky and ground that permits strong light to enter the building from unusual directions. On the interior particular attention is given to light at either end of the diagonal axis. To the north a brightly side-lit niche contains a tall statue of Mary holding the Infant Jesus,[21] which commands the view across the nave. To the south the hidden apertures around the upper corner of the chancel transform it into a kind of dramatically lit pointed apse.[22]

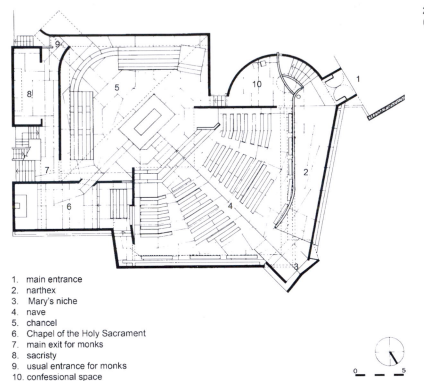

1. main entrance
2. narthex
3. Mary's niche
4. nave
5. chancel
6. Chapel of the Holy Sacrament
7. main exit for monks
8. sacristy
9. usual entrance for monks
10. confessional space

Lighting the geometry

As was said earlier, the monks drew on various sources for their understanding of light.[23] Yet curiously, classical and mediaeval light symbolism seems not to have been prominent.[24] Simplifying we may say that, in the Western tradition, light may basically be divided into two, according to the kind of shadow it produces. One has to do with the structure of reality, where shadow and matter are at the bottom of the hierarchy (the pre-eminent example being Dionysos Areopagita, whose Neo-Platonic light ontology was determinative for the rest of the Christian Middle Ages, as well as for the Renaissance and Baroque). The other kind of light has to do with understanding or morality, in which darkness signifies confusion or disorientation, intellectual or moral. What one sees in Plato's *Republic* (Books VI–VII) is that this second, psychological, shadow-light dialectic strives to be united with the first, the structure of reality. This has comprised the basic drama of light symbolism ever since: to reconcile the historical with the eternal, the human with the divine. Though rarely made explicit, these basic symbolic structures seem still to be relevant. We have light refracted through perspective (Cusanus to Alberti) and from that to physics and perceptual biology; and we have artificial light from domestic illumination to stadia (or Nuremburg), and from tiny warning lights to the strip of Las Vegas (i.e. as signs telling us to do something) and the manifold forms of artistic expression that exploit all of these. Yet in terms of light's capacity to offer something of mediation between earthly

2.10
Correa's explanatory
diagrams of the church's
plan, section and volumetric
massing.

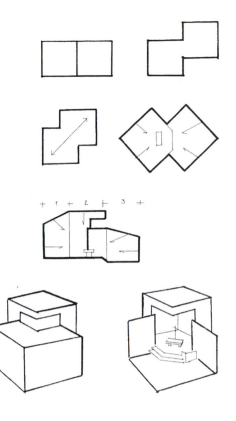

transience and something more lasting, natural light and its symbolic structures
seem still to be authoritative.

The designers of the church were working with this basic inheritance
(and against all forms of artificial light), and striving to find a vehicle in which it
would be most prominent. Furthermore they needed allusions to settings or
places, i.e. light cast on flat walls always suggests implicit rooms, as Appia had
theorized at the start of the twentieth century. They needed spatial discrimina-
tion and a structure of shadow and light which could be deployed to suggest a
place made by God, therefore of light (Gen. 1:3), and therefore also standing for
creation itself. In this regard the choice of the double cube seems arbitrary, a typically modernist point of departure, except for the possibility that God's building
needed 'ideal' geometry. The designers explain that one cube is for the monks,
the other for the laity, so they may perhaps be understood as two modalities of
being human before God. Whatever its derivation, the double cube lies at the
heart of a formalist dilemma – on the one hand, it appears one naturally relapses
into formalist vocabulary to describe its nature; on the other the design does
indeed display a cunning non-frontal use of cubes, but mostly because they are
not needed to understand the space. In other words, it is possible to participate
in this church without ever recognizing that cubes lie at its heart, though the over-
emphatic geometry they support is also why aspects of the design have a curious
awkwardness. Such a formalist dilemma is not unprecedented in the modernist
period. What saves the sacred spaces of Le Corbusier and Luis Barragan is the

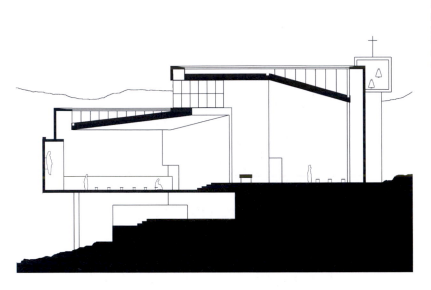

2.11
North-south section of the church cut on the diagonal, after the drawing of the project published in P. Gross F. and E. Vial B., *El Monasterio Benedictino de Las Condes* (1988), p. 121.

element of violence. This is also true here where it is the diagonal alignment of the double cube which allows it to act as the aggressor or *agent provocateur*.

On the negative side, the double-cube geometry, reinforced by aspects of the lighting, focuses all visual attention on the altar and its silhouetted cross at the centre (Fig. 2.15). While it can be argued that such an arrangement rescues the worshipper from disorientation in the otherwise diaphanous space,

2.12
The church entrance from the esplanade.

2.13
View towards the nave from the main public entrance to the church. The floor-level line of light and the brightly side-lit niche against which Mary's statue is silhouetted draw the eye onwards.

this seems too literal a response. The decision to make the altar/cross the only frontal element in the spatial order, and to position it precisely on the vanishing point, simply makes the design too explicitly oriented to the interpreting observer. And yet conversely the decision to crush the cubes together across the corners is decidedly provocative, as this compromises their ideal character, and adjusts them towards something like the reciprocity of monks and laity referred to above. It also means that the altar's location is in a fracture between spaces rather than at the centre of a space. Similarly, the diagonal emphasis suppresses the claims to ideal form, and turns the scheme into a single ambiguous reference to rectilinearity (and therefore propitious for the implicit rooms generated by shadow and light patterns whose role in subverting the geometry is outlined below). The cuts into the cubes for Mary's niche and the entry further compromise this ideal by asserting the claim of earth and of other places, while also supporting the implicit rooms of shadow and light. The diffuse, indirect lighting, however, suppresses the ideal in a different way – it suppresses all clarity of form and turns it into ambiguous locations of walls and ceiling while, because its source is natural, retaining the solar sequence of the day and seasons. And because this method of lighting also involves a separation of walls and ceilings, it begins to suggest a helpful dissolution of the cubes into separated planes.

The drama of light and the drama of the diagonal

Beyond this explicit fracturing and dismemberment of the double cube, light counterpoints the single-mindedness of the diagonal geometry in other ways.

First of all, there is the unusual topography of light and shadows referred to above, that in qualifying the geometry through the generation of

2.14
View across the nave
looking east. The window
to the Chapel of the Holy
Sacrament reveals the
golden illumination within
that heightens the whiteness
of the main church.

implicit rooms serves to make other readings of the space possible. Thus the nave may be experienced as a tent-like pavilion between two brightly lit 'exteriors', its transformation into a shelter defined by walls and a ceiling in shadow locating it between Mary's radiance at low level and the chancel's upper light of heaven (Fig. 2.21). The effect of this light distribution on the performance of the liturgy when a weekday lay congregation is in attendance[25] is interesting. On these occasions visitors naturally tend to occupy the benches beside the back walls of the nave from where the monks can most clearly be seen and where the light is strongest. Within the volume of the double cube the play of light across the end walls to north and south defines the space in which monks and congregation gather together. A wide space in which monks and visitors stand about 20 m apart, contained by the low dark horizon already described and the unorthodox walls at an angle to the orientation, separates and yet unites the group. In this setting the essential action of the liturgical drama is played out in the stronger light at the southern and northern ends of the church, the light supporting the act of worship by scaling the stage on which it is performed.

Secondly, as the following description of the entry sequence into the building indicates, the way in which light and enclosure are handled supports a persistent landscape metaphor that makes the church the endpoint of a journey away from the city toward the horizon, from within which it has been sculpted as a cave. It is the wandering line[26] of this journey that contrasts with the rectilinearity of the diagonal axis; the elaborate, decidedly not-a-cube intra-uterine entrance sequence an obvious counterpoint to the scheme's equilibration of axes. Other aspects of the design help to ensure that the intangible whiteness of the interior is tethered and brought into communication with the everyday. On the one hand a series of low walls, simple benches, choir-stalls and steps, drawn together by the polished grey concrete of the floor, ground the space within a

2.15
View south towards the altar
along the diagonal axis of
the nave.

2.16
View across the nave looking
west.

2.17
Beside the main entrance
door a roof-light provides
stronger, more directional
light. A window above the
door allows a glimpse out
from the nave towards
neighbouring trees.

darker head-height horizon.[27] On the other, three openings to the exterior and one
to the interior qualify its detached 'otherness', subverting the building's radical
interiority as they locate the building in its site. And so when standing beside
Mary's niche, for example, the abstract vision of light presented by the view of
the chancel from here may be exchanged for long views across the landscape
from the adjacent windows. From the same spot, but looking north-westwards
across the ceiling of the narthex, a view through a window above the entrance
reveals the verdant greenery of the trees outside.

As Guarda and Correa confirm, light is used to give the building's spatial sequence a definite hierarchy, a third aspect of the design which undermines
the single-minded geometry. In a series of carefully designed thresholds the
darker lower narthex naturally leads the eye into the higher brighter nave, and
from here a view opens towards the still higher and brighter chancel (Figs. 2.13,
2.15). In other words, from the harsh light of the exterior to the more controlled
interior, the journey is structured by instituting darkness at the beginning of
the sequence, and carefully releasing the visitor to greater openness and light.
Furthermore, Guarda and Correa realize this is not simply a matter of increasing
light levels along the route to the altar. Patterns of light distribution are carefully
handled to direct movement and heighten anticipation, so that subtle changes
in light quality can allow the more explicit drama of shadow and light at the start
to be succeeded by the more quietly lit space of the nave.

2.18
View towards Mary's niche
from the east side of the
nave.

And yet from the perspective of the monks such a lighting scheme does have its drawbacks. Sitting opposite the church's only large window, they are confronted and isolated by light: direct sunshine from the north that gives the chancel its strong light, but whose brightness contrasts strongly with the darker nave below (Figs. 2.19, 2.20). Unlike their lay visitors, looking across the nave is an uncomfortable experience for them.[28] It seems worth asking at this point whether these are acknowledged or unforeseen shortcomings of the design. Both the need to articulate monastic enclosure, and the fact that the nave's subordinate status is compounded by this aspect of the design (it was felt its emptiness on weekdays might otherwise be a source of distraction[29]) imply that the isolation effect is deliberate. Yet given the scale of the model it would probably not have been possible to locate the eye in the correct place to realistically assess this view. When asked to identify lighting issues that emerged following construction, Correa refers to these difficulties, confirming that the impact of the north facing window on the monks' view of the interior had not been foreseen: 'Here there is an excess of light, and so much so that you lose the interiority of the space, the subtleties of shadow.'[30] White curtains which filter the sunlight currently mitigate the problem, though Correa acknowledges their inappropriateness in the austere, otherwise bare interior. It is likely that if the glazing of the offending window was tinted or fritted the situation would be much improved.

Sunlight and the desert

This church evokes the desert, not only thanks to a romantic and superficial resemblance (a figurative representation of some of its elements), but in order to achieve a purifying effect on our soul.

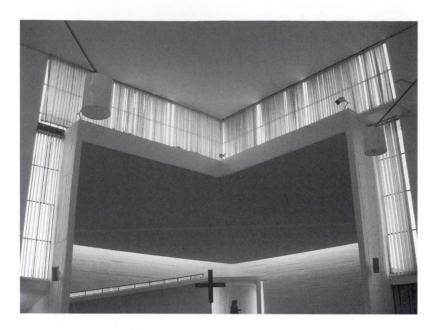

We desired to reproduce its silence, its simplicity, its nakedness, its vastness, its asceticism – in a word: its atmosphere …

This is the reason for the large white cubes, the sharp edges, the rough walls. That is why we have closed the exterior, and turned towards the interior.[31]

With its raw materiality and sophisticated modelling of space, the church has an extra-ordinary spatiality generated by extra-ordinary light. As this quote indicates, its authors explain this distillation to essentials as a quest to evoke the first home of the monks, the desert.[32] From this perspective they are using light to bring the desert to life. Material severity (restricted use of colour, roughness of wall texture, basic detailing, the use of just one construction material) and spatial emptiness are animated by a richly complex play of light and shadow. By 'transforming the rough walls into fountains of light',[33] it is as if they see themselves as fulfilling the monastic desire to create a vision of paradise from an arid desert. In fact the desert motif (Exodus, Deut. 32:10, Isa. 42:11, Joel 2:22, Matt. 4:1-11, Mark 1:12-13, Luke 4:1-13) is not inconsistent with techniques employed previously to re-establish architectural authenticity: the empty stage of early twentieth-century avant-garde theatre design[34] (Appia, Craig, Pirandello, Brecht); formalism (the regular need to resort to the terminology of axes, diagonal, form, cubes, space); and a highly ambiguous material spirituality (intimations of infinity, unclear horizons, direct communication between individual experience/ psychology and abstract space, matter turned into light) that were typical from early modernism onwards, through Le Corbusier and Kahn, to the Abstract Expressionist painters like Rothko. Given the building's similarity to the 'white box' characteristic of the modern museum, it would seem that there are two deserts (both metaphoric). The first is the inability to take anything for granted,

2.20
The monks' view of the altar
and the nave beyond.

except floor and altar. The second is the Christian one. The first is epistemological, the second moral. The first is an experience of doubt, the second an object of choice (deriving from Jesus' successful resistance to temptation). Like Le Corbusier and most of their contemporaries, Guarda and Correa are seeking to reconstruct liturgical space from the ground up. But in fact they do not reinvent it; rather they seek to further purify modernist space, to avoid becoming caught up in its commercialism and casual 'style'. In this sense, the chapel seeks to resist history, seeks to be a moment of stillness in a noisy, ever-changing world, as do certain works of Kahn and Le Corbusier. It is in this sense that the church is a silent desert of natural light asked to confront a noisy desert of artificial light, at the same time a refuge from fiercely strong sunlight (like every Chilean building) and a refuge from the city.

Between the perils of nostalgia – and of revolution – the dilemmas of rethinking liturgical space are well illustrated by the alternative interpretations to be found for the church's unorthodox north–south orientation. As the expression of an ideal orientation that separates the building from traditional churches, it launches the worshipper into a milieu where altar and cross are the only indication of the nature of the setting. Within this disposition, the decision to introduce a large north-facing aperture (even if, on completion, it was discovered to be too large) means that the strongest light is coming from a solar, not a Christian source. The consequences of this approach can be summarized as follows. Intentionally or otherwise, all efforts following the decision to employ cubes were designed to compromise them as cubes. They are there as references only, and in the last instance. In the final building the encounter is primarily with wall surfaces which are rendered in shadow-light that moves with the day,

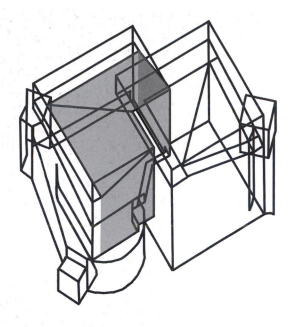

2.21
Diagram of the implicit space created by indirect light in the nave. The pattern of shadow and light implies that the nave is a dark pavilion set within brighter exterior spaces at the northern and southern ends of the building, after the drawing of the project published in F. Perez O. *et al.*, *Iglesias de la Modernidad en Chile* (1997), p. 186.

and have their brightest moment just before noon. It seems that this might help the monks think of their services in terms of different kinds/times of light but it also subjects the church to a temporality more redolent of history than eternity. Perhaps we are supposed to think of the worshippers as stranded, but in a situation that makes their vulnerability or finitude apparent. And yet the light imagery in the Psalms, the hymns that are sung at every service in the building and are therefore an obvious source for the building's implicit interpretation of light, suggest that another set of ideas are in play: 'God covers himself with light as with a garment' (Psalm 104), 'The entrance of God's words gives light' (Psalm 119), 'God is a sun and a shield' (Psalm 84), 'The Lord is light and salvation' (Psalm 27). In an evocation of the lighting ambitions of its designers, the words of Psalm 19 give the clearest indication of the powerful – and typically monastic – light symbolism that the building's unusual orientation and taut spatiality may be intended to celebrate:

> In them (the heavens) he has set a tent for the sun,
> which comes forth like a bridegroom leaving his chamber,
> and like a strong man runs into its course with joy,
> Its rising is from the end of the heavens,
> and its circuit to the end of them;
> and there is nothing hid from its heat.[35]

Notes

1 G. Guarda and M. Correa, as quoted in A. Mohler, ed., *The Church at Las Condes: Architecture at Rice 20*, School of Architecture Publications, Rice University, 1967, p. 16.

2 On a sunny day the illuminance at the north-east edge of the nave remains remarkably even, while the directionality of light in the middle of the nave is relatively low, indicating that the light is very diffuse.

3 Originating in the Roman Catholic church, this movement of scholarship and reform of worship has also affected many protestant and reformed churches and acted as a major influence on the ecumenical movement. See P. Hammond, ed., *Towards a Church Architecture*, The Architectural Press, 1962, chs 1–7.

4 Both the Roman Catholic directives for church building first formally set out in 1947 in a document produced by the German Liturgical Commission entitled 'Guiding principles for the design of churches according to the spirit of the Roman Liturgy' and the later 1957 'Diocesan church building directives' issued by the Bishop of Superior, Wisconsin, pay little attention to lighting issues. The two concerns they share are that the altar should be placed where the light is strongest, and that windows on the sanctuary's back wall should not be a cause of distracting glare. See Hammond, *Towards a Church Architecture*, pp. 246–262.

5 F. Perez O., P. Bannen L., H. Riesco G.and P. Urrejola D., *Iglesias de la Modernidad en Chile*, Ediciones ARQ, 1997, p. 176.

6 The principal sources for this chapter are an architectural history of the monastery by the Santiago architect Patricio Gross who collaborated with Guarda and Correa on the development and construction phases of the project (P. Gross F. and E. Vial B., *El Monasterio Benedictino de Las Condes*, Ediciones Universidad de Chile, 1988); an early monograph on the building produced by Rice University, Texas (A. Mohler, ed., *The Church at Las Condes*; a description of an earlier Chilean scheme in which light was a central concern, the Los Pajaritos Chapel project (A. Cruz C., 'Proyecto para una capilla en el fundo Pajaritos', *Anales de la UCV*, 1, 1954, pp. 219–234. Available online at http://www.ead.pucv.cl/1954/proyecto-pajaritos/); light monitoring studies carried out on site in October 2006; and a personal interview with Brother Martin Correa (M. Correa, personal interview, 2006).

7 Alberto Cruz, José Vial and Arturo Baeza together developed an ambitious scheme which restated the cloister walk as a linear path connecting existing and new volumes laid out zigzag fashion across the slope. See F. Perez O. *et al.*, *Iglesias de la Modernidad en Chile*, p. 177.

8 M. Correa, personal interview, 2006.

9 Ibid.

10 Ibid.

11 This was confirmed by Correa in October 2006.

12 A. Cruz C., 'Proyecto para una capilla en el fundo Pajaritos', pp. 219–234.

13 Ibid.

14 Ibid.

15 Ibid.

16 'I arrived at the minor dimensions that told me that amplitude in which the eye sees the space, the luminous reflected penumbra' (ibid).

17 P. Gross and E. Vial B., *El Monasterio Benedictino de Las Condes*, p. 120.

18 Ibid.

19 M. Correa, personal interview 2006.

20 Ibid.

21 Once money was available in the mid-1960s the statue was specially commissioned for this location from Francisco Gacitúa and Marta Colvin. Previously a 'Madonna del saco', a Madonna constructed by Correa from sacking had occupied the niche (ibid.).

22 Correa says of the curved wall that helps to create this corner, 'This curve is a trick, a fault. It makes sure that the source of light behind the wall is hidden from view. As an idea it makes me uneasy, but it looks right' (ibid.).

23 Though the use of natural light is a major theme in previous discussions of the building, only one direct and very brief reference to the Christian interpretation of light in a comment by Guarda and Correa on the significance of the changing pattern of sunlight penetration is quoted in the existing architectural analysis. In it they note the capacity of sunlight variation to give 'the liturgical cycles their full existential meaning'. See A. Mohler, ed., *The Church at Las Condes*, caption to cover image, back of front cover.

24 See further on these themes D. Vesely, *Architecture in the Age of Divided Representation*, MIT Press, 2004, p. 113ff., and Edgar de Bruyne, *Etudes d'esthetique medievale*, Livre IV, Lonrai, 1998, ch. 1.

25 At this relatively isolated church large congregations are expected only at Sunday Mass and the major religious festivals, and while the nave of the church is frequently empty for other weekday services, smaller numbers regularly attend Vespers in the evening.

26 F. Perez O. *et al.*, *Iglesias de la Modernidad en Chile*, pp. 179–180.

27 The horizons of sitting and standing relate to the height dimensions of the altar on the upper-floor level of presbytery. The upper surface of the altar table is at eye height for those standing in the nave, i.e. the same height as the low horizon to the north-east and north-west of the nave. The lower horizontal surface of the altar table/top edge of the ambo/pulpit is at eye height for those sitting in the nave, i.e. they sit within the lower horizon of the room.

28 Attention was also paid to the visual structure of the monk's view of the rear walls of the nave, but as Correa acknowledges, seeing into a more shadowy world in this context is difficult (M. Correa, personal interview, 2006).

29 P. Gross F. and E. Vial B., *El Monasterio Benedictino de Las Condes*, p. 108.

30 In Correa's opinion sun patches at the back of the nave can constitute additional sources of distraction for the monks, as can the light in the Chapel of the Holy Sacrament that becomes overpoweringly yellow during the afternoon. They could also both be addressed by changing the specification of glazing in the relevant apertures (M. Correa, personal interview, 2006).

31 G. Guarda and M. Correa, as quoted in A. Mohler, ed., *The Church at Las Condes*, p. 15.

32 In order to avoid temptation and escape persecution, early fourth-century monks sought out a place apart, an austere place of contemplation and renewal where they felt it was possible to be closer to God. In later centuries monastic renunciation of the world retained its primary significance but was more commonly expressed via the enclosure of the monastic community.

33 See Note 1.

34 See M. Esslin, 'Modern Theatre' and C. Innes, 'Theatre after Two World Wars', in J. Brown, ed., *The Oxford Illustrated History of Theatre*, OUP, 1995, pp. 431–444.

35 H.G. May and B.M. Metzger, eds, *The New Oxford Annotated Bible with the Apocrypha, Revised Standard Version*, OUP, 1973, p. 668.

Chapter 3

Deciding the colouring of things

Scarpa's Fondazione Querini Stampalia, Venice

What I want to say is that the sense of space is not communicated by a pictorial order but always by physical phenomena, that is by matter, by the sense of mass, the weight of the wall. That is why I assert that it is the apertures, openings and orifices that create spatial relationships. Modern architecture, abstractly stereometric, destroys all sensitivity to framework and de-composition ... we have created a void around things ... to achieve anything we have to invent relationships. But someone might tell me: "See? Decoration doesn't matter after all!". And yet I say there comes a moment when you have to decide the colouring of things ...[1]

Carlo Scarpa is perhaps most famous for his obsession with detailing, a close attention to every element, every junction, every surface of his projects. And yet what one is struck by on encountering the work are the demands on the eye – and hand – made by his carefully choreographed episodes, the unusually nuanced room-scale and building-scale theatre they frame. Here the experiential consequences of his reworking of an existing Venetian institution, the Fondazione Querini Stampalia, are given close consideration in a chapter which focuses on the close reciprocity between architectural strategy and detailed construction that Scarpa's approach to design represents. By identifying the themes and aspirations that inform its quiet yet visually arresting *mise-en-scène* it aims to show the degree to which Scarpa has a special sympathy for the local lightscape, an awareness of the charged encounters that buildings can stage through a re-narration of the light that is already there. At its close the consequences of this new construction of place, architecture considered as lightscape in intimate dialogue with a context rather than dramatically lit modernist form imposed on a rural or urban backdrop, will be briefly assessed.

Light and life
Although a charismatic teacher at the Venice School of Architecture for many years, writing about his work did not come easily to Scarpa. It should therefore

come as no surprise that he never composed a design manifesto of any kind. Instead his teaching emphasized thinking through drawing, and working through design ideas at a range of scales simultaneously. Just as importantly he encouraged his students to interrogate the architecture with which they were familiar, to become alert to the pragmatic visual lessons provided by buildings and landscapes that had stood the test of time.[2] And yet it is curious that despite a concern for the lessons of history and an obvious interest in framing a dialogue with the past, he hesitated to clarify such ambitions in interviews and lectures. When given the opportunity, and this is worth emphasizing, Scarpa chose instead to characterize the act of building as akin to 'furnishing', explaining that the architect's primary task is to decide 'the colouring of things'. In underlining the significance light plays in structuring spatial settings, and the architect's role in deciding such issues, he put forward the idea that the architect acts more like a theatre or film director than a product designer, and that architecture is more about reshaping and re-narrating territory than imposing form. Those who heard him lecture reinforce this point, emphasizing that light was a subject with which he could hold audiences in thrall, whether evoking a specific light quality or analysing how daylight might be tempered for a particular purpose.[3]

Equally significant is the fact that Scarpa frequently chose to describe his primary ambitions in terms of light. As his lecture on the strategy of his 1957 Canova Sculpture Gallery at Possagno indicates, his aim with this project

was 'to frame the blue of the sky'[4] in a way which would allow him to structure complex spatial relationships within an almost all-white world. In underlining the range of experiential issues that the design needed to address, the lecture remains an excellent illustration of the complex thinking that lay behind the subtle orchestration of light, space and movement he saw as his *métier*.

Venetian light

Before discussing Scarpa's work at the Fondazione Querini Stampalia a few words on Venetian light are in order. When viewed from across the lagoon, many writers have described the mirage-like appearance of the city: an insubstantial citadel hovering on the horizon between barely interrupted expanses of sea and sky. From its many quaysides on the other hand, constantly evolving interactions of light and water ensure the city never looks quite the same from one moment to the next. And yet despite the dramatic visual spectacle its waterways provide, Venice is also a dark city. Land in such a location has always been at a premium, and as a result the Grand Canal winds its way between islands whose tall, closely spaced buildings mean that many interiors have minimal access to natural light. It should not be forgotten that in much of central Venice alleys between four-storey buildings are only 1.5m wide, and the smaller canals only 3m wide. To exacerbate this situation further few larger squares or courtyards relieve the density of the urban grain, and gardens are rare: within Venice it is shadow that predominates.

Has this unusual climate of light shaped aspects of the way life is lived in Venice? Given the natural defence provided by the city's lagoon location, it has sometimes been argued that Venetian Gothic facades are more open to daylight than is usual in northern Italy. Typically demonstrating a greater playfulness

in denoting inside and out through the inclusion of balconies and loggias, they have always offered opportunities for an unusually fluid interaction across these thresholds. Accordingly, Hills has suggested that Veronese's decision to place his scenes of feasting beneath pillared arcades which form 'interiors' that are still open on all sides to the elements, makes reference to a typically Venetian engagement with transparency.[5] What is certain is that among the Venetian nobility access to light – and the visibility of a palace facade – has always been an index of political and social status. The *piano nobile* of Venetian palaces, it should be noted, is on the second floor where light is more plentiful, rather than the first. Contemporary advertisements marketing the positive features of Venetian apartments that describe them as *luminoso*, 'bright' or *luminosissimo*, 'very bright', confirm that it is access to natural light which still dictates property values today.

A palace in Venice

In the small *campo* of Santa Maria Formosa, just a few steps from the cathedral of San Marco, lies one of the most remarkable art institutions in Venice, the Fondazione Querini Stampalia. Founded on his death in 1869 by Count Giovanni,

3.4
Venetian darkness: the alley
adjacent to the Palazzo
Querini Stampalia.

the last descendant of the Querini Stampalia dynasty, this unusual institution occupies a palace that has been in the ownership of the family for more than six hundred years. From the outset the foundation's aim has been to foster the study of the arts, and in particular the artistic culture of Venice. Thus, above a first-floor library – that Giovanni expressly stipulated should be open at all the times and days that others in the city were closed – the artwork and furniture typical of a noble Venetian family are displayed in their original setting. In contrast, below the library is an interconnected sequence of interiors and exteriors devised by Scarpa to enable the foundation to mount temporary exhibitions and accommodate conferences. Though commissioned as early as 1949, the project was only finished in 1963, during the directorship of Giuseppe Mazzariol, a firm friend and supporter of Scarpa and the author of the first detailed appraisal of the project's defining poetics.[6]

Throughout Venice ground floors are prone to flooding during the *acqua alta* (high tides) of November, so Scarpa's task was framed as the conversion of potentially damp storage space into a series of permanently dry reception rooms. He began by eliminating most of the nineteenth-century

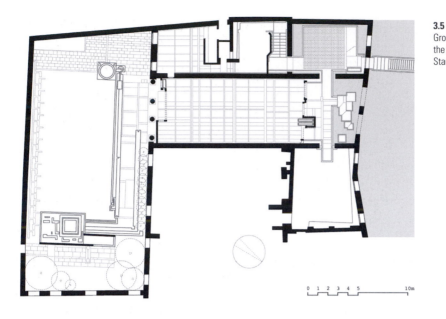

3.5
Ground-floor plan of
the Fondazione Querini
Stampalia.

0 1 2 3 4 5   10m

interior decorations and stabilizing the walls of the ground floor. This allowed
him to empty and lengthen the *portego* (the long central hall-passage[7] typical of
a Venetian palace) so that it could house the principal exhibition space. Enclosed
by glazed screens at each end that incorporate a pair of muscular radiators and
their gilded concrete housing, this room can be warmed in winter. Such a plan
reconfiguration meant that room for an exterior exhibition space and an interior
meeting area could be found in the north-west and south-east corners of the
ground floor respectively. They sit diagonally opposite one another across the
main hall. Changes were also made to the outside of the building: a new bridge
that enables direct entry into the palace from the *campo* was located at the front
of the palace, while at the rear Scarpa transformed an undistinguished courtyard into a verdant garden. How did Scarpa protect these rooms from flooding?
Counter-intuitively, the water still comes in, but only so far. His introduction of
a raised walkway linking the entry hall with the *portego* is the master stroke of

3.6
South-west–north-east
section through the garden
and main exhibition hall
of the Fondazione, after
drawings by R. Murphy
in *Querini Stampalia
Foundation, Venice 1961–63*
(1993).

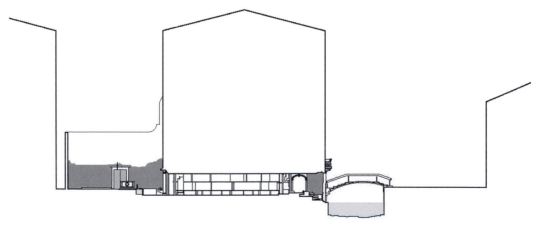

3.7
A canal of light: view of main exhibition hall looking south towards the garden in sunshine. The thread of stone/light embroidered on darkness that zigzags down the hall is very prominent in this photograph, as is the radiator beside the glazed screen between the hall and the garden.

the scheme.[8] (It is not a coincidence that he termed the walkway a *fondamentum*, a word which means both 'canal bank' and 'foundation'.) By allowing high water to enter the spaces just behind the facade, but preventing its entry into the main exhibition hall, this element transforms a climatic predicament into a source of spatial order. It enables the architecture to stage a potent alchemy of sparkle, gleam and shadow that establishes its primary theme: the emergence of order from chaos.

Strictly speaking, Scarpa's work at the Fondazione Querini Stampalia is not a restoration project. Rather, as Mazzariol has observed, through a careful meditation on the relationship between new and old it opens a dialogue with history by narrating a new passage through Venice. In his role as director of events, Scarpa choreographs movement and views along a route between the new access bridge, an existing but reworked entry hall, the *portego* and the garden, whose stages can be anticipated visually from the outset. Thus via the arched openings of the watergate an enticing glimpse of the garden – and its green lawn – is possible from the *campo*. In a typically Scarpian manner, the route followed to reach it then twists and turns, rises and falls, before arriving at a simple stone seat that borders the sea of grass.

Scarpa's assertion that his intention was 'to create a sort of luminous canal that also consecrates the spatial continuity inside the palace, putting the canal in communication with the space behind'[9] confirms that light was critical to his interlacing of themes at the Fondazione Querini Stampalia. What will be argued here is that this choice of words is not arbitrary, but a way of characterizing his intentions which shows that Scarpa saw the project as an opportunity to make sense of Venice and its history through a rewriting of its light.

The situation of light at
the north facade of the
Fondazione that looks
over the campo of Santa
Maria Formosa.

Entrance light

In Mazzariol's opinion, the new entry bridge leads the visitor into a space whose
colour and light is typically Venetian, where the elegant refinement of Scarpa's
work stands in contrast to the much rougher weaving of the existing brick walls
in the neighbouring *portego* (Figs. 3.11, 3.12). It is the first of a series of settings
in which Scarpa meditates on the specific qualities of Venetian light. Lining the
walls at ground level are a series of water channels whose flowerings of salt
record the floods that transform this interior into a 'ruin'. For a few days the floor

3.9
A palimpsest of artificial
light and natural light: view
through the watergate
into the ground floor of the
Fondazione from the *campo*
of Santa Maria Formosa.

3.10
The situation of light in the
garden at the rear of the
Fondazione.

3.10
The situation of light in the garden at the rear of the Fondazione.

becomes an island and the room a garden animated by glittering reflections. This metamorphosis is only ephemeral, but he restates the idea that Venice is a city hovering above – and by reflection – below the water in the detailing. Below, the ruffled water surface evoked by the marble tiling of the floor composes a bounded sea of light. Above, the ceiling suggests still, dark water: the deep Venetian-red polished stucco mirror turning the world upside-down to suggest watery depths extending upwards.[10]

A luminous canal

The main exhibition space occupies the garden side of the *portego* (Figs. 3.7, 3.13). Exactly how it is seen, what archetypes it evokes, are equally critical to Scarpa. Again, whether it is inside or outside is in question. While the long side walls are lined with slabs of polished travertine, and the soffit is of smooth stucco, the new floor surface is much rougher. Recalling the materials tradition-ally in use for exterior courtyards in Venice, a network of lines of polished Istrian stone threads between precast panels of rougher washed aggregate concrete. Scarpa describes this hall as a luminous canal. He gives it the walls of an honor-ific room. They are walls that allow Mazzariol to argue that Scarpa's adoption of layered construction recalls Gothic palace facades in Venice, and Dal Co to suggest that the interior of nearby Santa Maria dei Miracoli inspired Scarpa's use of travertine. In fact Scarpa's equivocation is quite deliberate. The exhibition hall is both an inner room and a public space. It is meant to be intimate, of human scale, a place of contemplation and measured conversation, and yet at the same time weighty, open to the wind and light, a place for argument. The pictures it exhibits are on the walls of the city: inside, and yet out in Venice.

3.11
The Venetian world turned upside-down. The entrance hall of the Fondazione with its dark mirror of a ceiling and choppy sea of a floor.

In a relatively shadowy interior of this kind, light reflected from shiny surfaces is more perceptible. Here the relative dimness of the space allows the wall and ceiling surfaces to gleam, and provides a foil for the network of lines in the floor and walls whose pattern evokes the vibrating shimmer of light off water. It is these polished surfaces that not only give the hall its quiet luminosity but help it to feel more spacious. Again the detailing re-narrates the light.

Composition, de-composition

In Scarpa's work continuities are made potent through discontinuities. What is light must also be heavy. What is straight must also be crooked. As Dal Co explains, although employing several of the same materials, the material character of the interior and the garden is deliberately very different. While an elusive play of light across surfaces gives a quality of lightness to the space within, it is weight and solidity that matter outside. This dialectic between continuity/discontinuity is also used to evoke the complex dance that navigating Venice requires, that between water and stone, wetness and dryness, to underline that in Venice water is both a source of light and a source of darkness, the reservoir of creative and destructive forces. To counterpoint the simple line of view between public square and private courtyard, Scarpa introduces a wandering route which demands the zigzagging movement typical of a journey on foot through Venice.

3.12
The choice of routes in the entrance hall. The principal route into the main hall is signalled by the brighter light to be seen through the portal on the left.

At right angles to the real canal outside, the *portego* creates a gleaming canal of stone that connects a bright ocean of paving with a more closely contained and intensely coloured sea of grass. Alternatively, the watery darkness of the interstitial passage that surrounds the main hall reinforces the reading that it, like Venice, is a luminous island of stone.

Broken light

Unlike at his Possagno Sculpture Gallery project, where an extreme articulation of space creates a restless discontinuity and what Holbrook terms 'the sensation of dis-enclosure',[11] here the basic calmness and gravity of a long simple hall is more subtly fractured by the scattered field of light it structures. To each side of the hall the travertine wall surfaces are divided in two by eye-height brass strips. Subverting this large-scale spatial order is a fragmentary field of broken lines of light. The artificial light sources embedded in the walls and the aforementioned lines of Istrian stone write equivalent networks of light across the room. Further strokes of light are added by the etched strips of glazing and the gilded edges of the screens at each end of the hall. The only continuous path of light meanders down the centre of the floor (a thread of stone light embroidered on darkness).

The empty room

Perhaps the most remarkable space/light in the project is the room towards which the walkway leads from the entrance (Fig. 3.15). Like the entrance hall, and the end of the *portego* adjacent to the watergate, it is actually flooded in November. Yet here, mysteriously, though the high tides recede, water is never absent. Presenting Venice as shadowy architecture on the brink of dissolution, the room, even when dry, stages flooded space. How Scarpa achieves this is not easy to explain. With its dark-green ceiling and small windows, the space is not expansive. Materials metamorphose in the low side-light, sectional relationships are imaginatively reinterpreted: the concrete floor becomes a body of water, the walkway a jetty that projects out into it. The view into the room is carefully orchestrated: looking from the entrance hall through the enfilade doorways at either side of the *portego*, one of two columns embedded in a rough brick backdrop is visible off-centre. The fact that these lines of movement and view are misaligned is quite deliberate. For Scarpa, visitors are not spectators but actors. Rather than standing outside, they must participate in the drama. Presenting Venice as a rhythmic architecture of stone hovering above the abyss, the arrangement asks them to interrogate what they see. An antithesis to the canal of light, it is a spatial sequence which sets forth dark emptiness. Venice is not only festive light. Here, in a dead end, is its shadow.

The L-shaped passage

Having underlined that Scarpa's design re-establishes the *portego* at the heart of the ground floor, it is worth emphasizing that the whole lateral passage is unorthodox with respect to Venetian palace conventions. It is an invented space, a gap in the customary expectations of arrival, penetration and ascent to the more decorous world above. This L-shaped passage has the effect of making the garden equivalent to the empty room just described, each at either end of

3.13
Main exhibition hall looking north towards the canal.

3.14
The north end of the canal
of light: the watergate
of the Fondazione in
overcast conditions.

the arms of the L that has the mosaic floor at its apex, and that frames the main hall (Figs. 3.15, 3.16). The placing of a well-head (the typical feature of a Venetian *campo*) on the arm of the L that extends to the garden also suggests that garden and *campo* are to be seen in relation to each other. The garden and empty room are experienced reciprocally – the empty room has a raised platform at the centre from which one looks outwards, the garden a higher periphery from which one looks inwards. The only explicit earth – that of the garden – is also the only place to get direct sunlight (establishing the reciprocity of earth and light which animates the whole); everywhere else is borrowed light. The apex of the L is therefore the dark corner, but it has the most luminous floor. The exhibition space is more boxed-in by glass than it is a layer in a sequence from canal to garden, though of course it is also that (wet canal–dry hall–wet garden). The floor of the exhibition room is, as it were, printed/cast from the travertine walls. As already discussed they are curiously similar to each other, even if also different. In fact the floor of the exhibition hall is the most humble of all the rooms.

Light and spatial order

What is Scarpa's *concetto* here? This study suggests that at the Fondazione there are two orders superimposed upon each other. One is 'orthogonal', and goes *campo*–canal–exhibition hall–garden–stream–garden. It is marked by the change from two-to-three openings (the two watergate openings to the three intercolumnar openings onto the garden), the suppression of lateral columnar openings, and by an ascent from canal to garden. This declares the customary movement from public life to the life of a palace. The second order is 'orbital'

3.15
The first arm of the L-shaped passage: a view through light towards the darkness of the 'empty room'.

about the exhibition room, and contemplative: it takes the other 'empty room' of the exhibition hall and declares it in terms of the key spaces of Venice, or of architectural order generally – the *campo*, the empty room with embedded columns (a potential or lost building), the garden. These are presented as 'pictures' meant to be understood from the apex of the L, the special room with luminous floor that one accesses from the bridge (the steps from the canal are more thematic than practical). That is, one leaves the density of practical life, crosses the water, and arrives on the skywater mosaic, at the vanishing point of echoes of that practical life and its settings. The orbital order gives the conditions for the contemplation of Venice's potential creativity ('art'). All this takes place in the darkness of the *sottoportego*,[12] an ambiguous realm of anticipation or preparation for the more decorous life above, vulnerable to the waters, marked by sounds of barrels and boatmen and the necessities of life, that is, in the dark, moist earth of a civilization more often characterized by luminous, ephemeral effects, nobles consuming wine from Murano glassware by candlelight and indulging masked conspiracies to music from violins and harpsichords.

3.16
The second arm of the
L-shaped passage: a view
through darkness towards
the light of the garden.

3.17
Light and heat: the radiator
in its gilded column between
hall and watergate.

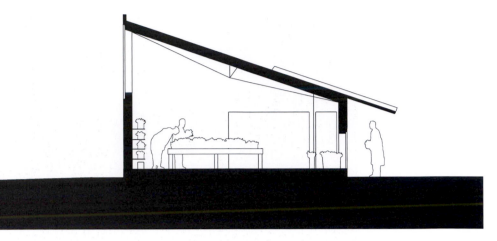

3.18
North–south section
through the 'empty room' of
Lewerentz's flower kiosk.

Light and heat

Curiously, if the scheme has a centre, it is the positively monumental radiator and its gilded columnar housing at the walkway end of the exhibition space (Fig. 3.17). A piece of equipment that reads as an interruption in the otherwise primordial setting, it is as if the concrete, gold and crystalline housing is desperately trying to pretend it is actually something like a reliquary. It could be that heat is a special experience with respect to the bitterly cold Venetian winters, and, like the lights, a mark of technical culture. This would go with the warm room character of the exhibition space. It might also be said, from a practical point of view, that the radiator is pushed across the boundary of the exhibition room in order to give a bit of heat to the passages which are otherwise 'outdoors'. There is no question the radiator has been given special prominence. It is mounted well clear of the floor as well as having been given such an elaborate housing. Perhaps Scarpa thought hot water in pipes a good thing to contrast with the cold water in canal and garden, much like the fluorescent and ceiling lighting contrasts with natural light. Or perhaps he felt it was important simply to be honest about Venice in the twentieth century. (In the 1958 showroom devoted to business machines that he designed for Olivetti in nearby St Mark's Square, a basin of water defines the threshold.) What seems likely is that amidst all the pastness/earthness of the other references, Scarpa is declaring with this radiator that the exhibition hall is a twentieth-century room, and that, by crossing the visitor's horizon of contemplation so abruptly with the plumbing, he is 'twisting' the water margins vertically, consistent with the use of water as marking passage but also consistent with technological violation of those natural conditions.

Changing attitudes to light

Whereas in the 1920s Le Corbusier speaks of composing with light, as if light is a universal medium, it appears that in the 1960s, beyond understanding design as a search for meaning through making, Scarpa sees himself as staging objects and people in a light he knows, a light whose daily and seasonal changes in character he can predict. The intentions behind the project discussed here have been closely examined, but the wider significance for architecture of a sensitivity to light

3.19
The flower kiosk at Malmö
in the early morning: in this
photograph the natural back
light is reinforced by artificial
light.

understood as the essential aspect of climate that shapes a shared way of life and its building(s) is worth airing. This issue is perhaps best explored through a comparison of the Fondazione with a 1969 project by a contemporary of Scarpa's whose career also reflected a lifelong engagement with the crafting of space and light.

During the same post-war period, Sigurd Lewerentz[13] was producing work in his native Sweden which demonstrates a comparable attunement to the local light and the role it plays in pacing spatial sequences and qualifying the relative weight and presence of different materials. Responsive to issues of visual and tactile perception, and establishing a language of construction that reflects a close familiarity with the physical and psychological weight of different components, his most famous projects of this period (St Mark's, Björkhagen, Stockholm, 1956, and St Peter's, Klippan, 1963) present closely studied assemblies of elements that generate provocative landscapes for worship in which violent chiaroscuro is deployed to articulate the situation of prayer. The ambiguous narratives of light and ground these buildings construct through their unexpected spatial and material conjunctions were pursued further in Lewerentz's final project for a flower kiosk at the Malmö cemetery,[14] a landscape for whose layout he was also responsible. This building is simple in form – a four-square concrete hut with an indented side entrance and a sweeping folded-copper roof – but with an unusual spatiality and memorable light dictated by the placement of its windows with respect to the ground, human eye level, and the sky.

A significant point of comparison between the two projects is that the primary space (the only space in the case of the kiosk) of both is a heavy casket, and that this is used as a receptacle for ephemeral things – drawings or flowers – and that therefore there is to both a reciprocity of death (or history) and resurrection (or renewal) (Figs. 3.7, 3.20). Both also recapitulate their contexts – urban Venice and rural Sweden – but in ways determined by architectural order (i.e. not literally, or through representation). The Fondazione Querini Stampalia evokes a city already a memory, and ever on the brink of collapse or

3.20
A rough casket of light:
sketch of flower kiosk
interior after an early
photograph.

drowning, while the kiosk is another masonry figure in a necropolis rendered in terms of Nordic landscape themes (romanticism/archaism). Scarpa's work is the more sophisticated (complex) of the two, but both deploy a primitivist horizon of reference so that the actual earth, for example, is not taken for granted but made thematic. For both nature is the ultimate referent, or rather a dwelling in nature that puts humans second, transient with respect to its primordial earthness and processes. This means as well that light and shadow are neither the consequence of openings, nor simply formal pattern on the walls or floors, but rather thematic as such – firstly as solar and weather cycles (temporality), then as hope, orientation. This said, the kiosk is, as it were, the ultimate reference of this kind, the horizon of dwelling on which the chromaticism and sophisticated elaboration of Scarpa's project can be developed. The closest affinity with the kiosk is actually the empty room of the Fondazione. However, the Fondazione Querini Stampalia is actually made up of three empty rooms: the one with the embedded columns, the exhibition room and the garden. It is possible that the entrance hall, with the mosaic, is a fourth – the room behind the window which grants orientation, where one pauses upon the intimations of sky/water from *cosmateschi* pavements but rendered by Scarpa as hesitating between constitution and dissolution. However this room seems to stand outside the others. It depends upon their earth rather than re-enacts it. It declares the ground as light rather than as earth, and it feeds the two transitional passages rather than being a place of arrival. On this reading, what the two projects also have in common is the motif of the empty room, and a mood that alternates between pregnant possibilities and loss.

Scarpa's reference to architecture as 'furnishing' relies on an assumption that there is a world already existing worth being furnished, and a way of doing things worth rewriting. Where modernism had prioritized invention, extolling the virtues of a brave boldly-lit and therefore best of all possible worlds, framing design as a series of problems to be solved via the rational application of technological principles given a reductive abstract dress, the basic position of Scarpa and Lewerentz is both more ambiguous and more realistic. They are less certain that such wholesale rejection of tradition is either necessary or helpful. What it is to evoke collective understandings, collective memories through the re-narrating of a shared history that makes telling reference to the past is key to their approach. Their buildings are not carefully delineated objects, but slow settings for action with deliberately reticent light. The taut spatiality of these interiors depends on a close appreciation of the relations between people, and the pacing of movement that architecture can choreograph with light, and for that very reason are not easy to photograph. They make sense because the relations they establish with their wider settings are carefully thought out and deserve more attention than modernist design principles would ever assume was necessary. Like good clothing this architecture makes it easy for its wearers to feel themselves because it acknowledges not only where they have come from, but their psychological and physical vulnerability. For Scarpa, as for Lewerentz, the world of things emerges from shadow. From their perspective light is invisible and cannot be pinned down and commodified. Essentially fugitive, appearances can only be glimpsed before they are gone.

Notes

1 C. Scarpa, 'Furnishings', an address whose text is published in F. Dal Co and G. Mazzariol, eds, *Carlo Scarpa, The Complete Works*, Electa/The Architectural Press, London, 1986, p. 282.

2 'History to him, as to Muzio (despite the great gap between the two generations), was a story put together day by day, by looking and examining and remembering, linking together two, three, or a dozen memories of different kinds and trying to find points of contact and deviation, explaining both the former and the latter in light of the relations which this approach or that particular resolution had with the place, the problem or the moment' (L. Quaroni, 'Scarpa's "lessons"', in F. Dal Co and G. Mazzariol, eds, *Carlo Scarpa*, p. 255).

3 'As a lecturer he made a deep impression on me and I shall never forget his account of how he solved the problem of displaying the Syracuse *Annunciation* at the exhibition of paintings by Antonella da Messina. Scarpa explained that this painting was so fragmented that the surviving pieces tended to be viewed separately from one another. Harsh lighting would have produced an undesirable clinical effect, making viewing like an autopsy. The light filtering through the drapery screening the window in the exhibition hall was a pitiless white, showing up the shreds of that glorious painting and making it harder to respond to the cold tones of the landscape and the severe construction of the interior. Weaving his hand about as if to make us feel the impalpable lightness of a drapery, the lecturer described how he had gone out to a haberdasher's and bought a nylon underskirt, very lightly tinted. This he set, at a suitable distance, between the exterior light and the window drapery, so that the light was mellowed without being dimmed' (C. Bertelli, *Light and Design*, in F. Dal Co and G. Mazzariol, eds., *Carlo Scarpa*, p. 191).

4 See detailed discussion of this project in D. Hawkes, *The Environmental Imagination*, Taylor & Francis, London, 2008, pp. 111–128.

5 See P. Hills, *Venetian Colour: Marble, Mosaic and Glass, 1250–1550*, Yale University Press, New Haven and London, 1999.

6 G. Mazzariol, 'Un opera di Carlo Scarpa:il riordino di un antico palazzo Veneziano', in *Zodiac*, no. 13, pp. 26–59.

7 Traditionally the ground-floor hall (termed by Mazzariol a *portego,* but strictly speaking an *androne*) staged the honorific entrance sequence of a Venetian palace. A passage that connected the public space of the canal to the private world of the palace interior, it led from the watergate towards an inner courtyard. From here visitors would have ascended an outside stair to the living quarters above.

8 'One morning in 61 at the Querini, when I was insisting that the high water remain outside the entrance of the palace where the library is housed, Scarpa, after a moment's pause, and looking me straight in the eyes, replied to my pressing request: "The high water will be deep inside – inside, as in the rest of the city. It can only be dealt with by containing it, by governing it, by using it as a luminous reflective material: you will see the plays of light on the yellow and violet stucco of the ceilings. A miracle!"' (G. Mazzariol, as quoted in G. Busetto, 'Carlo Scarpa alla Querini Stampalia: ieri, oggi, domani', in M. Mazza, ed., *Carlo Scarpa alla Querini Stampalia. Disegni inediti*, Il Cardo Editore, Venezia, 1996, pp. 9–20, p. 14.

9 C. Scarpa as quoted by F. Dal Co in F. Dal Co and S. Polano, *Carlo Scarpa: La Fondazione Querini Stampalia a Venezia*, Electa, Milan, 2006, p. 28.

10 When interviewed in 1990, Eugenio De Luigi, the artisan responsible for the plasterwork at the Fondazione, noted that Scarpa was deliberately trying to reverse the traditional sense of wall, ceiling and floor in this room by making the ceiling darker and the walls lighter. See E. Soroka, 'Restauro in Venezia', *Journal of Architectural Education*, vol. 47, no. 4, pp. 224–241, p. 241 n. 47.

11 T. Holbrook, 'Palimpsest and the Theme of Exile: Discontinuity in Scarpa', unpublished diploma dissertation, University of Cambridge, 1993, p. 19.

12 The Venetian term *sottoportego* refers to an alley that passes under a building, literally 'under the *portego*', and thus to a dark narrow passageway.

13 Originally trained as a mechanical engineer, Lewerentz founded his own architectural practice in Stockholm in 1911 following a period of apprenticeship in Germany. Heavily involved with the design of crematoria initially, he subsequently became disillusioned with practice. Turning his energies instead to the design and manufacture of modern building components, he set up his own factory in 1940 and chose to abandon architectural practice altogether for a number of years. After this hiatus it was not until the mid-1950s that he revived his professional career to produce the post-war projects for which he is now most famous.

14 See A. Worn, 'Communicative Construction: Sigurd Lewerentz's Flower Kiosk', unpublished third-year dissertation, University of Cambridge, 2004, for a thoughtful in-depth analysis of the themes of this project.

Chapter 4

Reading light at Seinajoki, Finland, and Viana do Castelo, Portugal

Aalto's and Siza's conspicuous conservation of daylight

One thing that upsets me terribly in architecture is waste, apparent even in the use of light.[1]

At first sight the public libraries of Seinajoki and Viana do Castelo are similar: white buildings of relatively simple form sited in park landscapes that from the outside give little away of their internal logic. For those who use them it is another matter. Although of a similar material palette, where the former has a reading room of almost complete introspection, the latter has a series of compartmented spaces sliced by views. At Seinajoki a connection to the surroundings is denied, and only glimpses of the sky are visible from the interior. Instead a cloud of light hovers above the books, an exuberant section helping to define an introverted space buoyed by light in which users are drawn to glance upwards when not immersed in reading. Here a complex play of light and shadow at high level is the counterpoint to an otherwise calm retreat from the world outside. At Viana do Castelo on the other hand, contrasting views to either side offer visual release to readers hard at work in a train carriage of bookstacks, and users lose themselves in reading between hill and water, town and sea.

These projects appear to represent very different ideas about the kind of visual setting a public library should provide. Alvar Aalto, the author of the 1963 Seinajoki building, places readers below a churning abstract sky, removing them from their everyday environment, whereas Siza, the designer of the 2008 building at Viana do Castelo, exposes them to a series of fragmentary views of the neighbouring topography which explicitly locate them above the everyday fray of the town. And yet Siza himself, when asked about his influences has particularly emphasized his debt to Aalto, underlining their shared willingness

4.1
Situating reading. Sitting
side-on to a window gives
good daylight for the visually
demanding task of reading
but some may consider the
view too distracting.

to act as 'agents of cross fertilization'[2] in the pursuit of design solutions responsive to place and climate.

    In a questioning of the 'circumstances' that matter to design, what
this chapter aims to explore is the extent to which Siza and Aalto share a philosophy of light, whatever the differences in outlook these projects might seem
to represent. To this end a detailed review of the thinking behind these designs
explores how decisions about daylight and its distribution are integrated with
other spatial intentions, and with the perspective of the users who need to navigate the building – to find information and read it – uppermost in mind. In the
process the impacts of both geography – the climate of light that shapes how
particular settings are experienced by users – and history – the traditions that
shape users' expectations of library spaces – are examined.

    With this in mind, what is good reading light, and what particular
lighting issues the situation of private reading in a public space raises deserve
discussion. Because access to enough light is now never in doubt whatever the
location, how architecture can create suitable light for reading might appear to
be an open question. How complex a question it is, and the extent to which it
involves a broad appreciation of how people respond to and interact with the
buildings they occupy is perhaps not immediately obvious. The phrase 'good
reading light' conjures images of a reader near a window, book to hand, with the
page in question turned to the light. What the phrase and the image would seem
to suggest is that what is critical to reading is enough light from the right direction
so that the fine detail of a text is intelligible and the page is sufficiently bright to
be the reader's natural focus. It implies that the relationship of the reader to the
light, the book and the room is important, i.e. that good conditions for reading
are a matter of spatial geometry as well as sufficient illumination.

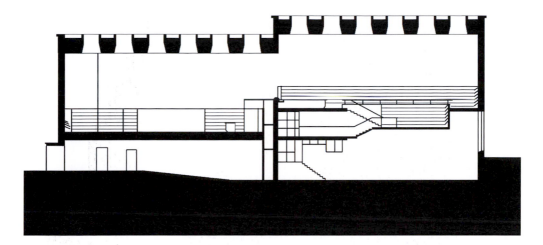

4.2
South-west–north-east
section through Viipuri
Library showing central entry
stair and windowless walls.

In older library buildings – where daylight is the principal source of task-light – the overall arrangement is clearly informed by such thinking. Typically the distribution of light shapes both the section and the plan in order to ensure that readers are located and oriented to make the most of the natural light. Since artificial light has become available, however, libraries of larger size, deeper plan and longer opening times have become possible, now that task-light can be readily supplied via desk lamps. While such light sources have the added benefit of not only giving readers control over their local environment, but helping them define their own private territory, the downsides of this innovation in lighting, for this building type and others, are often ignored. The very fact that turning on a light is so easy and so relatively cheap in economic terms means it can be argued that the very availability of artificial light has prompted and continues to prompt its conspicuous consumption. Throughout the developed world having all the lights on has now come to signal the 'openness' of public buildings to such a degree that even buildings designed to be daylit are artificially lit throughout the day, whatever the conditions outside. In turn many people have come to imagine that more light is always better light. Such profligacy has obvious downsides as far as energy consumption is concerned but arguably it also makes for more impoverished, less diverse interior conditions. This is because the ubiquitous use of artificial light not only mitigates the vitality that natural light variation brings but obscures its critical orienting role.

With their emphasis on minimum requirements, it is clear the way lighting standards are presently defined does not help. They assume that light can always be made available, confirming and fostering a carelessness with it. Moreover the very fact that the standard metric criteria for daylight (e.g. lux levels, daylight factors, brightness ratios, glare index, etc.) provide only a very narrow functional definition of the luminous environment, and one that can be met with significantly different qualitative effects, means that translating this guidance into daylighting principles is anything but straightforward.

Are there alternative perspectives that might help us to see – and use – natural light differently? Unusually the libraries at Seinajoki and Viana do Castelo *were designed to be* predominantly daylit, i.e. their intelligent responsiveness to

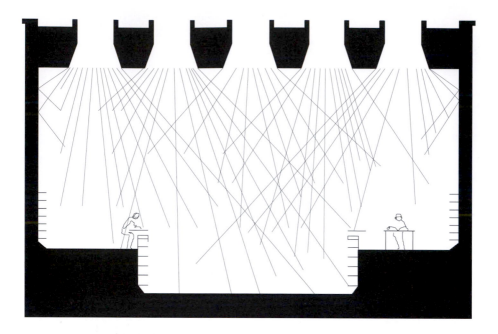

4.3
Rational reading light.
The conical roof-lights at
Viipuri Library that produce
even, shadowless light for
focused reading, after a
sketch by Aalto.

the local visual environment means that few artificial light sources are required during the day – even if these lights are now always in use, largely for the reasons already explained (and as many of the photographs of the Siza library indicate). What these projects may therefore be able to illustrate is what deploying natural light sensitively involves. This study began as a quest to explain Aalto's daylighting legacy for Siza but it has become more than that. In its exploration of a common concern to make the shaping of the visual environment a source of spatial order, it begins to suggest why Aalto and Siza's close observation of the relationship between the reader and his/her wider environment prompts their reliance on the sparing use of daylight. More than just an account of historical influence, what it aims to demonstrate is that their successful treatment of light as a 'precious' resource has wider implications for lighting design guidance and the way it is currently framed.

Lighting public libraries

As an index of the cultural life of a community, a repository of knowledge and collective information resource, the civic statement that a new public library represents has often been the focus of architectural analysis in recent years, as for example was the case with Alsop's 2000 Peckham Library, London. In these discussions what such a building looks like seems to matter more than whether its users find it an appropriate setting for study. And yet how such buildings perform in visual terms remains an important subject because their basic purpose – the storage of books and other media, and the provision of settings in which to read or view them – means that how space is organized with respect to light is always critical.

If such a building is to be predominantly daylit the potential access to natural light is obviously a critical issue. The long history of libraries as daylit

4.4
Romantic reading light.
*Wanderer above a Sea
of Fog*, by Caspar David
Friedrich, 1818. © Hamburg
Kunsthalle.

spaces offers many useful lessons on daylighting principles, and can clarify the site conditions, relative size and value of book collection and readership, for which a particular daylighting strategy is suitable. As this history illustrates, side-lights, clerestory lights and roof-lights, alone or in combination, help to shape the mood of a library setting and dictate what choice of location and view, what degrees of intimacy or publicity, are available to readers. Likewise it demonstrates how structuring daylight intelligently can improve navigability in a building type which often tends to the labyrinthine.

Is it possible to say what good library light should be like? The fact that people have different opinions on the ideal public setting for reading (especially in relation to the availability of intimacy or view) suggests that framing daylighting needs from the perspective of users is no easy task. It can be clarified, however, by returning to first principles and reviewing the different visual tasks – and kinds of seeing – that this light needs to foster:

1 Casual seeing in order to navigate space or communicate with others.
2 Concentrated seeing – seeing and thinking, reading, discriminating fine detail (need for few distractions, desire to define visual territory).
3 Looking but not seeing (daydreaming, inwardly reflecting).
4 Looking to find something: scanning the visual field and then locating an object within it (browsing).

To locate what they are looking for readers must scan a catalogue or the book-shelves (1, 4). In order to immerse themselves in reading they need to create

4.5
A grand precedent for the
Seinajoki Library lighting
strategy. Main reading room
of Asplund's 1928 Public
Library Stockholm. Source:
Holger Ellgaard.

a situation where they are more 'with the words' and less 'with the room', i.e. 'lost in the book' (2). In this situation a sort of 'withdrawal' from the immediate environment takes place in order to achieve visual and mental focus. When this concentration becomes tiring the kind of visual relief offered by more casual 'seeing into the distance' (3) can be helpful. Arguably, the aim of a library day-lighting strategy should therefore be to provide appropriate light for all these activities (enough light of the right quality), a range of spatial settings (a series of appropriately lit spaces and surfaces) that allow users to navigate the building and find their own seat – whether in a more intimate setting or larger room – and an overall ambience that allows for browsing while fostering concentration. What is worth emphasizing here is that devising such a strategy involves careful thinking about not only the amount and quality of light that arrives on the page, but also the way that light potentially structures and qualifies spatial experience for a transient population of readers, some of whom will be seated and some of whom in movement. From the individual reader's point of view it is for these reasons that light is a potentially critical factor in modulating the occupation patterns and, critically, the sense of locatedness, which assist private reading – and its other 'seeing', comprehension – in a public room.

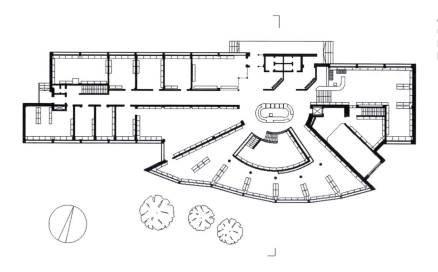

4.6
Ground plan Seinajoki
Library, after drawing
by Aalto.

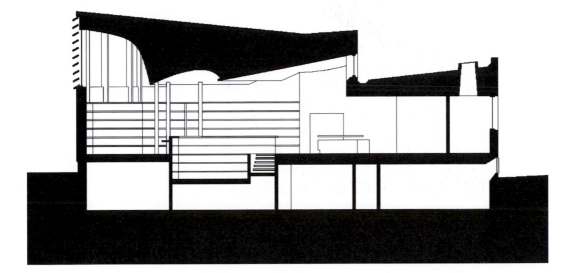

4.7
South–north section through
Seinajoki Library, after
drawing by Aalto.

Finally some reflections on library history are necessary. Apart from being places for study, libraries have always acted as depositories of the written historical record of knowledge, coming to symbolize learning over the centuries. In housing this record, and especially from the fifteenth century onwards, they have been expected to define a way of being with knowledge to which indirect daylight has been indispensable. In the seventeenth century, the golden age of library construction in central Europe, the books, their shelves and their access galleries structured the undulating walls of a vaulted chamber which promised to act as 'the soul's apothecary'. Views outwards via windows at floor and/or gallery level were possible from such rooms, but they were not the focus of movement or gaze on entry. Instead the books themselves were intimately united with the architecture to create an exquisite and self-contained casket of knowledge whose reading room borrowed from the church, uniting actual light with the divine light of theological wisdom (for example, St Gallen Monastery Library, Ottobeuren Monastery Library).

Public libraries on the other hand are a relatively recent phenomenon. Over the course of the nineteenth century and the first couple of decades of the twentieth, architects and librarians across Britain and the United States struggled to agree on how to make books and journals available to the public in municipal buildings whose decorum, navigability, and visibility were all a concern. The emergence of a building type whose interiors owe more to shop design and grand domestic precedents than to the archetypal monastic libraries of a previous era underlines the emerging shift in understanding about the primary aims of library architecture.[3] Whereas Labrouste's 'Renaissance' 1851 Bibliothèque Sainte Geneviève in Paris was one of the final libraries where readers were collected within (and dwarfed by) an authoritatively ordered wall of books, Koolhaas's 2004 Seattle Library, and Adjaye's 2005 Ideas Store in Tower Hamlets, London, represent the other end of the spectrum – the library as a café/meeting place with information resource attached, whose deliberately non-conformist and 'noisy' openness aims to generate community participation.

4.8
Northern entrance facade of
Seinajoki Library.

4.9
Central reading well. This
intimate refuge for reading
can 'see' enough of both the
north and south clerestories
to be adequately daylit,
while the height of the latter
means they are out of a
reader's line of view.

4.10
Librarian's view towards southern edge of main space in overcast conditions. At the centre of the room the ceiling is somewhat lower and perpetually in shadow, acting to shield library staff at the control desk from a view of the bright clerestorey.

Aalto's light

> The main problem connected with a library is that of the human eye … A library … is not humanly and architecturally complete unless it deals satisfactorily with the main human function in the building, that of reading a book …[4]

As Moore[5] and Millett[6] have emphasized, for Aalto library design begins with light. More than for any of his modernist contemporaries, they argue that light is a primary ambition, a primary design catalyst, but that this is less to do with the appearance of the building or the spectacle of light as an end in itself, and much more to do with the character of light the building shapes for users. In Aalto's mind a building is essentially a vehicle for light. In an environment where winters are cold and daylight is sometimes scarce, how architecture can provide an appropriate degree of shelter while making the most of the daylight available *to accommodate particular activities* is his key concern. What this means for his public libraries is that he gives explicit attention to how form, material and spatial sequence – at this latitude, and in this light climate – will together achieve a specific quality of light for reading.

In each of the public libraries he designed at Viipuri (1935) (Figs. 4.2, 4.3), Wolfsburg (1962), Seinajoki (1963) and Rovanniemi (1968), a room without a view is grounded by a kind of step well of books that is evenly daylit from above. White plaster surfaces (of deep roof-lights, or the walls and ceilings adjacent to clerestory windows) are deployed as indirect sources of daylight, exploiting the fact that in the overcast conditions predominating in northern winters, the sky is brighter at the zenith than the horizon. Sunlight is only allowed to enter directly, if at all, in winter, when it cannot cause overheating, and the section adjusted

4.11
Reading bays adjacent to
south wall of main space in
overcast conditions. Sadly,
additional bookstacks that
Aalto did not envisage now
make this area feel more
cramped than he intended.

so it does not reach desks and issues with glare can be minimized. This means
every reader can be given the shadowless light Aalto considers conducive to
visual concentration on a text.[7]

Intriguingly, in a reference to his design process for the library at
Viipuri, Aalto comments on this daylighting strategy as follows:

When I designed the city library of Viipuri for long periods of time …
I pursued the solution with the help of primitive sketches. From some

4.12
Creating intimacy with light.
Warm artificial light in the
darkness at the main desk.

4.13
Main space in sunny
conditions on a November
morning.

kind of fantastic mountain landscape with cliffs lit up by suns in different positions I gradually arrived at the concept for the library building.
The library's architectural core consists of reading and lending areas at
different levels and plateaus, while the centre and control area forms
the high point above the different levels. The childish sketches have
only an indirect connection with the architectural conception, but they
tied together the section and the plan with each other and created a
kind of unity of horizontal and vertical structure.[8]

Beyond enjoying good levels of diffuse light, the situation of reading, it would
seem has another dimension for Aalto. By denying his reading room a view, it
becomes possible to distil within it the wild openness of the Finnish landscape
under overcast skies. The adventure of reading is removed, distanced, to an inner
exterior where between an undulating ground of books and an unchanging sky,
enclosure and time are in question.

The problem of reading is more than a problem of the eye; a good
reading light permits the use of many positions of the human body
and every suitable relation between book and eye. Reading a book
involves both culturally and physically a strange kind of concentration;
the duty of the architecture is to eliminate all disturbing elements.[9]

As this quote illustrates, Aalto's 1940 paper 'The Humanizing of Architecture'
argues that architecture cannot be entirely rationalized in scientific terms, stressing instead that its ambitions should always remain firmly rooted in human needs.
Using his Viipuri Library to illustrate this approach, he suggests that an awareness of the local light climate has allowed scientific principles to be applied, and
technology tuned (the roof-lights are termed a daylighting system), to ensure that
a suitably daylit setting is provided by a deliberately austere and introspective

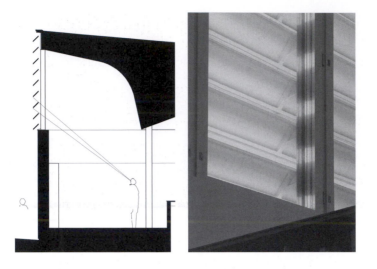

4.14
Humanizing architecture: a
veiled light-scoop formed
from southern clerestory
and curved ceiling provides
good diffuse daylight to
bookstacks below while
mitigating glare of overcast
sky for browsers, as this
diagram, after a 1964
drawing by Aalto, indicates.

room. From this perspective a library is an instrument for the interception and
redistribution of light for readers who seek isolation in private study. It is an
argument in which science, guided by thinking about inhabitation, rationalizes
decisions about form. What deserves emphasis here is the distance between
such a contention and his reference to the vision of a mountain landscape as a
source of inspiration for the room's sectional arrangement. Like Caspar David
Friedrich's 1818 'Wanderer above the Sea of Fog' (Fig. 4.4), each of Aalto's readers leaves the darkness below and climbs circuitously upwards to arrive at a high
viewpoint above a hillside of books. From this standpoint a library becomes the
setting for a personal encounter with the natural forces that a sublime direction-
less lightscape evokes.

As it turns out there are two particularly famous precedents for the
idea of a reading room lined with bookstacks below an arrangement of windows
and surfaces which allow the upper part of the room to act as a giant daylighting

4.15
West wall of main space
in November sunshine.
On sunny winter days,
when low-angle sunlight
is allowed to enter, the
small sun patches it throws
across wall, shelf and floor
surfaces make browsing
slightly harder but are not
a significant problem to
readers as they may choose
from a range of desks.

4.16
The crack of light in the direction of the sea in the changing rooms of the open-air swimming pool at Leça da Palmeira.

fixture for the whole. Wren's 1695 Trinity College Library in Cambridge is the first and most famous of these, though in this case the windows run down the east and west sides of a linear volume, with bookstacks forming reading bays to each side of a central aisle. More recent, and certainly a design that Aalto knew from personal experience, the main reading room of Asplund's 1928 Stockholm Library employs a comparable daylighting strategy for a space of much more imposing scale (Fig. 4.5). Here the enormously tall cylindrical volume at the centre of the plan is lit by a ring of clerestory windows rather than roof-lights, and the sky-like character of the upper region of the space is less abstract, the dimpling of the wall surface above the bookstacks a more literal suggestion of cloud forms.

Perhaps the significance of Aalto's more modest, and considerably less formal, public libraries is to have found a way to transpose this tune into a less emphatic key. In the projects after Viipuri, his libraries have a drama of light, but it is quieter, a charged stillness, rather than an imposing statement of taxonomic order or awe-inspiring vision of luminosity, and it is this more reticent architecture of light, architecture more closely attuned to the situation of casual browsing and reading, that allows the world of books to be opened to readers young and old in a less didactic way.

Siza's light

> … and I like to discover meaning in light, although sometimes that involves a degree of uncertainty.[10]

As with Aalto, Siza's buildings are famous for their light. Indeed it has been said by Vieiro de Almeida[11] that the common thread running through his work is a tactile, expressive light which represents the antithesis of the passive abstraction conjured by Le Corbusier's contentious definition of architecture as the play of forms beneath light. While such assertions elaborate what most commentators would agree with, i.e. the quality and studied control of light are

4.17
Light capture: the window
to the stair at the Centre
for Contemporary Art in
Santiago da Compostella.

a constant theme, they do not explain how he integrates this concern for light with other ambitions, or why he takes light so seriously. How Siza frames light as a design issue is a topic that deserves further exploration. While he may never have theorized his design process at length, a number of essays and interviews demonstrate he has much to say on the subject, his multi-faceted approach to light reflecting the stoic yet discerning pragmatism that colours his approach.

First, he is interested in light's role in perception, a sensitivity well illustrated by an early project where light is treated as an active protagonist, the agent for a transformation of mindset among users. In the changing rooms and open-air swimming pools at Leça da Palmeira (1966) on the Portuguese coast just north of Porto, Siza orchestrates an initiation rite of considerable subtlety in which immersion in a battle of shadow and light at the margin of land and sea prepares bathers to confront the ocean. After descending from a bleak coastal road to leave the city behind, circuitous movement through a dark and pungent interior pierced by blinding light precedes a slow return to the brightness and expanse of the sea. The word for threshold in Portuguese is *umbral*, a place of shadow, which precisely captures the goal of a project he chooses to frame as an exercise in light: ' … in a certain way this is more than anything a door giving access to the beach. In the gate of a wall, the transition is made through its own thickness, determining a time and a change of light.'[12]

A second instinct emerges in his comments on light as a natural phenomenon, a resource whose character decides how it should be deployed. The light he knows, the light he meets every day, is strong and mobile, erratic but vital, a source of damaging heat, and therefore something that requires close control because it is a potentially dangerous opponent whose precise effects on

4.18
The kind of traditional daylit
university library enjoyed by
Siza in which the bookstacks
are keyed to the windows.
Trinity Hall Old Library,
c.1590, Cambridge, UK.

fragile matter can be difficult to predict. Writing for example about the paradoxical
goal of museums in enabling both the display and protection of artworks, he por-
trays light as an 'implacable traveler who creates and kills with neither malice nor
goodwill'.[13] Likewise, reflecting more optimistically on the uncertain dynamism
of bright sunlight, he proposes elsewhere that 'it would be a fine thing to fix the
syntheses which are guessed at or assumed, to make universal the surprises of
light which the Southern sun allows'.[14]

One 'surprise of light' he enjoyed deliberating on at length, and that
demonstrates how he paces a trajectory by sculpting in light is the roof-light
stair-window at the heart of the 1993 Galician Centre for Contemporary Art in
Santiago de Compostella. In a reference to the light which skewers a complex
plan to make the aedicule of a stair landing the bright heart of the project, he
notes, 'One thing that fascinates me is to see how just a little incoming light can
be multiplied I don't know how many times'.[15] His coda to this statement: 'Light
is also important because it forces an uncoupling of the relationships among the
various elements of architecture'[16] underlines the destructively creative fracture
such a capturing of light allows.

Finally, not only does Siza frame the architect's role explicitly in relation to light, but there is the fundamental importance he places on the window
'as a selective way of capturing the landscape'.[17] Exhibiting a typical unwillingness to be prescriptive (while alluding to the incipient groundlessness of the
contemporary condition), 'Design', he asserts, is 'the catching of … or giving
geometry to a flittering image in all its shades.'[18] And yet it is locatedness he
is searching to establish through a restrained building with light. In this regard,
assessing what really matters in window design, he states 'It is a question of

4.19
A portal in a wall to the sea: Siza's library from the southern edge of the Viana do Castelo.

discovering a relationship in which the landscape and the control of natural light is decisive. There is often too much light in buildings made of glass or with huge picture windows, which is also an unnecessary waste.'[19] This sense of a magus-like role in fixing the unfixable, coupled with a fascination for 'balance' in exposure/enclosure (a fascination which explains his disdain for fully glazed walls), suggests he sees himself as wrestling with light to re-establish ground. And while he may once have declared 'It is very hard to make a window properly',[20] it is palpably clear that it interests him to try.

Sizan light is active for a purpose it would seem. Fierce and potentially destructive, its handling needs care. At this latitude a little light goes a long way, and wasting it is typically a matter of over-provision rather than not exploiting carefully the low levels available. Being measured with such light is an important goal, and in producing a body of work Frampton has termed 'an architecture of resistance',[21] Siza therefore sees himself as sculpting the everyday flow of life with just enough excoriating light.

Does Siza have anything more specific to say on library light? The challenging task that library architecture represents is well conveyed by a series of reflections on the design philosophy behind his 1994 Aveiro University Library. Unveiling a Bachelardian engagement with the history of reading and its settings, both grand and intimate, these thoughts reveal a deep distrust of the instrumental thinking driving much contemporary library design. Explaining his fondness for old university libraries (i.e. libraries that are not of an intimidating scale) he explains:

> I like the order of the shelves, the brass labels and the individual lamps in bronze and silk, anonymous, intimate; the ship's stairs and the narrow iron galleries, where going to look for a book can be a journey – not without its dangers.

4.20
Central courtyard and
entrance to the library
looking north.

> The modern library has lost this "attic-like" atmosphere and also the symbolic value, glorified by domes, by cylinders, by high modulated ceilings. It has lost that atmosphere of golden light – materialised by dust in the air – coming from unexpectedly high windows, always inadequate for efficient lighting, which needs the support of small green lamps.[22]

Where Aalto uses diagrams of light rays and a vision of landscape to organize his thoughts, Siza is keen to draw on his own experiences in library buildings. Yet what emerges from this more anecdotal analysis is a common concern with the inhabitation and navigation of library settings in relation to light, the complex matrix of territories and journeys a library represents. As for Aalto, library design for Siza is essentially the search for a particular kind of light that fosters reading. Without this light, or in his deliberately more romantic language, 'golden atmosphere', Siza implies that a library is only a scaled-up book depot with the potential to disorient.

Aalto's library at Seinajoki

The 1965 public library at Seinajoki forms one element of a civic complex designed by Aalto between the early 1950s and the late 1980s that also includes a church, a municipal theatre, public offices and a town hall. Fronting an urban square to the north and backing onto a small grove of trees to the south, the library appears initially to be nothing more than a modest, single-storey block. White walls, a linear form and heavily screened windows give nothing away of the carefully tuned sequence of space and light within. It is only on arriving at the main information desk inside that one begins to realize how a concern for natural light has structured its design and the visual fields that users experience.

In this library a series of ordinary rectangular rooms with ordinary

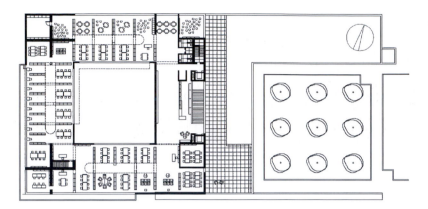

4.21
First-floor plan of Viana do Castelo Library.

side light are encountered alongside a taller and more inward-looking theatre of books whose complex ceiling modulates the daylight from high-level clerestory windows to north and south. Opening out southwards from the entrance hall, this much larger fan-shaped space holds the main lending library, accommodating readers among the books in an easily supervised arrangement. Library staff look over the book-lined reading well at the centre of the room into the radial bookstack bays beyond (Figs. 4.14, 4.9, 4.10). The ambition is to ensure the principal browsing areas are well daylit whatever the weather (the peripheral bays and the central well), and neither windows, nor the surfaces adjacent to them, are sources of glare. Sunshine is not entirely excluded however, an aspect of this room without a view which makes it a less austere setting for study than Viipuri. An otherwise cool interior glitters in good weather, either because filtered sunlight is allowed to enter (winter), or because the fixed external louvres to the southern windows themselves animate the view in this direction (summer) (Figs. 4.13, 4.15).

At Seinajoki Aalto considers not only how a particular quality of cool shadowless daylight can be deployed to create specific conditions for reading but how it can structure and pace the navigation of an interior. The colour and temperature of the light are as important as its pattern of distribution. This is a scheme where cool daylight predominates, but one which also depends on a judicious use of warmer artificial light for a specific purpose. On the one hand careful thought about how building surfaces disperse light to create relatively even daylight levels across the reading room determines the spatial hierarchy in which a complex ceiling is both an indirect source of daylight and a source of visual interest. On the other hand the landscape of light – artificial and natural – becomes a source of orientation that helps readers adjust to the quieter mood of a room for study whose status as a refuge Aalto is keen to evoke. In this case the overall plan of the building is centred on a librarian's desk that stands between the principal entrance and the main space (Fig. 4.12). It is the contrast between the lighting conditions in the middle of the building where it is located (relatively dark) and those at the far edge of the main space (much lighter) which articulates the route most readers will follow (Fig. 4.10). Against this backdrop the transformative power of an artificial light source is also tellingly in play. Whereas elsewhere the main light fittings are unnecessary in good daylight, the illumination to the

4.22
East–west section of Viana
do Castelo Library.

main desk provided by an array of downlighters is a permanent feature of the lightscape. Clearly Aalto is aware that given the relative dimness of its location, strong downlight will cause the timber of the desk to glow, transforming it into a key reference point – literally a beacon in the dark – for readers.

Before double and triple glazing became a possibility, windows were of course a potentially greater source of heat loss – and thus thermal discomfort to users – than is now the case. In this context Aalto realizes that integrating light, warmth, enclosure and pattern of inhabitation is crucial. He seeks to make the most of the available daylight while providing intimate shelter, a strategy whose thermal benefits do not prevent him from responding to the difficulties and joys induced by the local light climate (the frequency of overcast skies, solar geometry at this latitude which means low-level sunlight shines deep into buildings but also potentially straight into the eyes). Counter-intuitively, by locating readers below the centre of the space, he gives them a greater sense of refuge from what can be a bleakly uninviting (if luminous) snow-covered landscape in winter, while ensuring they still have good access to skylight and are not blinded by sunshine (Fig. 4.9). What the scheme as a whole demonstrates is that he considers daylight a precious resource not to be wasted, sunlight a much loved source of sparkle to be handled judiciously, a public library a democratic yet undogmatic setting where private study is aided by a largely diffuse sea of light.

Siza's library at Viana do Castelo

Viana do Castelo, the capital of the Minho region, is a small but handsome port-town on the coast of northern Portugal with a well-preserved medieval core. Below the belvedere of Santa Lucia, with its extensive Atlantic views, a series of densely packed streets of three- or four-storey buildings surround a series of larger interlinked squares on gently rising ground beside the River Lima. The replacement for a former dock area, its new library is part of a necklace of larger buildings strung out along the town's southern river edge which are renegotiating the town's relationship with the sea. Sited between a busy avenue that lies to the south of the old town centre and a new riverside promenade, the library is the furthest upriver of these new buildings, and stands at one end of a small tree-lined park. On this site, at this juncture, the new library composes and mediates a new boundary. Whether it is better described as a large docked object or a broken wall is difficult to decide (Fig. 4.19). It is definitely and defiantly white.

As a library, it is not immediately obvious how to enter. The building does not confront the street. It extends beside and hovers above it. But one realizes quite quickly that beyond framing a view to the river, the building itself

4.23
Entrance hall looking east
towards the stair.

acts as a monumental porch for its modest public entrance, a pair of glazed doors
to one side of a central void. Beside a two-storey L-shaped block which houses
an archive and the back-of-house administration areas, the reading rooms and
other public lending facilities occupy the series of bridges at first-floor level which
surround the void. To the east these bridges are supported by the ground floor
accommodation and to the west by two Herculean L-shaped pillars. In helping
to define an austere shadowy courtyard garden (Fig. 4.20) centred on a vibrantly
green lawn the whole arrangement creates a window at the scale of the town,
a giant aedicule that one slips inside.

     Within, the careful orchestration of movement through light and view
continues. Beyond an almost completely enclosed entrance hall, light from a
large window (Figs. 4.23, 4.24) at higher level draws one to the main stair. The
stair is a window. The window – a door height opening the length of the flight
of steps – is the stair. In this arrangement the ascent leads into the light/view.
On this slow journey away from the street (with its unpredictable rhythms and
unpredictable light) spatial compression and spatial enclosure precede an opening to light and deep distance. As Le Corbusier might have suggested, such a
window-stair invites the visitor to ascend to the view from a ship's rail. It is a
view one commands, a view one is encouraged to enter both literally (there is a
door to a terrace/deck at the top of the stair) and imaginatively (the eye searches
for life and light beyond the monochrome darkness), before turning to enter the
foyer. The library, and the possibility of study, one realizes, is beyond this view.

     Beside the stair, sitting with their backs to this upriver expanse of
water and sky, but side-on to a view of the street (a series of older terraced
houses and shops), the librarians command an interior lined with cabinets
(Fig. 4.25). In this room (the superimposition of two windows, one that is all
town, one that is all landscape) the history of the town is narrated in books and

4.24
View inland from window
at head of main stair
looking east.

printed images whose display is organized by the long blank wall which divides the foyer from the main reading rooms. Here in the half-light, half-enclosure that the two windows create, in a room which looks two ways, one is given a further moment to pause and get one's bearings. The noise of the street has been left behind. One is given the time and space to realize there is not a single route into the reading rooms but two. One can choose to circulate through the library clockwise or counter-clockwise. The route to the left leads towards the adults' library occupying the south and west bridges, the route to the right past the desk and towards the smaller children's library in the north bridge above the street.

Curiously, beyond the foyer it is difficult to say whether the library is one or many spaces. It presents a collection of rooms but also feels field-like. Such ambiguity, one comes to realize, depends on a carefully calibrated relationship of space and light that is determined not primarily by the interior walls (of which there are few), but, as in Siza's larger Aveiro University Library, by the bookstacks and their placement in relation to roof-lights and windows. As in many older libraries, the bookstacks are used to create a series of reading bays within which readers sit at tables side-on to the view (Fig. 4.26). In the larger bridge spaces, the bookstacks create four open-ended bays to either side of a central roof-lit aisle, in the corners, a series of small side-lit rooms, one bay wide (Fig. 4.27). In this scheme the continuous deep baffled roof-lights, which bring light deep into the bridge reading rooms, even out the light across the deep plan and articulate the larger scale order of the building's four-square geometry. The long horizontal windows on the other hand give readers useful side-light and access to a range of fragmentary views lacking in perspective depth, some of which are direct and some filtered by the building itself.

On this site, with this arrangement, it is a library with all the access to light it could want. In addition to its roof-lights it can and does have openings to the north, east, south and west. In other words it is not a library with a primary orientation, not a library whose readers are oriented to one particular light. Although generously daylit, it receives direct sunlight only rarely however. All openings in

4.25
First-floor foyer above
entrance hall from top
of stair.

relevant facades have fixed external shading devices, and as a result the light it provides for reading is relatively even and slow, that is to say not a light that changes significantly through the day. It is worth adding that the fractured views the building helps to frame have a particular power in the context of this simple timber and white plaster interior, with its rhythmical divisions and warm light.

In fine-tuning the building's unusual form to accommodate a library, order and disorder are knowingly, tellingly at issue. Arguably, this building offers the possibility of ordered wandering through a field of light to find a place in which to lose oneself in reading, or when the moment requires, a view. On the one hand there is no ultimate destination. No view is prioritized. Time itself, and passage through the library, is a circle. On the other, the whole library is measured out in intimate settings for study, each with their own specific set of views and thus character as territories. As the partial restatement of a familiar plan type (the centred gallery library) it recreates a recognizable landscape of reading whose simple symmetry and rhythmic repetition gives the hovering/floating bridge spaces a reassuring stability. In locating themselves at a table and before a view, readers are able to choose between greater visual austerity (the spare surfaces of the void), and greater visual distraction (the busyness of the townscape, the glitter of the water), that is, more or less exposure to the life of the town or the light and expanse of the sea (Figs. 4.28, 4.29, 4.30).

It is clear that the library at Viano do Castelo plays an important role in creating a new civic identity for the town on a site at the water's edge where this identity can be made most visible. In line with the concept that drives Tavora's master plan, Siza devises a library whose scale is between a building and a block, and whose precisely engineered form allows it to act as wall, window and terrace at an urban scale. The location and form of the library suggests that what citizens are being invited to do is to read inside a monument. This sounds

4.26
The west bridge
reading room.

daunting, particularly for children, and yet it cannot be emphasized enough that the quiet triumph of the building is the composition of a set of public interiors where visitors young and old can casually sit down to read. Siza is renowned as someone who is concerned with context (although being reduced to a contextualist is clearly something that irks him) and here he is constructing architecture in league with its setting through his handling of light – most tellingly in relation to both the unfolding of a journey away from the street (the window-stair) and the relocation of readers in their wider landscape in order to enable larger communal, and smaller individual, territories of study (the circle of reading rooms, the side-lit reading bays). Refinding their bearings in this 'golden atmosphere', readers can make the building their own, guided by a field of light that fosters their wondering and wandering between town and sea.

Reading light: the conspicuous conservation of daylight

They tell me (some friends do) that I do not have a supporting theory or method. That nothing I do points the way. That it is not educational.

A sort of boat at the mercy of the waves which inexplicably does not always get wrecked (also according to what they tell me).

I do not expose the boards of our boats too much, at least on the high seas. They have been split too many times.

4.27
Corner light: view of
town from children's
storytelling room.

I study the currents, eddies, I look for creeks before taking a risk.

I can be seen alone, walking the deck. But all the crew and all the
equipment is there, the captain is a ghost.

I dare not put my hand on the helm, when I can only just see the
pole star. And I do not point out a clear way. The ways are not clear.[23]

Despite their differences in approach to public library design do Aalto and Siza
share ideas about light? Is it useful to talk about a legacy in daylighting that
Siza has inherited from Aalto? What the buildings discussed here demonstrate
is that for both architects daylight is not just a source of inspiration for design
decisions or a resource to be deployed correctly but a critical subject for interpretation, that is, not a resource of which there must be a 'right' amount, but
an intrinsic aspect of spatial design. For both it is the inhabitation of light rather
than the vision given by or from the building that is the critical design issue –
inhabitation that is predetermined by, and therefore considered in relation to, the
local context. The nature of the settings they provide for reading may be quite
different, but the idea that a library is a kind of refuge from everyday life whose
'withdrawal' and 'otherness' is largely generated by the way daylight is regulated
by the building – and its locale – is common to both.

It seems worth noting that this approach is a more obvious – and a
more feasible – strategy when the climate of natural light, and the implications
this has for inhabitation, are thoroughly assimilated, rather then learned from
textbooks *in vacuo*. What the study has highlighted is that Siza and Aalto know
well the world of light they are distilling for readers, the circumstances of light
to which their work responds. The creation of appropriate shelter through the

4.28
Bridge light: view to
courtyard from aisle of the
south bridge reading room.

sparing introduction of light reflects their common instinct that light is not to be treated lightly, as it were. They are conservative with light because they cannot escape the fact that beyond being a natural, and therefore free resource, daylight situates a way of life, enabling the occupants of a library to become a community of readers. Siza, like Aalto before him, understands that natural light is oriented (physically, temporally), and that orientation is critical for understanding (knowledge is not merely disembodied fragments). Natural light is therefore the basis for good reading light.

Ray has argued that the arrangement of the main reading room at Seinajoki reflects an ordering principle in which Aalto 'maintains the specialness of a free geometry by setting it against an 'ordinary' orthogonal datum'.[24] In moving away from the austere, four-square stability of Viipuri, it is also worth noting that this organization echoes many early public library buildings in which a generously day-lit half-panopticon volume containing radial stacks was focused on the librarian's desk at entry. In time it was decided that views out from such rooms should be denied in a measure that matched a drive for economy with concerns about decorum. The argument ran that high-level windows allowed greater lengths of easily accessible shelving to be provided, while obliging users to focus on the task in hand. Beyond his predilection for certain formal relationships it would seem that Aalto's characterization of the library task – the emphasis on the individual, and his or her immersion in study – reflects the paternalistic philanthropy of the public library movement, in which the gift of 'perfect light' was intended to empower individuals through the self-improvement that reading achieved.

If the introspective character of Seinajoki can be framed in this way, it seems worth thinking about the aims behind the measured openness of Siza's building. The nostalgia he declares for old libraries is poignant, pointing as it does to the problematic impacts of the current obsession with the idea of the library as a knowledge resource centre. When an overwhelming focus is given to freedom

4.29
View to courtyard (and town beyond) from reading desk in the south bridge reading room.

of information and its rapid accessibility, concern for the character of setting that a library provides can easily be overlooked. In a gesture of quiet defiance, the intention behind the limited openness of Siza's enfilade interior, a distant echo of a previous plan type, is to create a recognizable territory of reading.

Siza's 1983 text 'Eight Points' quoted above eloquently foreshadows the dilemma of architects in the developed world at the end of the twentieth century. Uncertainty about the role of theory in reducing the haphazard wind-tossed process of design to a linear argument is the dominant theme, matched to the implication that collaborative dialogue over direction is the only sensible response in a situation where doubts about orientation (symbolized as ever by light) make navigation next to impossible. It is this unwillingness to rationalize an essentially iterative process that he – and others – recognize also in Aalto, which prevents them from being natural revolutionaries. Rather, Siza sees himself as following Aalto's path in fusing the lessons and motifs of remote architectures with his own more closely observed experience of indigenous building traditions. What seems worth underlining here is that it is a shared interest in the inhabitation of light that is critical to a creative interchange between the global and the local, between more widely recognized architectural traditions and the specific constraints and opportunities of place.

Finally, it seems worth touching on what the unglamorous ambition of modesty often adduced to both architects has to do with their approach to light. On the one hand modesty can be equated with unobtrusiveness, diffidence, the unexceptional. Yet, much more positively, modesty also suggests understatedness, a lack of pretension, the very opposite of all that is flashy, indeed, most precisely, *measure* (from the Latin *modus*). As this study has illustrated it is by being deliberately measured with light that Aalto and Siza achieve their radical aim of its conspicuous conservation.

4.30
View of town from reading
desk in the north bridge
reading room.

Notes

1   A. Siza, as quoted by K. Frampton in his introduction to A. Siza, *Alvaro Siza: The Complete Works*, London, 2000, p. 8.

2   A. Siza, 'Alvar Aalto: Three Aspects at Random', originally published in *Jornal de Letras, Artes e Ideias*, vol. 51, pp. 1–14, February 1983, and republished in *Writings on Architecture*, Milan,1997, pp. 98–104, p. 102. See also discussion by K. Frampton in *Alvaro Siza*, p. 59.

3   See O. Prizeman, 'Philanthropy and light: the formulation of transatlantic environmental standards for public interiors through Andrew Carnegie's library building programme 1889–1910', unpublished PhD thesis, University of Cambridge, 2010.

4   A. Aalto 'The Humanizing of Architecture', *Technology Review*, 1940, republished in A. Aalto, *Sketches*, ed. G. Schildt, trans., S. Wrede, Cambridge, Mass. and London, 1978, pp. 76–79, p. 78.

5   F. Moore, *Concepts and Practice of Architectural Daylighting*, New York and London, 1991, ch. 6.

6   M. Millett, *Light Revealing Architecture*, New York, 1996, pp. 32–33 and pp. 122–134.

7   Aalto discusses this attitude to library light in 'The Humanizing of Architecture' in *Sketches*, pp. 76–79, pp. 78–79.

8   A. Aalto, 'The Trout and the Stream' (1947) in A. Aalto, *Alvar Aalto in His Own Words*, ed. G. Schildt, Otava, 1997, p. 108.

9   Aalto, *Sketches*, p. 79.

10 A. Siza, as quoted in 'The meaning of things', *El Croquis*, no. 140, 2008 (Juan Domingo Santos interview with Alvaro Siza), p. 51.

11 P. Vieiro de Almeida, 'Álvaro Siza Vieira', July 1995, available online at http://www.cidadevirtual.pt/blau/almeida.html (accessed 26 November 2010).

12 A. Siza, *Writings on Architecture*, ed. A. Angelillo, London, 1997, pp. 194, 151.

13 Ibid., pp. 199–200.

14 Ibid., p. 203.

15 A. Siza, http://cgac.xunta.es/contenido/7/1/El%20Edificio, January 2010

16 A. Siza, http://cgac.xunta.es/contenido/7/1/El%20Edificio, January 2010.

17 A. Siza, as quoted in 'The meaning of things', p. 37.

18 A. Siza, from the prose poem 'To catch a precise moment of the flittering image in all its shades', 1979, as quoted by K. Frampton in his introduction to *Alvaro Siza*, p. 20.

19 A. Siza, as quoted in 'The meaning of things', p. 35.

20 Ibid.

21 Frampton, *Alvaro Siza*, 'Introduction', p. 59.

22 A. Siza, 'Libraries', Aveiro, 25 April 1995, in *Writings on Architecture*, p. 194.

23 A. Siza, 'Eight Points', Porto, September 1983, *Quaderns d'Arquitectura i Urbanisme*, no. 159, October/November/December, 1983, republished in *Writings on Architecture*, pp. 203–207, p. 206.

24 N. Ray, *Alvar Aalto*, New Haven and London, 2005, p. 178.

Chapter 5

Enlightening conversation

The Music Room and the Open City, Ritoque, Chile

It was neither with music or an acoustic, but with a sense of origin that we wanted to build the work. A work that seeks, is still in the seeking, in search of establishing a road.[1]

The Music Room was the first construction built at the Open City. It acquired this destiny simply through a gesture of the poet Godofredo Iommi throwing open his arms towards the horizon and declaring the magic words: Music Room. We had to begin by inviting the Muses. The opening, the poetic act of building was like this; according to the Greeks it would have been to make a poem. Perhaps this image led directly to the discovery of a symbolic lighting: the reception of light from the sky, from the zenith … together the architects achieved the building of this result, which takes a long time to explain because there were acts to initiate the study, find the site etc … the study of the way people listen to music, what musicians are seeking, and all human aspects from which architecture derives its dimensions.[2]

The Music Room of the Open City is a square single-storey room of lightweight timber construction which houses the weekly staff-meetings of the Valparaiso Architecture School. Sitting quietly and unobtrusively among the low vegetation and pine trees of coastal sand dunes, only the strange extrusions at each corner of its white diagonally boarded external surfaces give any clue to the extraordinary character of its internal environment. Lit by a narrow glazed courtyard at its centre and striated shafts of sunlight at its corners, the room reduces and transforms the strength and brightness of the Pacific light into a warmer more restrained cadence, as top-light and side-light is reflected and re-reflected off the raw wooden surfaces of the interior.

From the outside, the Open City is an unusual proposition, a 'city of the sand-dunes' that has dwellings, public meeting places, workshops, playing-fields, a cemetery and a church, but no streets, no boundaries, indeed no clear

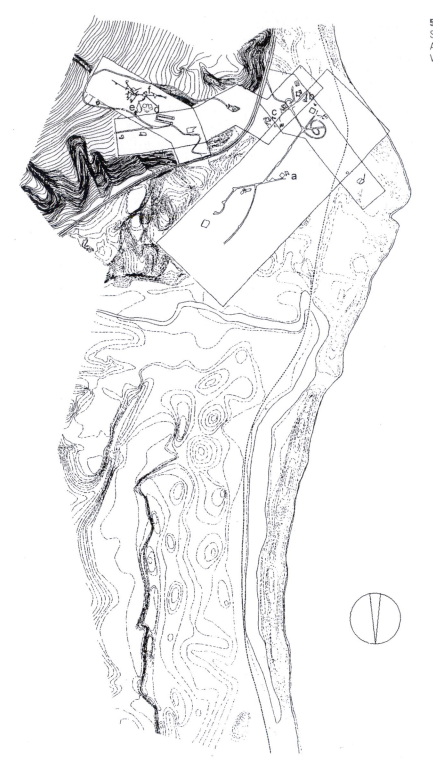

5.1
Site plan of the Open City.
Archivo Histórico José
Vial PUCV, 1996.

5.2
Aerial view of the Open City. Adjacent to a grove of pine trees, the Music Room is at the bottom right of the photograph beside the playing field at the edge of the settlement. The area of the site below the coastal highway is very exposed to wind and light, and, though divided from the shoreline by a high embryo dune, can never escape the ceaseless roaring of the Pacific breakers. On the plateau above a road winds between individual dwellings and their modest outbuildings. The major fissure in the plateau is the leafy gully in which the cemetery, church and amphitheatre are located.

'plan' at all. Dissected by a busy coastal highway and cut off from the shore by a single-track railway, it is a settlement without an obvious centre – or obvious connections – a 'city' whose reluctance to attempt any articulation of larger-scale order begs the question about what kind of city it can be. Only by living there does one discover that at one and the same time it is an open-air workshop and a city in the making: a large-scale architectural experiment that is continually being transformed by the teachers, poets, artists and architects who are its builders. And only after conversation with them does one begin to understand the more profound lessons of an unusual community whose shared goal has been 'to make art rhyme with life'. The collective authorship of architectural propositions or *trabajo en ronda* (work in a circle) that this 'open' settlement embodies is a form of cooperation which reflects a shared conviction that resonant design can only be achieved through collaboration. Building is considered a fundamentally collective act and conversation between the participants pivotal to the process of establishing the poetics of a project and refining and realizing these poetics in design. In line with this thinking, the authoring of projects is deliberately played down, all those involved in the dialogue being cited if authorship beyond 'The Open City Group' is elaborated. One of the first acts of construction in this city, and the act which marked its foundation in 1971, was the building of the Music Room.

What this unorthodox design practice offers is the opportunity to explore the relationship between light, designing, building and living. It makes possible a study of the central role played by light in a working environment – and a design process – pursued as a collective poetic act (design considered as

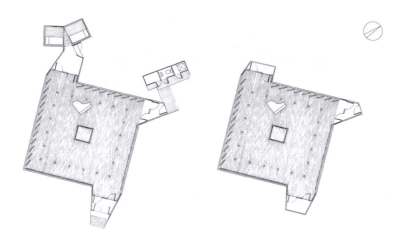

5.3
Left: Plan of the Music
Room, 1972. Right: Current
plan of the Music Room.

an open adventure, restrained by an ongoing discourse about how architecture
scales and locates everyday events). Through close examination of the progress
and direction of this discourse in relation to light, this chapter aims to explore a
number of issues. Do ideas about 'good light' change when design and construction become one and the same thing? In a context of this kind can ideas about
light generate design, or do they evolve in combination with other intentions?
And finally, what dialectic in light has this full-scale civic experiment revealed?

The philosophical foundations for the work-life of the Open City
were laid by a group of young architects led by the charismatic teacher Alberto
Cruz and the poet Godofredo Iommi in the years following their arrival at the
Valparaiso School in 1951.[3] An alternative approach to the teaching of design
which put emphasis on both learning through observing and learning through
making soon attracted the interest of other Chilean artists and intellectuals. It
enabled the group to open the kind of broader dialogue between architecture
and other disciplines to which their outlook on life and work was attuned, and
whose fruits their teaching was beginning to examine. Eager to engage in real
construction projects, it was quickly realized that it would be necessary to
create a suitable framework for cooperation if they were to extend the thinking
they were developing through teaching into collective research and practice.
Established at the school in 1952, the Institute of Architecture became the
first vehicle through which the group cooperated. The work it produced in the
following two decades reflects their preoccupations and acts as the clearest
manifesto of the design approach they continued to pursue at the Open City
from 1971. Since the construction of the Music Room the settlement of the
Open City has proceeded in piecemeal fashion, building by building, project by
project, family by family, and these works (and the extended collective of the
group itself) have evolved gradually over time. Certain other important insights
about what constructing buildings, constructing a life and constructing a city
have got to do with one another have emerged along the way that are also
important to the argument presented here. Brief analysis of a series of works
by the Open City Group, beginning with two important unbuilt projects from
the early 1950s and touching on other work completed more recently at the

5.4
Section through the Music
Room looking west. The
asymmetry of the ceiling
surfaces orients the interior
to northern sunlight.

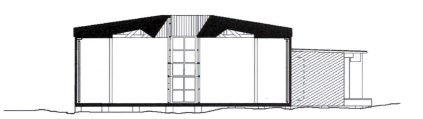

Open City, therefore preface a detailed discussion of the character of light and space provided by the Music Room and the lightscape that the city-wide project now represents.

Two early projects

While much of the early work produced by the group touches on themes that have remained important, two unbuilt projects were of particular significance to the development of a design discourse in which light and lighting issues were given a new emphasis. The first of these, the 1953 Los Pajaritos Chapel project, by Alberto Cruz and referred to in an earlier chapter, was for a small public chapel on a rural estate close to Santiago. The second, the 1954 Church of Santa Clara project by the Institute of Architecture, was for a church on an urban site in the Chilean capital Santiago, later constructed to an entirely different design.

In the Los Pajaritos Chapel project a series of simple cubic or almost cubic volumes are deployed to provide the necessary elements of the scheme (Figs. 5.6, 5.7). Steps lead up to a low platform on which a small aedicule containing a statue of Mary stands in front of the main chapel building. The plan's central east-west axis is marked by the steps and statue at one end of the platform and the altar and tabernacle within the chapel at the other. Between statue and altar stand the large chapel doors that in a reworking of a typical rural tradition may be opened on festival days to transform the space of the platform into a virtual extension to the nave. To the rear of the chapel a sacristy extends to the northeast beneath the cubic cage of an open bell tower. The main room of the chapel is a cubic volume elongated slightly in the horizontal direction whose main source of light is hidden: perimeter glazing surrounding the ceiling that allows indirect light to wash over the large uninterrupted wall surfaces from above. Contrasting with the evenly graded light of the white walls, the brightness of the small top-lit tabernacle niche in the wall behind the altar draws the eye, especially in the morning, and gives a primary orientation to the space.

In Cruz's theoretical text of 1954[4] which offers a detailed explanation of the ideas behind this unbuilt project, light is central to an argument that seeks to frame design issues from a new perspective. In a rejection of the modernist obsession with technology and the pursuit of form for its own sake, Cruz seeks to illustrate how insights derived from the careful observation of everyday life can transform the design process into an imaginative search for light grounded by practical experience. In this case he indicates how the chapel's design process

5.5
Music Room interior looking
north towards entrance; light
well open.

reflected his search to recreate a particular quality of light he had encountered during a service in a temporary chapel that had led him to identify light as critical to the circumstance of prayer:

> It was just before receiving the request to realize the chapel that I participated in a memorial mass in the estate house of Los Pajaritos. The windows were half-closed in order to separate the hallway from the living room and transform it into an oratorio. A soft, delicate luminous penumbra arose. A light that made one look at the space, and only at the space. No wall of any kind (it was a normal living room let it be understood: full of complications).

> The light, I said to myself. The light is the sand that enables being near to the sea of our praying. Today nothing appears more than the light. Today only the light catches the eye. The rest doesn't matter, it is not at all interesting, let it be what it wants.

'The light is the sand that enables being near to the sea of our praying' is of course a remarkable metaphor in its own right, crucial to what is called 'design' in this instance. Although being 'beside' or 'near' to prayer is difficult to interpret, the rest of the metaphor implicates the fundamental conditions of Chile in a more cosmological orientation whereby the light is the firm substance – earth – against which washes our restless, ever-hopeful praying. (Intriguingly this reverses Le Corbusier's metaphors regarding light and earth, though the link between water and language is not original to Cruz. In Near Eastern and then Greek cosmologies, the sea is traditionally that from which the solid earth grows; but Cruz seems to be implying that our life, and its prayers, is amorphous, restless, *desconocido*, i.e. unknown and unknowable, the unstable part of the relationship. Perhaps something of the wandering seafarer is also implied, with an even more distant reference to the arrival of Europeans to these shores and another ocean, in inverse latitudes.)

In the description that follows the idea that ambitions for light must

5.6
Los Pajaritos Chapel project,
photograph of model interior
illustrating 'equal light'.

be considered *specifically in relation to* the human acts and events they illuminate is given particular emphasis, as noted earlier. In this approach questions of
scale, geometry and form are not ignored, but always explored in relation to
how they affect architectural experience. ('I arrived at the minor dimensions that
told me that amplitude in which the eye sees the space, the luminous reflected
penumbra.')[5]

In analysing his deployment of indirect light for example, care is taken
to explain the significance for light distribution of the interplay between spatial
geometry, window location and surface colour. The argument is then extended
through detailed analysis of the role such a chapel may be expected to play in
the immediate physical and cultural landscape, both by way of defining an intermediate scale space between exterior and interior that engages the passer-by
and invites entry, and acting as a robust setting for the display of the flowers,
candles and other votive offerings of popular religion. Illustrating the central
importance of light and visual perception to design thinking and at the same
time demonstrating its circular mode of inquiry, the text deliberately ends with a
question rather than an answer. Opening the issue of lighting from a new standpoint it asks: 'But what will the confessionals be like in this cube of light? What
will be their light, the light given by the form of these small churches inside the
larger church?'

While at first glance the design seems to exemplify the modernist
predilection for the ideal form of the white cube, it becomes clear that decisions
about scale, dimensions and colour are in fact determined by the search to give
the chapel indirect light of a quiet, diffuse quality whose evenness helps to
ensure dematerialization of form. Cruz knows that a tall square monochrome and
evenly lit form will create 'square light', or in other words, a poised, 'equal', half-
light. Nevertheless, in answering the key design issue (as he frames it): 'What is
the form like inside of which one prays?', Cruz's marriage of geometry and light

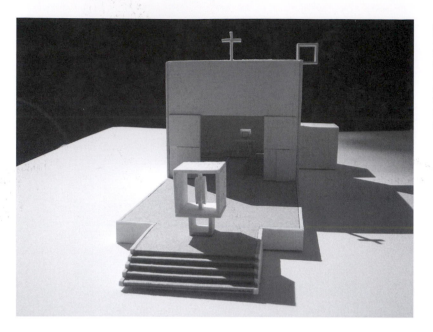

does not remain 'ideal'. The square plan is qualified slightly in order to give the chapel a stronger sense of orientation, one that also gives greater emphasis to the linear sequence between Mary and the altar/tabernacle when the doors are open. Here in a game of controlled tension, the timeless drama of the indirectly lit interior, with its one bright focal point, contrasts with the dynamic projection of Mary's shadow across the brightly lit surfaces outside.

The Santa Clara project on the other hand illustrates the kind of painstaking research the Institute was prepared to initiate to discover how a particular kind of light might be achieved (Figs. 5.8, 5.10). In this case it was felt that the light of a brightly daylit space should be made mysterious by concealing its source.[6] And so it was decided that the sanctuary of the church needed to be surrounded with 'walls of light' constructed in such a way that all the apertures were hidden within the walls and thus not apparent to an observer at ground level. Again the space in question was given a square plan in order to ensure the kind of evenly diffuse indirect light that dematerializes form, but in this case the walls were divided into a series of offset horizontal panels, with light entering between them from below. With its emphasis on the human perception of light and the visual environment, the unpublished paper 'Iluminacíon'[7] by Miguel Eyquem which explains the goals of the project and the various options that were considered represents an unusual marriage of the voices of science and art (Fig. 5.9). Adopting the terminology and diagrams of optics, but set out like Symbolist poetry, it abounds with references to architectural precedents (US, European, South American, traditional and contemporary) and the insights of personal observation (e.g. the diffuse quality of light under sunlit chestnut leaves, the impact of strong local colour on white surfaces, experiments with the light transmission properties of materials, the implications for light of liturgical ceremony), in order to clarify the ambitions for light that a rigorous

5.8
Santa Clara. Cut-away
perspective of interior
explaining indirect
lighting strategy.

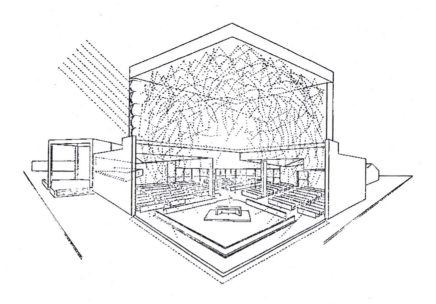

physical modelling process was intended to realize, as the following passage illustrates:

·   *north side of the Playa de*
  la Constitución:
      green trees
      red wall
      grey flagstones

The light that has gone through a strange diffusion and multiple filtration often arises in the sky of Chile.

At twilight on certain days when the rays of the sun cross a lot of atmosphere or soft clouds, it illuminates the cordillera

the snow
or certain
clouds

in certain sunny places in Miramar
the wall of stone loses its reality
of stone

as much as walls and houses (in Recreo, Miramar)

Certain houses of Valparaiso that face west.

This 'unusual marriage' of science and art deserves discussion. In principle of course, there is every reason for a continuity between nature and what we do or make. In practice, however, the claim of science has become a marriage or some other fusion because of the manner in which science frames nature, and therefore us as well. It is customary now to refer to material or constructional interpretation as 'technology', invoking all the benefits and worries of the technological manipulation of life, etc. Historically, one usually looks to the appearance of this sort of awareness of a need for a fusion with the advent of perspective and of scientific method with Galileo. When Ackerman traces the motif back to Milan Cathedral and the phrase 'ars sine scientia nihil est',[8] one must ask what counted for science in the fourteenth century. Here we find ourselves in the problem of a Latin translation of the Greek episteme, meaning a form of discourse that is internally consistent (like the statements of geometry) and true everywhere (fire burns the same in Greece and Persia, as Aristotle puts it). Aristotle reckons *Sophia*, the highest form of wisdom, as a combination of episteme and practical understanding which seems perfectly good, but it all comes down to how. Modernist architects and artists were particularly attracted to science (embrace of science was – and is – a way of being 'modern'), mostly the physical sciences (although there was a healthy enthusiasm for plant and cell analogies as well). The extreme form of this in architecture grew out of the hygiene and clarity motifs and a model of architecture that could be prosecuted wholly on scientific grounds. However, it comes as something of a surprise to find Kandinsky, precursor to Jackson Pollock, attempting to ground the most extreme species of lyric painting at that time in something like a perceptual psychology endowed with laws like those of physics (Point and Line to Plane). For Le Corbusier, the concept of law in science was that which granted contemporary access to 'cosmos'.

Whether one regards this as muddled thinking, characteristic of artists, or a symptom of a discontinuity that requires addressing, how recent architects have allowed this issue to influence their working practices, and more specifically the crystallization of their design ideas, is worth attention. In this case it is perhaps the significance of poetics to the working method of the Open City Group, manifested in Eyquem's document, that deserves emphasis. How they try to resolve what seems to lie between a protest against science – technology – and a cautious dialogue may be regarded as having its heart in practice, as a form of 'mixed' thinking that operates at several levels but uses poetics to find the 'truth' of a proposition (building, city, ephemeral installation) and 'science' to refine the results. As a result design propositions need only be 'good enough' from a scientific perspective and the idea that design should be optimized through science is entirely rejected. Cruz's assertion, 'So all origin of architecture is poetry. It has to be built step by step', reflects this embrace of an empirical poetics whose point of departure is discovery of a place and its

5.9
Three of Eyquem's sketches analysing light phenomena from *Iluminación*.

Left: light diffusion through leaves.

Middle: inter-reflections of light at a screened aperture.

Right: light reflection at the ground outside a building.

5.10
Santa Clara. Detail of section
through wall to sanctuary.
To achieve the seamless
enclosure by light envisaged,
a light scoop fixed to the
top of each panel helps
to focus what daylight or
sunlight is available onto the
gap between panels, and a
deflector located in this gap
redistributes the light evenly
across the panel above.

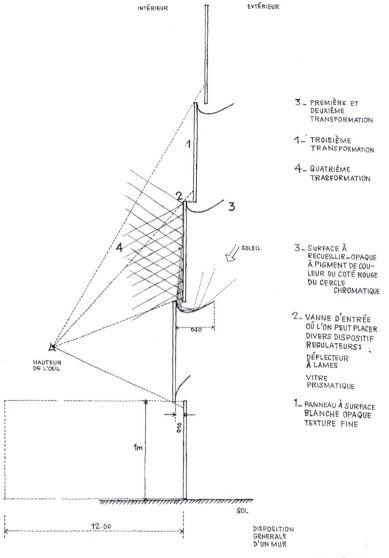

INTÉRIEUR   EXTÉRIEUR

3 – PREMIÈRE ET
DEUXIÈME
TRANSFORMATION

1 – TROISIÈME
TRANSFORMATION

4 – QUATRIÈME
TRASFORMATION

SOLEIL

3 – SURFACE À
RECUEILLIR – OPAQUE
À PIGMENT DE COU-
LEUR DU COTÉ ROUGE
DU CERCLE
CHROMATIQUE

2 – VANNE D'ENTRÉE
OÙ L'ON PEUT PLACER
DIVERS DISPOSITIF
REGULATEURS:

DÉFLECTEUR
À LAMES

VITRE
PRISMATIQUE

1 – PANNEAU À SURFACE
BLANCHE OPAQUE
TEXTURE FINE

HAUTEUR
DE L'OEIL

0.40

0.40

1m

SOL

12.00

DISPOSITION
GENERALE
D'UN MUR

1:20   ÉCHELLE

destiny through poetic action. The emphasis here is on a way of acting rather
than the imposition of preordained order. In this approach the design process
itself becomes lived poetry, a collaborative dialogue in which design ambitions
emerge through a consideration of a place and its environmental qualities in
relation to issues of inhabitation. Cruz's comment that 'The Open City wasn't
done in the sense of the work to complete but in the seeking of its generation'
further underlines this point.

Some clarification is perhaps helpful here. The design practice pursued at the Open City involves collaborators in a dialogue whose ambitions are
shaped by the words that members of the group are motivated to utter during
an initial exploration of a site.[9] This poetry that 'takes place' (*poesía del ha lugar*)

5.11
Hospedería de los Diseños:
the corridor looking towards
the kitchen dining area.

proposes the claim of place to generate the words which initiate a design direction. 'To return to not knowing' (*volver a no saber*), the recovery of child-like innocence in the face of design questions, remains the guiding principle of the *trabajo en ronda* working method.

The Open City

Following the completion of the Music Room, the projects carried out during the first twenty years of the settlement's existence have included eleven dwellings, two studio-workrooms, three workshops, one outside eating area, a cemetery, a chapel, an amphitheatre and 'agoras' (external gathering places for concerts or other improvised theatrical events), and several garden projects including the 'Palace of Dawn and Dusk' and its 'Faubourg', and a small cemetery. Easily dismissed as merely a symptom of the discontinuities of current culture (a romantic landscape park of monuments, an open-air architectural laboratory, or a species of primitivism that grows from urban sophistication), what is not always clear to outsiders is the way in which its founding principles reflect not only a creative antipathy to capitalism, but advocacy of a local culture and its practical art against globalized technological processes, and just as importantly the effort to recover orientation in a cultural milieu marked at its origin by immigration. As such it is a community whose politics and shared way of life has shaped its narratives in light, and it would therefore seem useful to outline these principles before analysing this light in more detail.

As Pendleton-Jullian stresses, the deliberate imposition of any kind of collective order has always been avoided, and yet a character, if not an 'order' in the formal sense, expressing the ideals of social interaction promoted by the group is nevertheless emerging. Thus, despite its mutability, the lower landscape

5.12
Hospedería del Estudio,
late 1980s.

of sand between the river, the railway line, the mobile dunes and the highway
is given an end-point and a sense of direction through inhabitation. Above
the highway, the quieter upper landscape is also acquiring a new larger-scale
structure. This centres on the subtle exchanges and unpredictable rhythms of
a stepped wandering conversation between earth and brick, tree trunks and
timber columns, sky and stretched canvas. On the path that negotiates its way
from a group of trees beside flat grassland into a leafy gully through a sequence
of gardens that end in a cemetery, uncovered tree roots or the sound of wind
in the trees matter as much as the dimensions of steps and terraces. What this
means is that the lower 'end' of the city (beside the Music Room and a student
workshop) is marked by a playing field. At the other higher 'end' lies an intimate
cemetery garden where the city's dead are buried and next to which stands a
chapel. Between the two, apart from the aforementioned agoras, a couple of
more prominent clusters are taking shape, one of dwellings and one of construction workshops, that create intermediate gathering places or working courtyards.

There are two guiding principles for this arrangement. First, all the
buildings deliberately turn their backs on an ocean defined as *desconocido*, i.e.
unknown and unknowable.[10] Unlike neighbouring developments they do not
'view' the sea. Secondly the significance of a 'life-in-common' is reflected in
the absence of any truly 'private' space in the city. A new dwelling type has
been developed whose name, *hospedería*, or 'inn', indicates the weight given
by the group to the concept of hospitality. Built collectively following agreement

of the whole community, these buildings are occupied but not owned by group members, and each family is expected to provide a welcome to guests who seek lodging. The houses also provide a setting for group celebration, ensuring that somewhere in each *hospedería* is a space large enough to stage a gathering of the entire community round a single table.

Two *hospederías* in the lower city

Examples of the two basic approaches to spatial order at the Open City, the two *hospederías* described below display an intermediate degree of enclosure and adaptability which gives them a kind of episodic 'broken' light. With its four views and complex accretive form, the Hospedería de los Diseños is somewhat more open and adaptable; the Hospedería del Estudio, with its two views, and much simpler form, somewhat less so.

- At the centre of the Hospedería de los Diseños[11] a small roof-lit entry hall rejoins the major volumes of a building split by a narrow brick corridor descending across the dunes (Fig. 5.11). A long dining space that runs perpendicular to the corridor across the full width of the building is created by opening the glazed doors to either side of this hall. French doors at each end of the dining 'passage' open views along the dunes so that from the centre of the building one can see out four ways. From this intermediate level the building itself climbs casually down into the sand in a series of steps. Below its fractured sloping ceilings further apertures for light in the lightweight outer walls mean that the warm fragmented interiors (polished concrete, unplastered brick and timber boarding, with areas painted white), though not especially bright, are always lit from more than one side.
- In the Hospedería del Estudio,[12] a relatively simple, relatively closed volume

5.14
The segmented brick
walls of the Palace of Dawn
and Dusk.

divided by an oblique partition is given a complex roof form that together
with a tall window in an end wall, stages a dramatic battle of light across
the upper walls and ceiling at the start and end of the day (Fig. 5.12). In a
plan of considerable economy the transition between a more public entry
passage the length of the building, and a more private bed space that is
its width, hinges on the placement of a table in the brightest corner of the
room where the two spaces overlap. The painted interior is predominantly
white with some light grey ceiling areas.

Four projects in the upper city: The Cemetery Chapel,[13] the Palace of Dawn and Dusk,[14] the Faubourg of the Palace of Dawn and Dusk,[15] the Cemetery Amphitheatre[16]

These are a series of open-air structures that rework the relationship between
interior and exterior, ground and light, built form and sky on a more civic scale.

- The gathering space of a wall-less chapel is loosely defined by an array of
  timber columns and the shade created between them by a bright 'roof' of
  white mesh sails (Fig. 5.13).
- With its non-orthogonal plan, and monolithic yet rhythmic form of construction (brick walls of identical height composed of multiple units, each
  of which is the same arc in plan) the Palace of Dawn and Dusk offers an
  enigmatic expression of openness and closure, beginnings and ends, the
  emergence and dissolution of architectural order. A landscape of 2.2 m high
  fractured walls (rooms roofed by the sky) calibrates the extensive views
  towards the horizon that are available from the level cliff-top site.
- In its lee, an alternative 'garden' setting for community meetings, the
  'Faubourg' of the palace, dispenses with walls and roofs altogether, concentrating solely on the role played by furniture in setting up the conditions for
  fruitful dialogue (Fig. 5.15). Here a small-scale landscape of fixed furniture

5.15
Faubourg of the Palace of
Dawn and Dusk.

offers opportunities for the seating of an informal meeting whose dimensions and arrangement reflect the idea that everyone in such a setting should be able to look naturally at one another.

- A further mode of spatial containment that focuses on the boundaries of nature and artifice, is explored in the Cemetery Amphitheatre. Partly contained by groups of dark, relatively dense pine trees, and partly by the grassy sides of the gully itself, an intimate arena defined by a series of shallow-ramped brick terraces round a deeper irregularly shaped central area has been deftly configured from the natural landscape. Though two paths descend into it, and one away from it, no orientation predominates and people are able to group themselves informally, the slope of the terracing offering a range of possible seating and lying positions.

A public interior at the edge of the city: The Music Room

Sited at the eastern end of the playground, at the very edge of the fore-dunes that offer it shelter from the south-easterly wind, the Music Room is preceded by the level forecourt it shares with a diminutive service building. On entering this forecourt the sound of the breakers almost disappears and the sea is no longer visible. A group of pines under which cars may be parked locate this territory in the wider landscape.

The Music Room has a square, i.e. centred, non-oriented, form (Figs. 5.3, 5.17, 5.18). From the outside it presents itself as a simple white box wrapped with diagonal timber boarding whose colour is comparable to the sand, scrub-grass and pasture which surround it. Only one of its three corner porches is now in use as an entrance (although formerly all had equal importance). This porch is the central one of the three and faces north towards the sun. The building does have windows, but these are heavily suppressed, the wall and windows merging as a result of the fact that where the boarding crosses the windows, every other board has been removed (Fig. 5.20). Its ordinary door is painted white like the rest of the walls and is therefore not obvious from a distance. In this way, despite the prominence of its form among the undulating sand dunes, it is presented as an act of concealment.

5.16
Sloping upper step of
Cemetery Amphitheatre
looking east towards
the chapel.

After this ambiguous welcome, the warmth of the timber-lined, one-roomed interior is quite unexpected. Here, in a relatively dark space ringed by columns, diagonally filtered side-light from three corners is balanced by a stronger source of top-light at the centre. Below an opening in the roof four columns define a narrow light well that occupies the middle of the room. Equipped with triple-hung sash windows whose uppermost panes glow brightly in the darkness, this tiny courtyard orchestrates not only light and ventilation, but also the space available to users. The room contains a stove, a piano and some tables and chairs, and now it is used most frequently as a meeting room, two of the original porches having been made into cupboards. Lining the walls are a series of panels, surfaced on one side with reed matting and on the other with blackboards, whose fixings allow them to be reversed if the acoustic of the room needs adjustment. The key interior horizon is that created by the tables, the whiteness of whose surfaces is prominent in the relatively dark interior.

This project was authored by Godofredo Iommi, Alberto Cruz, Miguel Eyquem and Juan Purcell in 1971 following a poetic act of foundation (a *phalène*) constituted by a walk around this area of the site, and Iommi's declaration that its destiny was to be 'a place for music although there are no musicians amongst us'.[17] The sense that the purpose of such a room should remain open to interpretation, i.e. that beyond providing an arena for musical performance it should act as a forum for discussions about community life, was identified at the outset (Figs. 5.21, 5.23). Since its construction it has always been held in common, its versatility demonstrated by the range of uses found for it. Beyond the recitals of music its name would suggest, it has accomodated the staff meetings of the Valparaiso School every Wednesday for the last thirty years, several design studios and in the 1970s the poet Ignacio Balcells even used it as a dwelling, though this did not prevent it from remaining 'public' since he was happy to host poetry recitals to which all were invited. It remains the venue not only for major

5.17
Music Room and its service
building from the north-west.

festivities like baptisms, birthdays and marriages but the regular meals at which guests are formally given welcome to the Open City. According to David Jolly, the former Head of Architecture at the school, and a co-founder of the settlement, it is therefore 'the public interior of the Open City par excellence'. It is the unusually nuanced interplay of light and sound that has allowed it to accommodate this diversity of uses that is worth discussing at length.

Achieving a poetic synthesis of light and sound

> A light-size is divined
> The highest instance of form
> constructs the balance of what is seen and touched
> with what is not touched and rarely seen,
> the plan is not given a fixed orientation,
> the room is without a predicted orientation for people and objects,
> so that it can stage poetic acts
> with their unforeseeable orientation.
> In the centre, as a result of a thermodynamic phenomenon,
> small raindrops scarcely fall,
> A column of a rare, rarefied space is formed.
> Thus we hear music.
> Spatial divination and not technical light calculation.
> Because of the urgency of the moment of foundation,
> Confident that on the shore the mildness is auspicious.[18]

As this statement confirms, thinking about the mutual impact of sound and light was always critical to the design of the Music Room. According to Cruz, while its designers always saw light as a 'gift' of place and of latitude, they realised that the goal of creating a room with a particular acoustic meant a guiding principle for light's deployment was required. As he explains, the aim was to create

5.18
Aerial view of the Music
Room. Note the asymmetry
of the roof.

a calm inward-looking room of evenly distributed light sources and therefore concentrically even or 'equal' light[19]:

> We were thinking that the visual was important to what must be done. We wanted the almost impossible, the utopic moment of all works: that light would not illuminate the objects, that light would show itself. There arrived a moment when all this had to be referenced (*recogido*) – as the horizon references the visual. We realised that we should construct a vertical horizon at the centre, and the rest had to be a *penumbra* – luminous half-shadow. The extremes (the corners) had to have light so the light from the centre does not fade away.[20]

What is interesting is that Cruz describes the major light source at the centre as a 'vertical horizon'. It is the light source that controls how the space is perceived and against which the relative brightness and therefore visibility of the rest of the room is measured. (The upper part of the light well is a source of glare, but because it is just above eye height and thus out of focal vision in a room of this scale, this is not problematic. In its presence the modulated ceiling surface and the walls recede into shadow.) His sense of the more vertical sunlight at noon as 'equal' or 'even' light (in his view, 'light that illuminates things as things'[21]), clarifies why the lighting intention was 'almost impossible'. The intention was to make top-light ('equal light') 'show itself' on a permanent basis by ensuring it helped to create the relatively even shadowless light (the *penumbra*) beyond the centre of the room.

A refuge not only from the light and the wind, but also from the breathtaking views over the Pacific available outside, the room creates an adaptable stage for gatherings. While it originally presented a choice of entrances and still offers alternative acoustics, as already noted, its central light well can

5.19
Atrium of house of Gaius
Secundus, first century AD,
Pompeii.

be rejigged to transform the space and light it provides to users. Helping to dictate where a musician is located in relation to an audience, or how furniture is arranged for an event, the room may be one large semi-external space or an interior centred on a light well, depending on whether the light well sashes are raised or lowered. (According to Eyquem, musicians have generally preferred to locate themselves in the windowless quarter of the room. This may be because this corner is least likely to be disturbed by comings and goings, or because the top-light is slightly stronger here as a result of the fine-tuning of the light well discussed below.) Arguably what this suggests is that although lacking an *impluvium* (rain exits the courtyard/light well through the gaps between the floorboards), as a simple introverted space with a square oculus, the room is usefully compared with the entrance hall or atrium – the 'space of decisions' – of a patrician Roman house (Fig. 5.19).[22]

The detailed design of the central light well confirms that the goal of building 'equal' light overrode that of building 'equal' form. Though one's dominant impression is that the main space has four-square symmetry, on closer inspection one sees that the ceiling surfaces adjacent to the light well differ with orientation (Figs. 5.4, 5.18). In order to respond to the sun's path across the northern sky, those on the north sides are flat while those on the south sides are sloping, an adjustment which allows the light well to refocus the sunlight towards the centre of the space while moderating its impact as a source of glare. (On entry from the east, north or west one can see at least one of the sloping surfaces above the south-east and south-west sides of the light well, surfaces whose brightness is intermediate between the interior and the exterior.) Tellingly the process of thought behind this 'counterbalancing of the direction of the sun' is spelt out by Cruz as: 'To see the light, to think the light, to educate the perception. The education of vision.' What 'education' the strategy represents is hinted at by Puentes when he frames the significance of this detail as follows: 'The building sustains its own orientation, a concentric body which establishes *its own north* through the lantern.'[23] The effort to recover orientation for the postcolonial cultural milieu that South America represents – a primary aim of the Open City Group – reflects their view that an authentic South American architecture

5.20
Broken views and mitigation
of glare. The brise-soleil of
the western lantern porch.

will only emerge if its makers understand better and reflect their 'place' in the world. At the Music Room this development of a 'thesis of one's own north' is constituted by its enigmatic architecture of light.

Cruz suggests that the primary goal of the conversation prompted by this *trabajo en ronda* was to 'produce, understand and interpret a tension, an interpenetration, of sound and light'. But perhaps more significantly for this discussion he also goes on to describe the architectural intentions in the following terms:

> From someone being there with the light illuminating the room, we wanted to build a situation of being absorbed. Absorption is the idea of not having a past or a future … At the same time we wanted an openness, a psychological weight (*pesadumbre*).

It seems that the answer to a search for the environmental correlates of time-lessness was an introverted building which stops time half-way through the day at a perpetual noon, with its vertical, 'equal' light. In a room without a view (or rather a room with only broken glimpses of its immediate setting) a concern with absorption is linked to that of openness (the opening of opportunities for inhabitation) and the weight of shadow.

Paradoxically the Music Room is both light and heavy. Though constructed of lightweight materials its relative darkness gives it weight, especially in this location where so much light is available. It is, as Cruz says, 'simple, unitary, elemental', a square enclosure centred by light. And yet this stability is subtly undermined by the interplay between the building's orthogonal and diagonal geometries that guide how the building is encountered. Not only does the external

5.21
Music Room interior with a
staff meeting in progress.

skin of diagonal boarding give a dynamic spin to its basically stable form, but by painting the exterior onto the interior, it folds the outside inside, winding lengths of sunlight round and into the building. On the interior the diagonally oriented corner roof trusses and corner columns quietly counterpoint the orthogonal plan, whereas the corner porches key the diagonal geometry more emphatically to spatial encounter, and thus to experience. On entry they offer and attract the long diagonal views (each a *veduta per angolo*, an encounter with walls at an angle to the view) that deny confrontality and invite wandering into the space.

On the surface the Music Room says very little. As a public room it is reticent, undemonstrative, anti-monumental, transient. Not powerful through size, weight, or material sophistication but because it is ordinary and at the same time extra-ordinary, familiar and yet unforeseen. Its authors have described it as a musical instrument. More light-heartedly it might also be seen as a device for measuring the weather, or more profoundly as a lightweight cave. It is all these things, but, before this, it also aims to be just a cabin on a beach where people meet, or as its designers frame it, 'a space inside of which music can be heard' whose 'light-size' informs its orchestration of place.

Enlightening strategy

> To live together in the world means essentially that a world of things is between those who have it in common, as a table is located between those who sit around it; the world like every in-between, relates and separates people at the same time.[24]

Like the earlier Los Pajaritos and Santa Clara projects, the design process for the Music Room may be described as an inventive search for 'equal' light. And yet together with the work which followed, it represents an even more emphatic turning away from modernist ideals. Though a square plan form remains a starting point and austerity a guiding principle, the concern is no longer to offer a fixed hermetic solution, but rather an open-ended response to the demands and

midday 2.00 pm 3.30 pm

5.22
Spatial divination, and not the technical calculation of light, was the aim in the Music Room. Close attention was, however, paid to the geometry of the light well with respect to sunlight. Heliodon studies of a model of the Music Room interior showing the variation in sun patches across the afternoon at the spring/autumn equinox.

opportunities of assembly. The seamless white planes and ethereal 'cubes of light' are succeeded by raw timber boarding and measured darkness where the time and space of the event or gathering are subtly choreographed to create a versatile public room oriented by light rather than view.

An appraisal of the many different threads of conversation concerning light that have been developed at the Open City is not possible here, but an outline of some key themes illustrates the eloquent dialectic the settlement now represents. One spectrum of possibilities is reflected in the venues created at the Chapel, the Cemetery Amphitheatre, the Palace of Dawn and Dusk and the Music Room. As stages for public theatre, they offer a range of degrees of enclosure, and therefore also of closure and level of formality to the events they shelter. The Music Room is the darkest, most contained, most controlled and most formal of these stages, the church the lightest, loosest and most open to interpretation through performance. On the other hand, the series of settings for conversation represented by the Faubourg of the Palace of Dawn and Dusk, the Hospedería de los Diseños, the Hospedería del Estudio and the Music Room articulate variations on a theme concerning exposure to view. In this case it is the degree of exposure and the fixity of furniture that are in question, ranging

5.23
The Music Room with a meeting in progress.

5.24
Good light on a suitably
located table in the
Hospedería del Estudio.

from the most open but also the most fixed setting at the Faubourg to the least exposed, most flexible arrangement at the Music Room. In the former the furniture locates a conversation open to time, weather and the horizon, in the latter the room orchestrates and orients more focused but potentially open conversation in time stilled through light.

Though deliberately divorced from the metropolis and the market forces to which professional practice must respond, the Open City is much more than a brave social and educational experiment. In showing how 'art may rhyme with life' the lessons it offers have wider political import than might at first be assumed. The emphasis it has placed on generosity and hospitality, rather than the doubtful promises of individual freedom or total flexibility, the effort made to see building as a collective open-ended dialogue, and the resulting work as offering salient degrees of choice and the potential for transformation underline what 'openness' now needs to mean more often. It is an 'openness' that relies on a serious conversation about the reciprocity of spatial order and light, one which sees light as essentially generative in design synthesis. Acknowledging that how architectural questions are framed is critical, its 'living poetry' is a form of practice which underlines that the 'truth' of the situation – the direction of architectural interpretation – can be an intuitive response to circumstance dependent on both nuances of culture and the lessons of practical experience. That the ambition for light in the Music Room, and at the Open City more generally, may be better characterized as good light for conversation (good light on a suitably located table) rather than either the meeting of technical guidelines or the production of striking effects is a potent statement of this philosophy. Essentially, as if for generals at war, it is the well-lit tables of the Open City that locate and structure the intensely fought debates over strategy that mark the building of this unusual community. Finally, that this civic project rightly sees the interpretation and deployment of light as a political act is worth emphasizing, demonstrating as it does that through the sympathetic staging of events, it is good light – not abstractions like form or space – that constructs the city.

Notes

1   A. Cruz, personal interview, 2006.

2   M. Eyquem, personal correspondence, 2006.

3   The major study in English on the work and philosophy of the Valparaiso School (the School of Art and Design at the Pontifical Catholic University of Valparaiso [UCV]) is A. Pendleton-Jullian, *The Road that is Not a Road and the Open City, Ritoque, Chile*, MIT Press, 1996.

4   A. Cruz, 'Proyecto para una capilla en el fundo Pajaritos', *Anales de la UCV*, vol. 1, 1954, pp. 219–234, published on the web at http://www.ead.pucv.cl/1954/proyecto-pajaritos/, December 2010.

5   Ibid.

6   M. Eyquem, personal interview, 2006.

7   M. Eyquem A., trans. M. A. Steane, 'Illuminacion. Study to establish the illumination for Santa Clara', unpublished paper, 1957.

8   J. S. Ackermann, '"Ars Sine Scientia Nihil Est": Gothic Theory of Architecture at the Cathedral of Milan', *The Art Bulletin*, vol. 31, no. 2 (June 1949), pp. 84–111.

9   'The poetic act comes into being after an assembly where the poet proposes the unfolding of a game that has as a fruit the emergence of words spoken by the participants, be they guests or those who are there by chance and have agreed to participate. The game is based on the silence proposed by the rules of play that have been agreed at that moment by the participants. With the words that originate from the act the poet forms a poem, adding only connecting words between the spoken words. The act terminates with a reading of the poem which is left as a gift in the place' (D. Jolly, 'Arquitectura Efímera', unpublished essay, 2010).

10 D. Jolly, personal correspondence, 2006.

11 Open City Group, 1977. The Hospedería de los Diseños has subsequently been extended. This description is of the original unextended version.

12 Fabio Cruz, David Jolly, Juan Purcell (1987).

13 Patricío Cáraves, Jorge Sánchez, Juan Purcell, Open City Group (1999).

14 Alberto Cruz, Jorge Sánchez, Open City Group (1982).

15 Isabel M. Reyes, Tomás Browne, Patricío Cáraves, David Jolly (1983).

16 Jorge Sánchez, Juan Purcell, Open City Group (2001).

17 Escuela De Arquitectura, UCV, Esposicíon de la Ciudad Abierta en los 30 años de la escuela, Museo de Bellas Artes, Santiago, 1982, as quoted in M. Puentes, 'Sobre La Sala De Música', unpublished essay, 2003, p. 21.

18 Open City Group, *Origen Poético*, Presentacíon de la ciudad abierta, UIA, Barcelona, 1996, as quoted in Puentes, 2003, pp. 6–7.

19 'We were thinking we were wanting the light to illuminate things equally, that's why the central part of the building is regular. We made it regular in plan so that it could illuminate regularly. With no double shadows. Unitary, restricted, elementary. Trying to avoid all irregularity' (A. Cruz, personal interview, 2006).

20 Ibid.

21 Ibid.

22 It has also been compared to a *solar*, a traditional Chilean rectangular dwelling type with both external and internal galleries (*corredores*). The latter surround a central courtyard (Puentes, 'Sobre La Sala De Música', p. 12).

23 J. Purcell, private conversation as quoted in Puentes, 'Sobre La Sala De Música', p. 18.

24 H. Arendt, *The Human Condition*, The University of Chicago Press, 1958, p. 52.

Chapter 6

Seeing the light

The Poole House, Lake Weyba, Queensland

James Bichard,[*] ed. Mary Ann Steane

> We must have the ability to create simple spaces and volumes, which can raise the spirits of those who inhabit them and accommodate the different generations of a family within a house, providing them their own privacy and dignity. Wouldn't you agree, that if a child can sit in his or her room, well lit, well ventilated and observe the sky, the birds, the passing clouds and the changes of light and texture that they can produce, he or she has a better chance of smiling or laughing and looking forward to what the day may bring … than a child confined within a box like space, with one window looking onto the wall of an adjoining house, poor light, and inferior ventilation.[1]

> The houses, which have taken over the market, are generally, gross – but do satisfy for their occupants, what I call the three little pigs syndrome … if it is brick and tile, it is security and pretty much to hell with the rest.[2]

When the Commonwealth of Australia was formed in 1901, its founders were concerned to avoid the pitfalls of the Old World in their creation of a new harmonious and egalitarian nation whose observance of democratic procedures would be above reproach. The unique blend of established traditions and new influences this initial consensus has helped to foster both shapes how the nation is now viewed internationally and reflects the promise and threat posed by an ancient but fragile landscape that is home to both the world's oldest continuous cultural traditions and a richly complex mix of migrant cultures. And yet despite the recent emergence of an increasingly confident post-colonial culture, particularly in dance, music, film and literature, what constitutes contemporary 'Australian' architectural expression still remains obscure to outsiders. Although home since 1973 to the world's most recognizable public building, Jørn Utzon's Sydney Opera House, it is only latterly that the search for a more resonant – and more distinctive – Australian architectural identity has been given new impetus.

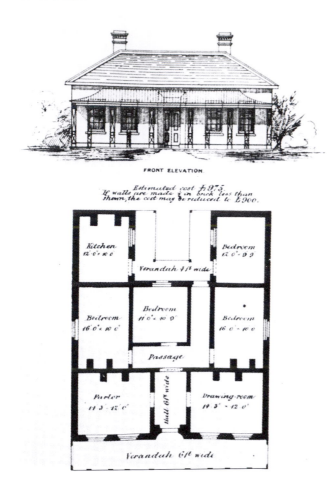

FRONT ELEVATION.

6.1
Imported ideas about
dwelling. A nineteenth-
century Australian
house with a veranda by
T.J. Crouch, 1856.

The result of a process in which longstanding relationships between physical and social geography are being renegotiated as the vulnerability of the country's natural resources are becoming more apparent, this new architecture is aiming to respond to international concerns about global warming and sustainability as it reinterprets the idea of dwelling in relation to local conditions. A key figure in the development of this new approach to residential building is the architect Gabriel Poole.

This chapter argues that it is possible to link Australian identity not only with the landscape but also with the thermal and, specifically, the visual climate of the country, and examines the implications of this idea for the way that dwelling is conceived and organized. As it explains, the lightweight, tent-like building type being championed by Poole represents the inversion of the closed, heavyweight European models that have prevailed in most Australian residential development since the arrival of the first British colonists in the eighteenth century. Critically, these new buildings respond to the local light very differently, giving careful consideration to how people see – or not – in the potentially blinding Down Under light by challenging what materials and forms of construction are proper to dwelling. In making light and air more of a priority than a vision of

6.2
The changing appearance of the typical residential street in Australia. (Diagram after the image on p. 89 of *The History and Design of the Australian House* (1985) by Robert Irving.)

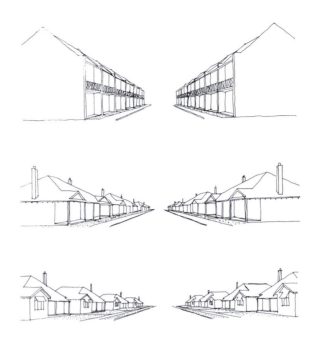

permanence or the provision of security, in reworking ideas about what a house should look like and how it should relate to the landscape, it would seem that Poole is proposing a new and very different response to the environmental setting Australia represents. It is one whose broader cultural relevance deserves attention, a subject to which the chapter will return at its close.

Inventing identity

The universal visual art, the art of shaping the human environment, is an intellectual, ethical, and emotional exercise as well as a means of expression. It involves the strange sort of possessive love with which people have always regarded their shelters and does not always make sense in wider environmental terms. It should therefore come as no surprise that the imported building traditions which have been a predominant influence on the appearance and character of Australia's landscape might have had a detrimental impact on its quality (Figs. 6.1, 6.2, 6.3, 6.4). What Boyd refers to as 'Australian ugliness'[3] has been the consequence of a fear of reality, a denial of the need to respond to local conditions when shaping the everyday environment of dwelling, a satisfaction with veneer and cosmetic effects.

Human occupation of the Australian subcontinent predates the white colonists arrival in 1788 by up to 50,000 years. The Aborigine population made their way south onto the land when the seas were lower and it was possible to traverse the channels between the Papua New Guinea Torres Strait and the northern reaches of the Cape York Peninsula. By remaining migratory, these nomadic peoples survived the continent's irregular and unpredictable weather patterns which prevented any permanent architecture and, hence, any discernible aboriginal culture in the eyes of foreign European settlers. Although their lack of visible culture led Europeans to consider them naive and uncivilized, the

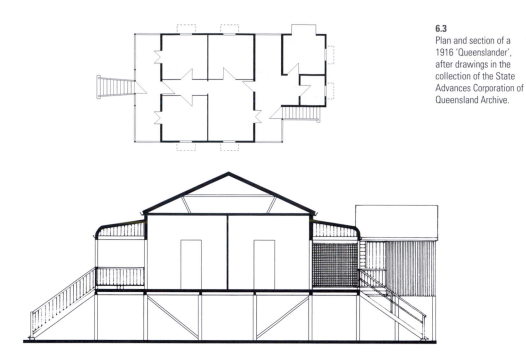

6.3
Plan and section of a
1916 'Queenslander',
after drawings in the
collection of the State
Advances Corporation of
Queensland Archive.

Aborigines were an advanced product of their environment, an environment whose possession they had secured not through land ownership, but by imaginatively taking it into their consciousness. In other words as they occupied the land they effectively sang it into existence. Every feature was sung into a rhythm, and these rhythms crossed the land, endowing it with meaning. For the Aborigines the act of passing through the landscape became more important than tangible connection to it. They chose 'to touch this earth lightly' and in the process these 'songlines' became the equivalent of an artificially constructed human habitat. Having no need for permanent architecture, the Aborigines used them to legitimize the vastness of the continent and give it a human scale.

Between the late eighteenth century and the 1970s the genocidal practices of Europeans almost eradicated the indigenous population. In addition to losses incurred in violent conflict, forcible displacement from their traditional lands was often fatal, particularly to native communities already weakened by exposure to the new diseases the settlers introduced. Their decrease in numbers meant that the new colonists faced little opposition to their imposition of an imported European culture on the Australian landscape, an imposition that fostered the emergence of Australian 'ugliness'. Under this security blanket of Europeanness, the fledgling towns and cities that began to expand adopted architectural styles directly from Europe. Meanwhile the new settlers spread over the continent in search of gold and minerals or land suitable for agriculture. But little across the vast landscape suited the techniques with which their farmers were familiar, and the population congregated around the shoreline, where rainfall was more generous and relief from the intense heat and sunlight was given by cooling sea breezes.

6.4
A 'Queenslander' in
Brisbane: a lightweight
dwelling type more open to
the breezes than traditional
European house-types.
Source: Wade Johanson.

It is clear that early Australian architecture adapted poorly to the new climate. Arguably the first cultural medium to respond with more sensitivity to the harsh environment was painting, although even this was not until after nearly a century of white occupation had elapsed. As Hughes explains, the status of their frontier culture meant that Australian painters were not initially in a position to record accurately the new light – and life – to which they were being exposed:

> English painting techniques of the early nineteenth century were being applied to an environment which they did not 'see' clearly … Society was governed by English law and enlaced by London's standards of morality, taste and etiquette. In short, the idea of an 'Australian' culture was unthinkable … The chief merit, perhaps the one function, of art in Sydney was that it strengthened the cocoon of Englishness needed for survival.[4]

But this was not always to be the case. Half a century later, after word spread back to Australia in 1874 of the first Impressionist exhibition in Paris, European influence began to foster a greater awareness of the peculiarities of the antipodean environment. While living in London, the young Australian painter Tom Roberts was strongly influenced by the concern for light that the Impressionists in France shared with Constable and Whistler in England. Returning to Australia in 1885 he set up an artist's camp outside Melbourne. The Box Hill 'Impressions' he recorded there led two other painters, Arthur Streeton and Charles Condor, to join him at a new camp at Heidelberg, and together they worked feverishly to produce the set of paintings which would become the first Australian art manifesto (Fig. 6.5). In emphasizing the steely intensity of Australian light this work made people look again at the world around them. William Lister-Lister, for example, observed later, '… after seeing Streeton's work we began to observe that the colour and atmosphere of the landscape were brighter than we had previously realised'. In Streeton's work, as Hughes confirms, Australian light and landscape took centre stage:

> Man was not the measure of landscape: for Streeton in the nineties, Australian landscape existed on its own terms and with its own

6.5
Seeing the antipodean light.
Tom Roberts: *A Summer
Morning Tiff*, 1886, oil on
canvas. © Art Gallery of
Ballarat, Victoria.

unique grandeur … Streeton experienced the Australian bush as a
romantic … he was obsessed by the stillness and remoteness of the
Australian landscape, its blinding light, and the contrast between its
fertility and ageless indifference to man.[5]

Lent authority by European Impressionism, the Heidelberg School began to
legitimize the Australian landscape in the eyes of the young nation, and thereby
lay the foundations for an Australian identity. It should come as no surprise that
a sense of place lay at the heart of that identity, for Australia was conceived of
from the first as a *place* of exile, a place to which the convicts of Britain could be
banished. It was critical therefore that all its people should come to terms with
this new-found place, seemingly devoid of culture yet teeming with a surplus
of nature. Finding space in the vastness of the land was never a problem, but
what this new movement declared was that grasping its light, embracing the
unique character of its environment, would be pivotal to the authenticity of any
independent culture which might emerge from it.

In more recent years Australian visual culture has been dominated
by two mainstays, Uluru/Ayers Rock and the Sydney Opera House. Anchoring
Australia on the coast, the Opera House has become a symbol for Sydney and
the other Australian cities, its complex geometries and five facades a potent
attempt at symbolizing a unification of culture, architecture and place. In contrast,
at the very centre of Australia, Ayers Rock stands as a permanent symbol of
mighty natural architecture. Its mass provides a tangible centre for the vast continent. Between the two is what suburban Australians refer to as 'the Outback'.
This term has found a way into Australian mythology, the definition of the space

6.6
Suburbia Palladia. A typical
Australian suburban dwelling
ill-suited to the climate and
therefore heavily dependent
on mechanical servicing.

between the coast and the centre, a space imbued with meaning, full of nature, but empty of significant white settlement.

What could be achieved through art, i.e. the recognition and celebration of what was fundamentally different about the antipodean world, was not so easy to achieve in architecture. Adapting Northern European building traditions to the Australian situation was much more difficult. This is because Australia's most southern regions share a climate similar to Barcelona, while her northern extremes are like those of Nigeria. In contrast to Britain, the extreme harshness of the light demands a building type which neither shuts it out completely, nor admits it so readily that glare and heat cause discomfort. Yet despite this, the only changes made to the closed-box housing models imported by the new settlers were the wide eaves and Indian-inspired verandas that were sometimes tacked onto facades (Figs. 6.1, 6.3, 6.4). As had been the case for earlier British colonists in other regions of the globe, a recognizable architecture that helped to quiet unease in face of an unfamiliar – and therefore unpredictable – environment was deemed more important than architecture which helped adjustment to the new climate. As elsewhere, the forms of dwelling that were adopted represented an uncertain hybrid of imported assumptions about how life should be lived and building practices adapted to the manpower and materials available. In such colonies the establishment of a sense of locatedness has always meant the built environment has needed to have the shape of 'home'. Whether such imported models have provided the most suitable set of living conditions in the brave new world of a frontier culture has usually been considered unimportant. From this perspective the idea that the early colonists of Australia failed to see that the light they were living with had changed so radically, is perhaps less surprising. What seems more startling at the start of the twenty-first century however is the way in which this blindness and these anxieties are not only continuing to influence dwelling design and settlement patterns, but the way life – and place – is imagined and lived at these latitudes.

As free-settler immigrants began to outnumber convicts, so the suburbs started to spread around the cities. The lure of unlimited space in the

6.7
Gabriel Poole's Tent House
at Eumundi.

new nation sparked the Australian dream: that any new immigrant could afford to buy a plot of land on which to build their own house. At first houses were simple single-storey affairs with small gardens at the front and back, but as the nineteenth century progressed the ideal shifted from simple shelter to comfortable home. By this point 'comfort' was denoted by an increase in scale and closer imitation of European models, i.e. rather than representing a change in the conditions within, it was a matter of appearance. It should therefore come as no surprise that by the end of the century style rather than amenity had come to be the major architectural concern.

In the twentieth century the relentless expansion of suburbia continued apace as another influx of European and American immigrants arrived, bringing with them their own ideas and building traditions. In response to this demographic pressure identical speculative housing has begun to mushroom in every Australian city. Typically these buildings manifest a European obsession with weight and solidity. Solid brick boxes that lack porches or any other means of providing shade, they tend to stand within a conspicuously artificial environment: a carefully subdivided landscape of fences, weeded beds and trimmed lawns completely shorn of native shrubs and trees. This artificiality is crucial in understanding Australian attitudes to housing from the 1960s to the 1980s. European immigrants sought this artificial neatness and similarity to home to protect them from what lay beyond the back fence. To belong to the city and not the frontier society of the bush was crucial, and the unreal suburban world in which they lived was deliberately designed to cut them off from the sights, sounds and rigours of Outback existence.

It is an outlook which still predominates. 'Suburbia Palladia', in which brick driveways navigate manicured lawns towards whitewashed cement block villas whose tiled roofs conceal continuously whirring fans and air-conditioning units, and whose small tinted windows remain firmly shut to retain

6.8
Evening light at Lake Weyba.

coolness, remains characteristic of the majority of new housing developments in recent years.

Challenging banality: The work of Gabriel Poole

Some dissenting voices have nevertheless emerged more recently. Now based in Toogoolawah, Queensland, architect Gabriel Poole has been developing a design philosophy which challenges the standard approach to housing by implementing the lessons learned over a long career in practice in this region. Having realized that lightweight buildings provide the most comfortable conditions for occupants in the local climate, his work seeks to capture the bright Queensland light and the cool Queensland breezes in exactly the right combination. The overriding principle is to make the stifling summer sun more bearable and to establish an integrated microclimate of house and site that makes the experience of dwelling more enjoyable. Arguably, in aiming to create a living environment more in tune with the climate and more open to the landscape, his work is seeking to reject the radical introversion of atomized suburbia by rethinking its light.

The differences between Australian and Northern European light are worth clarifying at this point. In contrast to Britain, at Australian latitudes the sunlight can be dangerously intense not only on occasional summer days but for much of the rest of the year too. Noosa lies just south of the tropics, so midday summer sunlight passes almost directly overhead at an altitude of 87° above the horizon. The equivalent winter sunlight angle is 60°, i.e. the maximum summer sun angle in London. Furthermore, atmospheric conditions with comparatively low pollution levels result in clear skies free of smog, haze or dust particles, which is why Australian skies are so blue and one can see such a long way.

Another critical factor affecting the visual environment is that the strength of the sunlight and the predominantly clear sky conditions mean that when viewing the landscape in Australia, the majority of the glare and brightness is typically coming from the ground. Relatively speaking, the sky, although bright, is not as hard to look at as the land. Moreover at these latitudes there are particular problems associated with the entry of direct light into dark interiors. In

6.9
Plan of the Poole House at
Lake Weyba, after drawing
by Gabriel Poole.

such circumstances the prevention of glare by orchestrating the relative brightness of adjacent surfaces within the field of view can be crucial to the shaping
of appropriate visual conditions within buildings.

Poole's other major aim has been to make this lightweight housing
affordable. From the outset a search for simplicity of form and structure and a
willingness to exploit prefabrication has led to the achievement of lower average
building costs through the use of a repetitive module and standardized, mass
produced fixings. Following projects such as the 1983 Lewis House and the
1985–1986 Noble House, in which these goals were successfully pursued, Poole
embarked on the design of a house for himself and his wife on a twenty-hectare
site of wild bush at Eumondi, half an hour inland from Noosa (Fig. 6.7). Seizing
a chance to evolve his lightweight housing further, Poole proposed a slender
steel structure that supported a raised house with few solid walls. Via a tent-like
building he sought to provide the closest possible contact with the landscape,
and a set of living conditions in tune with the natural environment. Again it was
intended that the house should be the prototype for prefabricated housing, and
be the vehicle for developing a kit of parts which people could take away and
rebuild elsewhere. The steel frame was designed to be unbolted, dismantled
and moved. A PVC roof that acted like a fly-sheet shaded the inner roof, producing an envelope that was passively cooled in summer by air movement. Only
the bathroom, closet and kitchen had fixed walls. The rest were either stretched

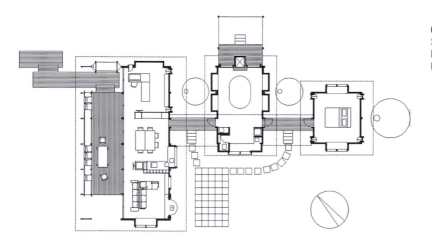

6.10
South-east elevation of the
Poole House, after drawing
by Gabriel Poole.

6.11
Section through Poole House
Living Pavilion, after drawing
by Gabriel Poole.

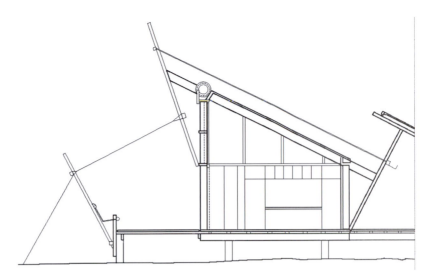

clear vinyl doors which could be slid back, or canvas sheets that could be rolled up. Embodying an ephemeral lightness, the house was reduced to a living platform in the landscape. Recalling the years he lived there, Poole reflects on the consequences of this attitude, concentrating on the unusual degree of interaction it allowed between the house and its context:

> It was truly a joy, and a wonderful and extraordinary living experience. Light steel frames moved like yacht spas in the wind, and the translucent walls created ever-changing patterns of light and shade. With the floating tent forms ... cool space was created in the building. Roll-up walls and windows and clear vinyl sliding doors opened our home to the environment and created a living experience like no other I had known.[6]

Capturing the Australian imagination in a way no previous house of its kind had done, the project not only won three prestigious architectural awards, but formed the Australian exhibit at the 1991 Venice Biennale. Funds given by a Queensland newspaper even allowed a permanent replica to be purchased for the Brisbane Botanical Garden. And yet it failed to have a significant impact on the suburban landscape. Although prompting as many as 3,000 enquiries from prospective buyers, not a single house was subsequently ordered. Complete with skeletal turrets and swaying flags, the project tellingly demonstrated some of the benefits of reversing Australians' 'castle' mentality, but in the end prospective occupants judged it a provocative experiment rather than a realistic solution to the problems they faced. In the end what they saw was an enchanting but fairytale house-of-cards, not a dwelling in which they could live.

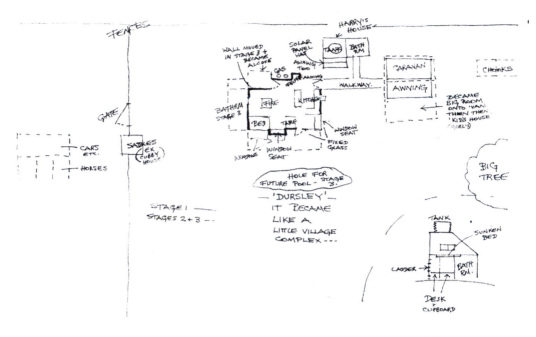

The Poole House: Making light work

6.12
Gabriel Poole's sketch of
his own dwelling at Dursley
whose informal living
arrangements in-and-out of
doors were an inspiration for
the environmental approach
taken at the later Lake
Weyba Poole House.

Elizabeth said, "Well, wherever we are in this new house, I want to be able to see the sky." She said, "The builders and everyone will come along and they'll stuff up everything around us but the thing they can't stuff up is the sky". And so that's how we got the great big tilt-up and then we put garage doors up on the top of it so that we could close that down or open it up. The whole thing right down to the toilet, you could be anywhere in the house and you could look at the sky.[7]

Despite the fact that the 'Tent House' nearly ruined him financially, in 1996 Poole proceeded to develop its interplay of ideas about lightness and openness in the next dwelling he designed for himself and his wife Elizabeth. As these telling comments of Poole indicate, his latest theories on house design were thoroughly explored in their ongoing dialogue about what relationship a house should establish with its environment.

Set in an area of natural coastal wallum or scrubland near Lake Weyba in Noosa, the tent-like aspects of this building are less obvious, although it too challenges the idea that a house must have a secure castle-like form. The atypical formal/spatial strategies it adopts reflect Poole's perennial concern to marry lighting and ventilation strategies while challenging assumptions about dwelling and its relationship to the land. How it frames light and topography in order to ground inhabitation by orchestrating fluid relationships between interior and exterior deserves close scrutiny.

Cleverly situated to one side of the site, and slightly raised, the house overlooks the expanse of adjoining grasslands, its floor level with the dancing

6.13
Poole House seen from
north-east across the
low horizon of wallum
scrubland grass.

grasses in front. Divided – unusually – into three single-storey blocks whose
steep skillion roofs open northwards to the sun, it approximates the height of
the gently swaying gum trees behind. Like the trees, the pavilions are visually
lighter towards the top while the crispness of their base scores a dark shadow
beneath each one. In between, below a frieze of vertical wooden battens, the
crisply folded steel cladding that wraps around the blocks is punctured only for
a door or a window. Despite their obviously lightweight construction, this makes
the pavilions seem sturdy, yet room is left for light and the northern coastal
breezes to pass through, carrying the smell and colour of the bush, and relief
from early morning mugginess.

Approaching the house from the road, one must walk up to the edge

6.14
Poole House from the
northern approach at
twilight. The steel exterior
wall cladding may have been
bright at first, but over time
it will return to the dull grey
of the wallum bush. Likewise
the upper fibro panels of the
side elevations are painted
a light purple that evokes
the shade cast by the gum
trees or the colour of the
sky at dusk.

6.15
View down veranda on entry.

6.16
View through living pavilion
to the bush.

6.17
Dining area beside living and bathing pavilions.

6.18
Bathing pavilion.

6.19
Heliodon studies of bathing
pavilion showing morning
sunlight penetration.

of the grassland surrounding the house. Here a boardwalk extension to the veranda which runs the length of the nearest – and largest – pavilion steps across the grass. It is from this point that an oblique view through the house is possible towards the second but not the third, more private, pavilion beyond. Arriving at one end of the veranda one looks down its length into the bush.

Where is the door? The house does not have one. Instead an entire wall lifts up to negotiate a threshold between bright sunlight, glowing half-light and coloured shadow. Above the grasses and below the foliage, the veranda decking floats between two horizons. Under the shade of its canopy, breezes from the north can pass unhindered across the deck and into the house. With the front wall raised (a series of garage doors), there is no division between inside and out, a continuous floor surface emphasizing the seamless juncture between the two. In fusing together the site and the house, a seat of steel mesh running the full length of the veranda edge takes its support from the building's structure but is literally suspended over the landscape.

In the first and largest pavilion, the central area is reserved for the kitchen and dining room. Here the sectional arrangement means that seasonal changes in solar geometry can be addressed intelligently. In winter low-level sunlight comes streaming through the clerestory windows, striking yellow surfaces located to highlight the sun's path, and bathing the dining room in warmth. In comparison, on humid summer days, the interior is protected from the high-level

6.20
Possessing the landscape of light. View of the living room looking north, with its ceiling of moving light and shadow.

midday sun by the double roof. As with the Tent House, the twin-layered roof structure of each pavilion helps to negotiate the contrast in brightness between the inside and out (Fig. 6.11). But in this case a tarpaulin outer layer shades the interior and a stiffer, more secure, polycarbonate inner layer insulates the interior from the sun's heat. Again because both layers are translucent, the contrast between light levels inside and out is reduced, allowing the visual connection between them to be maintained without difficulty. This makes it more possible to see what one is doing, more possible to see where one is.

In marked contrast to most suburban houses not only do all the windows of the house look out onto some form of untamed landscape, but unusually a raised walkway leads out of one interior into a fragment of that landscape before entering the next. Here the house's collision of artifice and nature, its creation of intermediate enclosure defined by broken light and shadow, continues. In these spaces the steep high-level sunlight reflects off the pavilions and onto the ground, animating the dark underneath of the house with continually changing light. Without destroying it, Poole seeks to humanize the landscape by splintering its light. Intentionally his half-way territories construct wild rooms.

The central pavilion contains the bathroom, the final pavilion the bedroom, further inside-outside spaces where the interaction of enclosure and light draws the landscape into play. In this house Poole and his wife were not sure they wanted an internal bathing pool, and so here it is made more or less external via its relationship to door openings. From within the plunge pool bath, the views northwards though these doors is of trees or grassland. The trees on

the horizon stand on a plane of grass which runs in turn up to the edge of the deck. This means that when one sits in the pool, it feels as if the landscape is running straight inside the room. In the final pavilion the close proximity of the trees means that from midday onwards dappled light is cast onto its canvas roof. Lying in bed below, this makes it possible to see the breezes moving the trees, and thus to feel more strongly how they are keeping the house comfortable.

Looking backwards: Evolving the 'Queenslander'

Although, as already discussed, early Australian architecture did not usually respond well to the climate, the 'Queenslander', a local lightweight housing type, breaks this rule in several respects, and has therefore helped to shape Poole's thinking (Figs. 6.3, 6.4). As he knows well, it is a design which deals somewhat better with ventilation issues than with light. Typically these timber dwellings are raised high off the ground to provide a shady area for storage that optimizes the capture of breezes. At night the house cools down faster, and intentional gaps between the floorboards mean that, even on still days, cool air can be drawn from below to make the interior more comfortable. The wide overhangs and partial screening of the veranda shield the interior from the hot summer sun and allow it to provide cooler sleeping space at night when the climate makes this necessary. Finally, a central corridor running through the house from one side to the other exploits the Venturi effect and helps to ensure good cross-ventilation through every room (when a wind speeds up in passing along a narrow breeze-way, it increases its cooling effect). Yet, as Poole is also aware, this precedent has shortcomings which affect both visual and thermal comfort. Not only are the wide eaves of the veranda seldom properly ventilated, trapping heat beneath their ridges in uncomfortable air pockets, but just as significantly, interiors are dark and gloomy, so that views out are hampered by strong contrasts in light levels and disabling glare from veranda surfaces.

Drawing on the positive and negative lessons of the 'Queenslander' and of the cattle stations where he worked in his youth,[8] Poole makes his house in Noosa a complex working of breezeways and intermediate territories. In doing this he is seeking to address some of the lighting issues the vernacular house type had failed to resolve as he proposes a new relationship between his dwell-ing and the bush. Importantly, the design retains the idea of the central corridor as an axis uniting all the elements, and one which ensures each room can be readily cross-ventilated. And yet the 'Queenslander' plan is not repeated but deliberately pulled apart so that the house embraces its natural setting – and the setting in turn infiltrates the house. In order to emphasize this breaking down of form, rather than running the inside-outside space of the veranda around three sides continuously, Poole uses it only where necessary, i.e. to view the grasslands, to draw the landscape up to the edge of the bathing pavilion, or to extend the living pavilion into the bush.

> I can always remember riding home at night with the smell of the bush in the air. Those beautiful moonlit nights in the bush with the dingoes howling … That sensitivity and awareness is reflected in my house designs. It's inviting all that beautiful stuff out there into the

house. There's the feeling of being in here (the Poole House) but being able to push those walls up and you can almost reach out and touch what's outside. It's that – it's living with it and being able to retain it.[9]

Between the constantly moving horizontal plane of the grasses and the vertically swaying background of the bush, the Poole House becomes another platform for observing nature, another dwelling in league with the landscape. Once more, in order to make the humid climate of the tropics more comfortable, Poole opens his building up to it, rather than shutting it out. This inside-outness demands an architecture that combines complex moveable walls (the double height north wall of the living room) and screen walls (walls interrupted by ventilation slots) with inchoate, thicket-like natural lines of enclosure (the bush). As a result it has more or less of a physical presence depending on the place from which it is viewed, or its state of openness or closure. Interestingly it also suppresses – but does not totally deny – frontality. In overlaying the precise grid of the machine on nature's tangled web Poole has arrived at a proposition which can be encountered as a string of closed individual elements or a series of half-open stages. Attempting to answer more realistically the Australian desire for security while not compromising an embrace of the bush, Poole proposes a house which is both more – and less – hidden. When viewed at a distance across the grassland the house has a clear form, but from nearby its materials and loose spatiality allow it to merge with the landscape, to recede in the light.

Light camouflage

Poole terms the basic obstacle to any serious improvement in the quality of dwellings in Australia as the 'three little pigs syndrome': the idea, dear to many Australians, that a house must above all else be a secure closed box, a small-scale individual fortress whose weight and fixity shore it up against wind, weather and interference from any quarter. In the houses he has constructed in Queensland, in a climate of searing light and sometimes cloying humidity, the measures he has taken to open life to the breezes and to veil, rather than block out the sunshine, illustrate the experiential poverty of this point of view.

Like the Tent House before it, the Poole House is an antithesis to the brick dwelling. Despite its lack of air conditioning, ceiling fans or framed doors Poole has succeeded in demonstrating that it is possible to make a stimulating, comfortable and sufficiently secure house in a tropical climate. What is unusual about this architecture is that the roof is a mediator of glare rather than a source of shadow, a glowing, rather than a shaded, surface, a projection screen rather than a bulwark against the storm. With such a roof the architecture acquires the spatial character of the woodland, an interplay of glowing surfaces and skeletal shadows, that is neither truly inside or outside. In this architecture of half-light it is worth underlining that it is the act of seeing and a vision of security that are potentially in conflict. For Poole, framing the brilliant light appropriately to foster a way of life in tune with the landscape is more important than delivering an image of stability, yet he knows that insecure-looking houses do not sell. In fact, with its polycarbonate ceiling and stiff walls, the Poole House is somewhat more robust physically than its canvas predecessor, but it also establishes an edgy compromise between closure and openness that allows for its evocation of fixity and its opposite, potential dissolution.

Realizing that affordability is the key to making an impact on the domestic housing market, Poole has subsequently produced a series of web-based house designs and specifications which draw from the experiences of the Poole House, and are an economic alternative to Suburbia Palladia. It is as if he has realized that the Poole House is still too radical for many Australians, but that it remains an important initiative for him personally. Unlike courtyard housing, he is aware that it does not provide the obvious model for a more dense suburbia, and yet its radical embrace of spatial adaptability offers a series of lessons on how the house might be rethought for this climate and this landscape. In rethinking how life might be lived with, rather than without, the Outback, it has also illuminated the particular difficulties and opportunities that Australian light will always raise for designers. It is these aspects that have made this building and others like it a critical catalyst in the debate about how Australians 'see' Australia: how they engage with, and develop respect for their environment.

In this house suburban ideals are inverted: what was closed is opened, what was formal is dissolved; where there was heaviness there is permeability. And just as importantly where the divide between occupied land and wilderness was crystalline it is now blurred. Poole reverts back to an Aboriginal understanding of the land, breaking down the built environment, potentially at least, to houses of uncertain enclosure. He does this by building with the light, by thinking closely about how seeing is made possible here. In pursuing these intentions he creates a dwelling that is deliberately camouflaged rather than revealed by light, a dwelling which thereby suggests provisional encampment rather than permanent occupation, in order to 'possess' the landscape at last.

Notes

*   James works in Sydney, Australia, as a Commercial Property Project Manager specialising in the delivery of leading edge sustainable developments by the private sector. Originally trained as an architect, then chartered surveyor, James has continued his studies into sustainability leadership, and in particular, models for strategic partnerships that can deliver long-lasting change to a more sustainable future.

1   G. Poole, 'A.S. Hook Address', given on the occasion of being awarded the RAIA Gold Medal, September, 1998. Available online at http://www.architecture.com.au/i-cms?page= 1.13429.19.51.5101.447 (accessed December 2010)

2   Poole, 'A.S. Hook Address'.

3   R. Boyd, *The Australian Ugliness*, 2nd edn, Cheshire Pty Ltd, 1961, p. 143.

4   R. Hughes, *The Art of Australia*, 2nd edn, Penguin Books, Australia, 1970, p. 36.

5   Ibid., p. 61.

6   G. Poole as quoted in P. Hyatt, *Local Heroes – Architects of Australia's Sunshine Coast*, Craftsman House, Australia, 2000, p. 80.

7   G. Poole, January 2004, interview whose transcript is available online at http://www.abc.net. au/built/stories/s1111482.htm (accessed 26 November 2010).

8   Poole's inventiveness in expanding his first house at Dursley seems also to have been a key precedent for the thinking behind this project. Making do initially with a caravan, Poole and his wife added canvas annexes and awnings with a shade cloth over the top. Gradually more buildings were added incorporating a screen and roll-up walls, connected by walkways and a courtyard. As he notes, the place became like a little village.

9   G. Poole as quoted in B. Walker, *Gabriel Poole – space in which the soul can play*, Visionary Press, Australia, p. 12.

Chapter 7

O'Donnell and Tuomey's lessons in the history and geography of light

The Ranelagh Multi-Denominational School, Dublin, 1998

> Instead of considering time as divided in linear chronological art-historical categories, with old buildings suspended in a petrified past and new buildings projected in a volatile future, we prefer to think of all buildings co-existing in the context of the living present.[1]

Unlike many current architects O'Donnell and Tuomey have little to say about light. Neither as goal nor justification does 'light' figure large in an analysis of their own motivations. They choose instead to focus on 'responsibility for form', a responsibility they see as the design of buildings responsive to their surroundings, architecture which does not erode the character of the urban or rural neighbourhood it constitutes, interventions that do not seem 'out of place'.[2] Alongside this concern for circumstance, they also see their work as a nuanced response to programmatic issues, citing conversations with clients as an important source of inspiration. This means that a building is always a collaboration in their view, an ongoing dialogue attentive to the demands and goals of everyday use as well as to broader contextual issues. What they do not discuss – and yet what helps make their work compellingly resonant – is that this is an approach which depends on carefully structured relationships in light. By examining the ramifications of the practice's ambition 'to build something completely new that feels like it was already there before we started, as if we had discovered the scheme rather than designed it',[3] this chapter demonstrates that light is a contextual issue. Through an analysis of the eloquent lighting strategy in O'Donnell and Tuomey's project for the Ranelagh Multi-Denominational School in Dublin (1998), it considers the character of an institution, the nature of a community, and a sense of history, in relation to the structure of light.

Irish architecture and the Irish climate

The tentative thesis of this chapter is that many architects' intuitions about the light they know – and the visual character a building will possess in that light – come from lifelong experiences of which they are not always conscious. After all, every architect spends his or her life experiencing the local climate, observing how people behave in and around buildings and becoming aware of the variable settings they provide depending on the time of day or season. They draw on these memories when imagining the potential opportunities for inhabitation that a new building may offer, especially in projects where intermediate threshold environments have greater significance, and where easy exchange between interior and exterior is a basic requirement.

Even more influenced by the warm waters of the North Atlantic than Britain, Ireland has a mild changeable climate with no extremes of heat or cold.[4] Snow is rare, as are days of uninterrupted sunshine. As a consequence, with its milder winters, and cooler and cloudier summers, sunny days are remarkable (it is sunny for only approximately a third of daylight hours in Ireland). Two points about Irish light deserve attention here. First, there is the relative frequency of low gloomy light conditions produced by overcast or even very overcast skies. Secondly there is the speed of weather variation, typical of maritime climates. Although anecdotal, the following attempts to convey the impact of these ever-changing conditions establish the environmental drama penned by Ireland's ever-changing light.

7.2
Sketch after photograph
on p. 6 of Tuomey's
Architecture, Craft, Culture
(2004) of the main window to
the living room in the house
Barragán built for himself in
1948 in Mexico City.

In my past life I have known cases in which a very plain human face looked beautiful because lit up by a brilliant intellect. The mind within, like a lamp behind a picture, made the features luminous and attractive. Such also is the effect of sunshine in Connemara.[5]

Nowhere does light vary so constantly, or play such a part as a beautifier. An Irish scene might be painted many times like the haystack in Monet's picture, with the changing light on it, the real person in the picture. That light has the richness of the air, of the earth below, constantly watered by soft rain. It is a liquid thing. I have seen it come in to a grey Dublin street, straight from the Western sky over the mountains which were framed in the last houses of the short street, to splash the high walls, as if someone had taken a paint brush and dipped it into a pot of pale gold.[6]

How might such a climate influence people's attitude to shelter? Two effects seem likely. First, the low light levels and cool, very flat light quality of overcast conditions make access to daylight and the provision of visual warmth a priority, along with access to the animating drama of sunlight whenever possible. And secondly, because severe cold is so rare, a particular advantage is gained from investment in the design of thresholds and other sheltered external space to offer protection from the weather while allowing exposure to fresh air and natural light.

7.3
Johannes Vermeer
(1632–1675), *Woman
Writing a Letter, with Her
Maid* (*c*.1670), oil on canvas.
© National Gallery of
Ireland.

Windows and light

As it turns out, evidence for O'Donnell and Tuomey's oblique yet thoughtful
approach to light emerges in their discussion of windows. Tuomey's book
Architecture, Craft and Culture begins with the memorable image of the heroic
four-square opening Barragán devised for the studio space at the centre of his
house.[7] Musing on the view it must once have provided of its author at work,
sitting at a table and looking out towards his wild garden, he succeeds in evoking
this window's ambiguous status as a mediator of worlds, as an eye,[8] a room and a
virtual garden; a vehicle of exposure and enclosure (Fig. 7.2). Quoting Barragán's
analysis of his (Barragán's) meditative state as 'between introspection (time
lived) and idleness (enchanted space)',[9] it prompts the insight that windows are

7.4
Sketch after photograph
on p. 17 of Tuomey's
Architecture, Craft, Culture
(2004). Sketch of Le
Corbusier's 1925 Pavillon de
l'Esprit Nouveau, Paris.

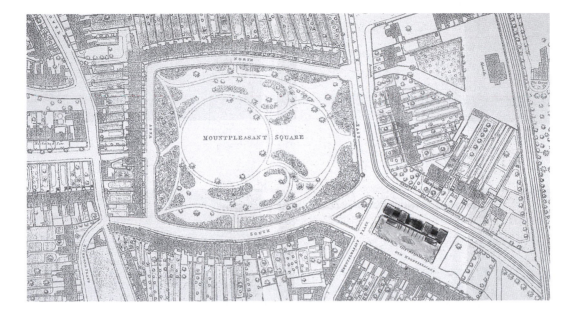

7.5
Site plan. The playground
is sited to allow for a
continuity of open space
in front of the terrace of
Old Mount Pleasant.

perhaps 'a way of seeing into the architects' intentions',[10] a lens onto 'the secret life of architecture'.[11] Later in the book he builds on this thinking to highlight the intrigue of the captured garden at the heart of Le Corbusier's 1925 Pavillon de l'Esprit Nouveau[12] – also a deep window with the scale of a room and a threshold that creates spatial ambiguity. As he notes, it was this project which provoked Aalto to ask, 'Is it a hall beautifully open to the exterior, or is it a garden built into the house?'[13] A subsequent chapter devoted to man-made landscapes betrays an interest in the principles that govern such relationships between space and light at larger scale. Through close analysis of the way in which vernacular architecture is influenced by 'the engagement of construction with context', Tuomey concentrates here on the unusual formal and spatial possibilities these topographies provoke, the way they challenge accepted landscape-to-building relationships. But importantly, what this discussion also illustrates is an awareness of how environmental concerns are carried latently by vernacular architecture, the

7.6
Finding more light for the
neighbourhood.
Above: Section through the
'tin church'.
Below: Section through
O'Donnell and Tuomey's
new school. Diagrams after
drawings by O'Donnell and
Tuomey Architects.

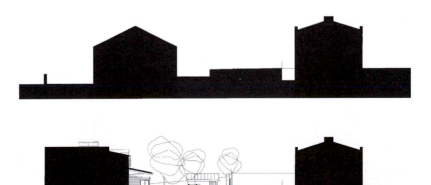

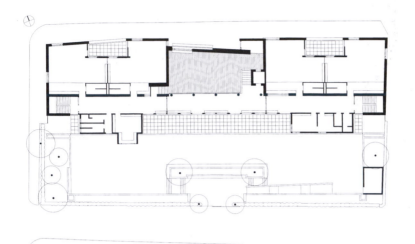

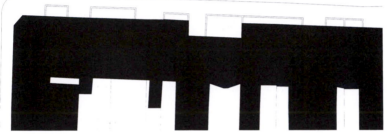

7.7
Ground-floor plan. The
reception-class children
begin their passage through
the school in the classroom
at the north-west corner.

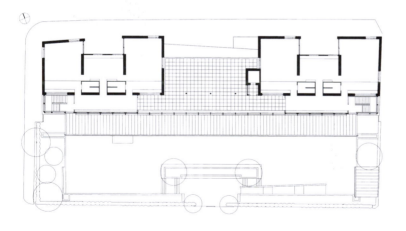

7.8
First-floor plan. The final-
year children occupy the
classroom at the north-west
corner which opens up
the best views over the
surrounding neighbourhood.

7.9
Typical rural Irish National
School from the 1950s.

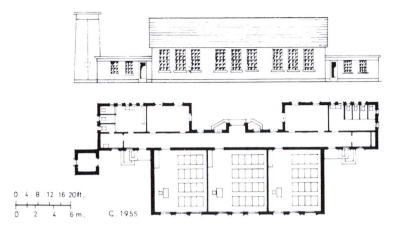

0 4 8 12 16 20 ft.

0   2   4   6 m.   C. 1955

underlying reciprocity they exhibit between climate/topography (outside) and construction/patterns of inhabitation (inside).

O'Donnell and Tuomey's implicit concern for light re-emerges in an interview they gave prior to the 2004 Venice Biennale.[14] Reflecting on the work of the seventeenth-century Dutch artist Vermeer, they point to a concern with how deep space is represented on a flat surface; the depth and complexity of light that stems from where window, shutter and pane of glass sit within a wall; the sense of interiority and mystery of an interior. Vermeer is most famous of course for the side-lit Dutch interiors he rendered as timeless theatres of graded light, and it is to these intimate interiors (the bulk of his *oeuvre*) which these comments clearly refer (Fig. 7.3). What O'Donnell and Tuomey are again hinting at here is an interest in the way windows qualify enclosure/exposure, the spatial reconfigurations that adaptable windows can generate. As Rasmussen notes in his chapter on daylighting in *Experiencing Architecture*, the variations in spatial mood of Vermeer's interiors are largely determined by the subtle transformations of light made possible by the shutters and curtains of traditional Dutch window design.[15]

Finally, the lessons for O'Donnell and Tuomey of the window arrangement in one of only two exteriors painted by Vermeer are also worth citing. As they explain, it was the subtle misalignments in the fenestration pattern of *A Little Street in Delft* (shifts which give the work its understated yet charged visual balance), that prompted the thinking behind the facade design for their Ranelagh School Project:

> There were shifts in the facades Vermeer painted – which we had already been working on in the Ranelagh School – that resonated with us. The way the openings and their proportions shifted became really useful to us in thinking about how to deal with the different scales of activity inside the buildings we were designing there.[16]

Why this carefully ordered facade represents an admirably fine-tuned reciprocity of light, building design and urban grain is the subject to which the discussion now turns.

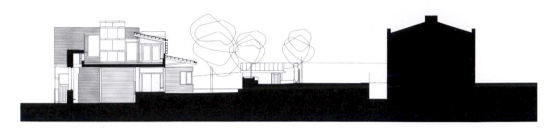

7.10
Cross-section through
the school looking
east, indicating how its
playground and hall spaces
are embedded within the
slope of the site.

A school in the city

> The scale and material of the new structure was established out of a careful process of negotiation and analysis, and the long game was guided by the principles of street and garden, which make the urban form of this part of Dublin.[17]

Located at the corner of Mount Pleasant Square, between a main road from the centre of Dublin and a quieter Georgian terrace to the south, O'Donnell and Tuomey's Ranelagh Multi-Denominational School represents the most substantial addition to its suburban neighbourhood in 150 years (Fig. 7.5). The community's strong attachment to the buildings it replaced and local concerns over the potential impact of a modern structure on its prominent site stimulated lengthy discussions over the scale and character of the new school. As O'Donnell and Tuomey themselves recognize, their final design therefore represents a slow, and by implication more measured, response to the physical and social complexities of the context than is often the case in projects of this kind.

Not a building which calls attention to itself in either material or volumetric terms, the school sits easily with the small-scale gentility[18] of the neighbouring residential streets.[19] The indented two-and-a-half storey brick facade to the major road at the north receives a stepped descent from the opposite side of the block (Figs. 7.10, 7.12, 7.13). In the morning, the children arrive through a gate in the wrought iron railings on the south, and descend through flowerbeds, hedges and small trees to an expansive courtyard-playground. This descent continues through a transverse portico, and then passes through a lateral corridor supporting a bench, canopy and walkway to the upper level terrace, descending one last time into the major public 'forum' of the school, the hall, whose back wall is the formal, north, wall. The 'front', formal facade is also the back, most chthonic wall of the garden-descent. This intelligent conceit allows the formal facade to do its institutional duty while allowing the life of the school to develop from the more informal, garden side of the site. If the order can be read as a garden descent from south to north, it is also a civic ascent from north to south; thus the public spaces always carry a double reading of town and garden.

The eight classrooms dictated by the brief compose the four house-like forms whose bold fenestration helps to give the brick facades their muscular rhythm. Separated by narrow courtyards, these 'houses' have been grouped in pairs along the main road to form two larger blocks to either side of a lower

7.11
A Scottish source of Inspiration for O'Donnell and Tuomey's organization of space and light. Charles Rennie Mackintosh's Glasgow School of Art (1897–1909).

block at the centre that holds the main hall. The younger children occupy the lower classrooms, the older children occupy the classrooms on the floor above. Above the hall, and hidden from the road, is a partially sheltered roof terrace. Beside the hall to the north is a small porch that acts as its formal entrance. To the south the staffroom and the principal's office lie to either side of the main portico. Organized internally by generous east-west corridor spaces at ground and first-floor levels, the layered plan is deceptively simple. A careful interweaving of inside and outside space inspired by the character and grain of the area gives it unexpected complexity and richness. The reassuringly confident civic presence to the main road shelters behind it a landscaped area that is actually a garden for playing pretend civic life. As O'Donnell and Tuomey are at pains to point out, this garden is also an element of their urban thinking. 'The new school is intended to provide for a continuity of open space in front of Old Mountpleasant, so that the landscaped playground can be understood as part of the setting.'[20] In this way the building's Janus-like character expresses the school's essential purpose as a forum of community life: an institution that does not just seek to accommodate, but actively constructs, its neighbourhood.

That the school should be aiming to build its own sense of community was a goal established during initial discussions between O'Donnell and Tuomey and the teaching staff, as the following set of comments by Joan Whelan, the school's principal during this period, confirm:

> We didn't want necessarily uniform classrooms that were eight individual boxes that the teacher went into, disappeared into and didn't come out of again until half past two in the day. And if you are looking at the curricular side of things, you will notice that we have a much more fluid approach to education in Ireland, particularly primary education, team teaching, children working in groups in and out of rooms, that sort of thing. So we wanted the sense that the school was a community. So it's things like being able to see other classrooms if

7.12
School and its south-facing playground from Mount Pleasant Place.

you're working in one place, being able to see into and out of other classrooms, being aware of the traffic, but not distracted by it, being aware that we are in an urban environment here, a heavily built up urban environment, rather than tucked away so we don't see the outside world from the beginning to the end of the day.[21]

What Whelan has to say here about the structuring of visual relationships within a school is the point of departure for a discussion of the sensitive approach to context that the building's daylighting strategy represents. How O'Donnell and Tuomey strove to address the questions she raises, not only through the nuanced design of its facade but also through their introduction of intermediate garden

7.13
North facade of school to Ranelagh Road.

7.14
Offset facade order. West
elevation of school to Mount
Pleasant Place.

spaces illustrates why thinking out light at a range of scales – and from a range of perspectives – can be critical to a successfully integrated neighbourhood. The argument begins with an extended explanation of the thinking behind the relatively unusual lighting strategy adopted for the classrooms which reflects the architects' perceptive synthesis of all the social, educational and physical (light/ noise/topography) considerations in play on this site.

Classroom light

Classroom lighting has always been a major consideration in school design, but as ideas about how children should be taught have changed over the last 150 years, so have ideas about the kind of environment a classroom should provide. Importantly it is a history that demonstrates some of the difficulties involved in an attempt to optimize design by quantifying it, i.e. to frame effective, genuinely beneficial environmental guidance that doesn't provoke more design conflicts than it solves. It also shows why discussions between educationalists and architects about classroom spaces (the activities they should be designed to support, their degree of enclosure, their relationship to the wider environment) remain fundamental to the design of stimulating places in which to learn.

The twists and turns of the debate in the UK over whether class-rooms should be oriented to take advantage of north or south light is a case in point.[22] In the second half of the nineteenth century strictly regimented class-rooms were typically designed to take advantage of north light in order to avoid glare from south and west facing windows. In contrast, in the years between 1900 and 1940 increasing awareness of the importance of fresh air and sun-light to the health of urban children prompted the open-air school movement. This new educational philosophy suggested that schools should be oriented in a southerly direction and designed so that teaching areas were exposed to fresh air and sunlight, and movement between the inside and the outside of the building was encouraged wherever possible. In the years immediately fol-lowing the World War II this emphasis on the positive benefits of light led to a demand that minimum daylight levels must be available throughout classrooms to ensure that no children were disadvantaged by working in poor light (this 1945 UK regulation stipulated a minimum 2 per cent daylight 'sky factor', with a recommendation that this should. rise to 5 per cent sky where possible). In many cases, however, the only way of achieving such a high level of daylight was through highly glazed facades, and they became the norm for many British schools constructed in the 1950s and 1960s. Because they were often thermally inefficient lightweight structures, such buildings overheated in summer and suffered from high rates of heat loss in winter, and as a result their classrooms,

What impact does the order of the facades have on the education the school can provide? Although their largest windows are north-facing the fact that these classrooms are lit from elsewhere is an important factor in how the school is experienced by the children. In each classroom further east or west side-light comes from windows onto narrow courtyard spaces located next to Ranelagh Road, and depending on their location, they also have other windows that face east, west or even south. As has been noted before, this reflects an approach to classroom design which follows a middle path.[29] Where other designs have sought either to establish a standard, repetitive unit flexible enough to take account of the full range of ages and teaching requirements (an approach typical in many early Irish primary schools), or to fine-tune each classroom to the educational needs of its age-group, O'Donnell and Tuomey's master stroke has been to devise variations on a theme through light. The effect of this degree of diversity (comparable to that of the variegated terrace structure of Georgian

7.17
Lower-floor classroom and one of the small shared courtyards to Ranelagh Road.

7.18
Upper-floor classroom.

7.19
View across the hall
looking east.

Dublin) is to give vitality to the simple plan, a vitality that helps different class-groups claim ownership of their own domains. This ploy is successful not only because it allows the possibility of negotiation between territories, but because it allows each territory to relate well to the whole institution, confirming Joan Whelan's view that intelligently organized light and views can orient and order social relationships. In other words, as spaces for learning the classrooms are sufficiently withdrawn to establish focus, yet sufficiently connected to establish a sense of community. On this urban site they not only strike a reasonable balance between exposure to noise and movement, and exposure to light, but offer opportunities for expansion that allow activities to be overlaid without difficulty, as if the life of the school has been thought of as a complicated dance. In these circumstances the daylight they provide it should be emphasized, while not of a very high level, is good enough.[30]

Finally, before appraising the contribution of the school's other windows to its architecture of light, this analysis of the classroom daylighting strategy is not complete without some comments on O'Donnell and Tuomey's measured attitude to colour. Despite the fact that white always makes for lighter interiors, it is their view that untempered whiteness can make for a very bleak ambience, particularly in the overcast conditions so frequent in Ireland. This has meant that while they have sensibly painted the major (street-side) walls of the classrooms white, elsewhere (and as in the streetscape of many Irish towns), accents of strong colour are deployed for warmth and diversity. Not only does this relieve the greyness of the remaining concrete-block walls that were stipulated by the brief, but it articulates each classroom's spatially layered plan. Inspired by the earthy palette of Italian Renaissance frescoes (which was also Le Corbusier's colour-range in the 1930s), the walls between classrooms are mid-lilac blue, the sink areas a lively apple green, and the bathrooms a strong terracotta red.

7.20
Bench in lower corridor
with houses of Old Mount
Pleasant in the distance.

Light in the streets and the squares of the school

As a block of interdependent, tightly interlocked components, the school has often been compared to a miniature city, as Tuomey himself is aware.[31] In his view it is more of a hill town, a reading which makes the general-purpose room on which it is centred its public square. With a floor half a level below the playground, this multi-purpose space and *sala terrena* that acts as a (formal) entry hall, place of assembly and market hall (it houses a farmer's market each weekend) can receive south light from both its portico entrance and a long roof-light in the ceiling, and north light from a window to the street (Fig. 7.19). In other words, this is the one teaching space in the school which has full access to the potential drama and warmth that a southern aspect brings in the northern hemisphere. It is also a room whose views reveal the project's active dialogue with its surroundings, and one which therefore makes concrete O'Donnell's idea that the school should act as a measured introduction to, and interaction with, the wider environment. (He has also suggested that a primary school should be 'a university of small life'.[32]) Looking southwards from beneath the roof-light, a series of screens (a row of columns, the glazed screen of the portico, the hedges and railings that surround the playground) both filter the light and structure the room's deep horizontal view of the Georgian terrace to the south. In this framing of the sunny garden shared between the terrace and the school, the street is inevitably drawn into the design, and the boundary between school and neighbourhood is made to disappear. Seen from this perspective it is the facade to the terrace which acts as the final wall of the school (Figs. 7.20, 7.23). While this view distils the idea that the school is essentially a large walled garden, and thus a world centred on play (intimate yet not out of sight, with a scale between the domestic and the civic), it also states that as a shared opening within the neighbourhood it represents an expression and embrace of community life.

7.21
The sheltered terrace above the hall in use.

Other aspects of the orchestration of light and views in this room, the corridors and the first-floor terrace manifest neighbourliness through careful attention to the messages that thresholds convey. Looking northwards for example, it becomes clear that a timber shutter may be slid across the hall's other window to close off the view to Ranelagh Road. Not only does this allow teachers to modify the visual and acoustic environment to which the children are exposed, but it transforms the hall from a side-lit 'cave' oriented to the garden into a more typical street-side space with a direct relationship to the city. On the first floor immediately above the hall is a garden 'room' which echoes Le Corbusier's Esprit Nouveau pavilion discussed earlier, in being partially covered and partially open to the sky. Now in use as a playground or outside classroom for the younger children, this terrace is sheltered from the road by a deep wall and cleverly concealed from view on the playground side by a robust timber screen. It is the design of the latter element which ensures not only that filtered sunlight animates this area but that an appropriate level of separation is established between the busy school and its quiet neighbours. It is also worth adding that windows to either side allow the light and space of this terrace to be borrowed by the upper classrooms, and yet despite the size of these openings the space doesn't feel overlooked. Tautly planned, the deep 'window' constituted by this 'secret' terrace creates a tranquil intermediate environment that in Dublin's mild climate can be occupied throughout the year. Finally, the generous scale of the corridor rooms provided by O'Donnell and Tuomey was appreciated by the staff and children from the start. Well side-lit from the south on the first floor, but darker below, they are connected at the east and west ends of the site by highly glazed staircases whose provision of extensive views over adjacent gardens opens the school to its surroundings in a manner not possible elsewhere. On the tightly packed site, such spatial release has a particular potency at a location all users of the building are able to appreciate.

The city in a school

An elegantly structured microcosm, the school composes a successful new corner of Dublin through its implicit response to light. The sharing of sky, orchestration of views and careful manipulation of enclosure generate a building whose construction of its urban situation is attuned to the needs of the children and their teachers, whether they are inside the classroom or outside at play. What is particularly admirable in this building is the way the window design in the classrooms judiciously balances the potentially conflicting requirements for enough light – and an appropriate degree of interiority – with a concern for the visual order generated by the whole building, rather than adherence to a priori assumptions about orientation. In not making daylight quantity or orientation an overriding priority and giving sufficient attention to the spatial relationships its apertures structure, O'Donnell and Tuomey's achievement is a project which asserts what a school should always be: not just an effective setting for learning, but a structured set of windows on the world.

Windows as urban theatre

> A critical issue for us as architects has become the recognition of those conditions of the situation, which could give significance to our choice of construction, embedding an initial sense of strategy which would remain evident in the eventual experience of the actual building.[33]

Like the paintings of Vermeer, Ranelagh Multi-Denominational School asserts the value of everyday life in a light that avoids both clinical precision and sentimental or sacramental overtones. It is an approach that depends on an attunement to the climate allied to a deep appreciation for the way contextual relations should impact not only on the form but also the environment of buildings. In repeatedly describing architecture as a kind of excavation, O'Donnell and Tuomey give

7.23
View from sheltered terrace looking south at the end of the afternoon to Old Mount Pleasant, the other wall of the school.

emphasis to the concept that architecture is discovery before it is invention. This vision of design as comparable to archaeology, i.e. a matter of painstaking detection and imaginative reconstruction rather than the self-expression of the artist or the potentially reductive analysis of the scientist, allows us to find Dublin in the school and to appreciate its quiet but compelling lessons in the history and geography of light.

Notes

1   J. Tuomey, *Architecture, Craft and Culture*, Gandon Editions, 2004, p. 30.
2   Over the last decade O' Donnell and Tuomey have published several volumes on their work: S. O'Donnell and J. Tuomey, *Transformation of an Institution*, Venice Biennale exhibition catalogue, Gandon Editions, 2004; *Profile: O'Donnell and Tuomey*, Gandon Editions and the architects, 1997; S. O'Donnell and J. Tuomey, *O'Donnell and Tuomey. Selected Works*, Princeton Architectural Press, 2007. See also K. Rattenbury, *Archaeology of the Air: O'Donnell and Tuomey, Architecture*, Trieste, Navado Press, 2004, for a thoughtful discussion of how the issues with which they are engaged impact on the work and its reception by clients.
3   Tuomey, *Architecture, Craft and Culture*, p. 41.
4   Climate data sourced from E.A. Smith and C.G. Smith, *World Weather Guide*, Helicon Publishing Ltd, 2000, pp. 190–192.
5   Revd H. M'Manus, *Sketches of the Irish Highlands*, London, 1863, as quoted in T. Robinson, *Connemara: Listening to the Wind*, Penguin, 2006, p. 191.
6   P. Hinkson *The Light on Ireland*, Friedrich Muller Ltd, 1935, pp. 9–10.
7   Luis Barragán, architect's own house and studio, Tacubaya, Mexico, 1947.
8   The Old Norse term, *vindauga*, or 'wind-eye' is at the root of the English terms 'window' and its Irish equivalent 'fuinneog', an elegantly compact etymology which expresses the dual role of windows as apertures for air as well light, while at the same indicating their role in the configuration of facades.
9   L. Barragán, as quoted in Tuomey, *Architecture, Craft and Culture*, p. 8. See also A.R. Martinez, *Luis Barragán*, Monacelli Press, 1996, pp. 106–108.

10 Tuomey, *Architecture, Craft and Culture*, p. 8.

11 Ibid.

12 Ibid., p. 17.

13 A. Aalto, as quoted in Tuomey, *Architecture, Craft and Culture*, p. 17. See also 'From Doorstep to Living room', in *Alvar Aalto: Points of Contact*, exhibition catalogue, Alvar Aalto Museum, Jyvaskyla, 1994, pp. 9–12.

14 O'Donnell and Tuomey, *Transformation of an Institution*, pp. 48–49.

15 S.E. Rasmussen, *Experiencing Architecture*, MIT Press, 1959, pp. 198–206.

16 Sheila O'Donnell, Shane O'Toole interview with Sheila O'Donnell and John Tuomey in *Transformation of an Institution, Venice Biennale Pavilion Catalogue*, Gandon Editions, 2004, pp. 40–50, p. 49.

17 Tuomey, *Architecture, Craft and Culture*, p. 36.

18 The characteristic dignity of Georgian domestic architecture anticipates a dialogue with small institutions.

19 As O'Donnell is aware, the streets in much of suburban Dublin have particularly low height-to-width ratios as a result of a very open urban grain (O'Donnell, personal interview, 2007). In this situation facade openings can potentially see considerably more of the sky and therefore provide more daylight per unit area, an important consideration in a climate with predominantly cloudy or overcast conditions. By locating the new building on the north side of the site and restricting its height and depth the access to light of the terrace is not compromised, indeed it is potentially improved.

20 S. O'Donnell and J. Tuomey, 'Multi-denominational School, Ranelagh Road, Dublin 6, O'Donnell and Tuomey', *Irish Architect*, no. 142, November–December, 1998, pp. 14–20, p. 14.

21 J. Whelan, personal interview, December, 2000, as quoted in S. Honeyball, 'Defining and designing the school environment: what role does the architect play?', unpublished third-year dissertation, Cambridge University, 2001, p. 46.

22 See *Passive Solar Schools: A design guide.* Building bulletin 79, Department for Education, Architects and Building Division, HMSO, 1994, pp. 7–8, on which this summary of the history of daylighting in purpose designed classrooms is based.

23 'The existing ridgeline of the "tin church" was adopted as the limit of the height for the new building and the north wall of the "tin church" was adopted as the limit of the distance from the terrace to the new building' (S. O'Donnell and J. Tuomey, *Irish Architect*, November–December, 1998, p. 14).

24 In Georgian architecture sash windows were employed, whereas O'Donnell and Tuomey's tall windows are fixed lights. They include a timber shutter for ventilation to one side of the glazing, and their external reveals, unlike those of traditional windows, are not painted white to increase the amount of light entering the interior.

25 See N. Roche, *The Legacy of Light: A history of Irish windows*, Wordwell Ltd, 1999, p. 38.

26 'Proportion was the essence of the Georgian idiom and the simple discipline of facades created a generally unified, yet deceptively varied, terrace streetscape … Spacious windows were practical in Georgian houses because they permitted maximum light penetration along the sometimes dark and gloomy canyon like terraces' (K.C. Kearns, *Georgian Dublin: Ireland's Imperilled Architectural Heritage*, David and Charles, 1983, pp. 31–32).

27 See Roche, *The Legacy of Light*, p. 13.

28 Ibid., p. 18.

29 See C. Slessor, 'Brick-and-mortar modern', in *Architecture*, August, 1999, pp. 76–83; and H. Campbell, 'Lesson Plan', in *RIBA Journal*, December, 1988, pp. 28–35.

30 As all the school's ceilings are currently fair-faced concrete (a stipulation of the brief), an improvement to the daylighting could be made in future by giving these ceilings a white plaster finish.

31 Tuomey, *Architecture, Craft and Culture*, p. 36.

32 S. O'Donnell, personal interview, 2007.

33 Tuomey, *Architecture, Craft and Culture*, p. 43.

Chapter 8

Inverse light?

The vulnerable openings of Libeskind's Jewish Museum, Berlin

A highly embroiled quarter, a network of streets that I had avoided for years, was disentangled at a single stroke when one day a person dear to me moved there. It was as if a searchlight set up at this person's window dissected the area with pencils of light.[1]

I remembered a story told by a survivor in Yaffa Eliach's remarkable book *Hasidic Tales of the Holocaust*. The woman who later lived in Brooklyn, recalled being transported by train to the Stutthof concentration camp and just as she was abandoning all hope, she managed to catch a glimpse of the sky through the slats of the boxcar. In the sky, a white line suddenly appeared, and she saw it as a sign that she would prevail. Through two horrific years in the camp, she clung to that sign as if it were proof that a miracle would occur and enable her to survive.[2]

It is easy to forget the shock generated by Daniel Libeskind's competition-winning entry for the Jewish Museum, Berlin (competition 1989, completed 1999, opened 2001). Just looking at the drawings and model photographs made many architects uneasy about how such a provocation could be justified. The design appeared to disobey all the rules. It had no right angles, no vertical walls, no obvious windows, no obvious entrance, and an anarchic zigzag form whose aggressive rupture of urban decorum violently scored through the existing streetscape at the same time as it drowned out the unassuming yet distinguished voice of the adjacent Berlin Museum[3] (the institution of which it was supposed to be the extension). Everything about it was disorienting. A wilful transgression. The closure and angularity of its broken shard-like forms meant it had no scale, no recognizable face. On closer inspection its interior seemed to have no spatial hierarchy, or certainly not one that could easily be read or that related to any previous museum typology. As a result while some asked whether it should be permissible for architecture to do this to a city, others wondered if this 'lightning bolt' could even be called a building.

In reducing the project to a list of defining elements Libeskind has focused on both its overall goal – the architectural integration of Jewish history

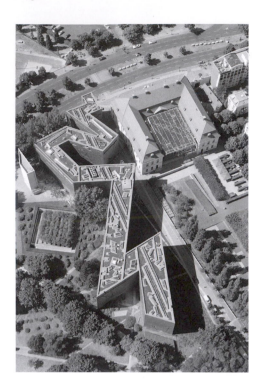

8.1
Aerial view of the building.
The sequence of voids is
representative of Jewish
absence while the zigzagging
line is analogous to Berlin's
sometimes tortuous
historical development from
city of enlightenment and
learning, to artistic hub of
the Weimar Republic, to
seat of Nazi power.

into Berlin's rich, multi-textured history – and its attempt to evoke for visitors something of the scarcely imaginable trauma of the Holocaust, enabling, even encouraging them, 'to feel what had happened'[4] (without indulging aestheticized trauma). In his view, the key elements of the project are: its zigzag form; the Void, 'a kind of cut in which there is nothing'[5]; 'a passage to a dead end'[6]; the route to the main stair leading to the upper floors which ends abruptly at a wall; the Holocaust Tower, whose only light comes from a slit in the roof barely visible from below and which is so dark people cannot even see their feet; a garden where the vegetation is 'out of reach, oddly tilted, making visitors feel disoriented, even sea-sick'[7] (the E.T.A. Hoffmann garden); the fact that the building has no front door, being entered instead by way of a stair that descends into its basement from the entrance foyer of the Berlin Museum. By ensuring that visitors encounter the fundamental if hidden union of the original museum and the new extension, Libeskind is wishing to establish that: 'Though the two histories contained in their respective buildings might not always be visibly connected, they are inextricably bound, and will forever exist in the foundation of Berlin.'[8] On this evidence, light doesn't seem to be a major concern in the project, and yet it is clear from his autobiography (in which a whole chapter is devoted to light) and from the comments of Hélène Binet, the architectural photographer who has documented several of his projects and published her own photographic essay on the building,[9] that he is always thinking about literal, symbolic and metaphysical light. His deliberate transgression of the conventions of building suggests that he is concerned with the premeditated subversion of assumptions about how light should be thought in architectural terms. At stake here are the

8.2
Planning counter-light.
According to Libeskind,
the relationship between
Germans and Jews was
inscribed into the building
by plotting 'an irrational
matrix that makes
reference to the image of a
compressed and distorted
star, the yellow star that had
historically been worn by
Jews on the same site'.

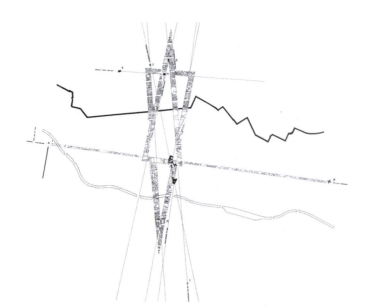

ancient metaphors of goodness and orientation – light, home, ground, path –
whose mobilization under the Nazis led to the Holocaust. Derrida declares 'each
time there is the sun, (idealising) metaphor has begun'[10] and with that the possibility of coherent discourse (and philosophy). The Jewish Museum Berlin makes
contingent this fundamental metaphoricity of architectural order. For Libeskind,
windows, the balance of light and shadow they generate, the concepts this balance articulates, the narratives it writes, are never taken for granted but always
in question. Whereas we are generally familiar with buildings whose windows
both orient, establish and pace some of the key rhythms of architectural encounter (four-square windows at one and the same time bring light into the interior,
give stable views, reinforce an orthogonal spatial order, and pace movement,
and as Le Corbusier would emphasize, 'give human scale'[11]), it is clear that the
apertures of the Jewish Museum challenge, subvert and rework expectations
about their purpose. At the same time they rewrite what light is possible and

8.3
Ground plan of Jewish
Museum. Diagram based on
a Studio Daniel Libeskind
and Udo Hesse drawing.

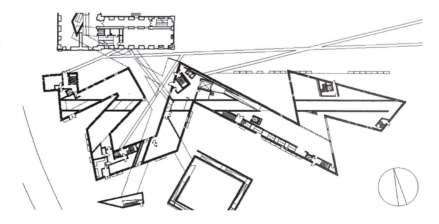

8.4
The entry route: a descent
into the basement from the
Berlin Museum.

therefore what light can say. What do they illuminate? What do they obscure? How do they situate the observer? Clarifying the character of light proposed by the building, and the role it plays in Libeskind's architectural thesis – an analysis of the chiaroscuro of the project's actual and conceptual interior – is the primary goal of this study.

Hieroglyphs of light

Libeskind's statements that 'there are a lot of ends in the museum', and yet 'no space in the building to get away to'[12] encapsulate his intentions for a project where 'standard exhibition spaces and traditional public spaces have been dissolved and disseminated along a myriad of complex trajectories'.[13] After its singular beginning (the entrance stair down into the basement through a tall concrete shaft he terms a 'voided void'), the museum can indeed best be summarized not as a series of spaces, but spaces that act in series,[14] offering a range of possible choices, possible narratives, unfolding in light.

Immediately on entry, at the foot of the first stair, a choice of three apparently identical paths, the so-called 'Axes'[15] of Continuity, of Exile and Emigration, and of the Holocaust, are offered at a crossroads.[16] (This is a simple map of the Holocaust dilemma carved out of the earth and reinforced by insistent lines of artificial light; it presents the museum as a set of catacombs, a columbarium, a labyrinth of equal lines.) The shortest of these paths leads to a dead end, the raw darkness of a concrete tomb, the Holocaust Tower, with its remote line of light high above the ground. Entering through the narrowest of vertical cracks, this light is hopeful and a source of orientation when everything else is unreliable.[17] The middle path allows the visitor to escape into daylight (sunlight if it is available, as this route exits from the south side of the building), and an enclosed upside-down garden at a disconcerting tilt. A contrast in light levels means one is potentially blinded on exit and on re-entering the museum at this

8.5
The crossroads in the basement, looking towards the exit to the E.T.A. Hoffmann garden.

8.6
The Holocaust Void interior with its remote chink of light.

8.7
The view through the
E.T.A. Hoffmann garden
towards the facade of the
Jewish Museum.

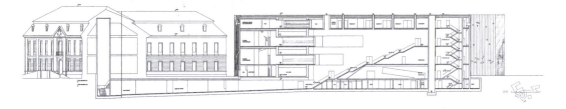

8.9
West–east section through
the main stair of the Jewish
Museum Berlin, after a
drawing by Studio Daniel
Libeskind and Udo Hesse.

point. Outside, views framed by the garden's columnar grid are towards the giant blade of the museum's facade.

The longest path leads to the main stair to the upper galleries on the first and second floors.[18] In a series of three sequential flights this stair rises though a trapezoidal crack from artificially illuminated darkness towards a brightly daylit but blank wall. On this section of the journey light is not an unadulterated blessing. It does give reassurance but it also shocks and confuses. On the one hand, the building's longest horizontal window offers momentary orientation by way of a long and very narrow view southwards over Berlin at the top of the stair, an edgy panorama that is the only traditional 'view out' from the museum (Fig. 8.11). On the other, the light that enters by way of this window and a series of one-storey-deep roof-lights, slashes through the ceiling and along one wall, throwing into silhouette the obliquely oriented beams that crash through the space below (Fig. 8.10). The dissolution of precise spatial enclosure that this achieves means that one climbs, as it were, from the darkness of the labyrinth towards an explosion of light and matter. Again light is hope[19] – and orientation – but a source of hope that is also equivocal and potentially dangerous.

In a sense the long stair is the least-expected element of the project because it is the most expected, i.e. it is at the same time an unforeseeable and foreseen necessity. One expects a primary route into a museum. As it turns out, the route upwards affirms and denies the normal decorum of the museum stair-hall, i.e. a stair which leads gracefully upwards from the darkness of ignorance towards the promise of light and knowledge. It takes place in an interstitial fissure rather than a four-square hall. It has the light but not the usual grace expected of such an ascent, appearing to provide the way out of the cave and yet thwarting onward movement at its summit. One must turn away from the light and view to continue. It is worth noting at this point that grand straight staircases of this type are relatively unusual. At the Munich Alte Pinakothek a pair of stairways each ascend to the first floor from the entrance foyer in two opposed straight flights (Fig. 8.12); the grand entrance into the Vatican for heads of state, the Scala Regia, has three flights in one direction and one return flight; while the archetypal staircase of this kind, the Scala Sancta, at the church of the same name in Rome, is a single flight of twenty-eight steps. According to Roman Catholic tradition, these steps had formed the staircase leading to the *praetorium* of Pilate at Jerusalem, and were hence sanctified by Christ's footsteps during his Passion. Recalling judgement halls of this kind, rather than the foyer spaces expected in a museum, the structuring in light of the Jewish Museum's main stair divides the world between light and shadow, the saved and the damned. Light may be hope. It is also always accompanied by shadow, its dark sibling.

8.10
View down the main stair from the top landing. An artificial line of light at the handrail. Natural light from the side and above.

There is no primary route through the galleries on the upper floors. Described by Libeskind as 'active paths', these spaces have exterior wall surfaces that are sliced, punctured or otherwise fragmented by light. His narrative for the origins of this design makes the motif of continuity manifest through its opposite, a splitting of walls:

8.11
View over Berlin from the horizontal window at the top of the main stair.

8.12
The stair in the Altes Pinakothek, Munich. From 1946–1957 Hans Döllgast, a professor at the local Technische Hochschule, played a major role in the preservation of this famous gallery. Transcending the war damage the building had suffered, he inserted floors in the wings where the stairs had originally been located and created this prominent transverse staircase in plain brickwork on the inside of the north facade. In Germany such a staircase is known as a *Himmelsleiter*, literally a 'ladder to heaven'.

The windows are the physical manifestation of a matrix of connections pervading the site. These cuts are the actual topographical lines joining addresses of Germans and Jews immediately around the site and radiating outwards. The windows are the 'writing of the addresses by the walls of the Museum itself'.

As the following comments make clear he is fully aware that the disciplined indiscipline of this 'writing' transforms the status of the windows and gives them a new role. They do not command long views over the city, but offer oblique and unpredictable glances into it. They also fracture what appears to be the bearing wall of the building.

The light which comes in and out of the Museum doesn't come through normal windows, as there are no conventional windows in the building. Of course there are places where you can see the sky, where you can see the street, and where you can look across, but they have never been conceived as traditional windows, as holes in the walls, which are there to look out of. They were generated by a completely different logic of openness. It is not the openness of an elevation that an architect could plan. Nor is it the openness of a system of geometric compositions. Instead, it is the openness of what

8.13
Facade calligraphy.
Exterior Star of David
Matrix window cuts.

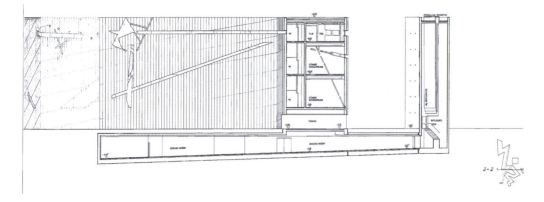

8.14
South–north section through
the Jewish Museum Berlin.
The Holocaust Tower is on
the right of this drawing.

remains of those glimpses across the terrain – glimpses, views, and glances that are sometimes very accidental, yet are the disciplined longitude-latitude lines belonging to a projection of addresses traversing the addressee.[20]

Whereas from the outside the windows (crosses, slashes, bands, irregular shapes, lines that wander, lines that intersect) are dark hieroglyphs scored into the otherwise sheer zinc facade,[21] on the inside they are oblique lines of light that slice apart and generate alternative three-dimensional spaces, after the fashion of Lissitzky's 1923 *Proun* compositions. Whatever the weather conditions, the haphazard intersections of the windows with floors and ceilings create brighter patches of light that randomly animate the otherwise flat whiteness of the box-like galleries. In sunshine spatial order is further undermined as precise lines of light are projected across the interior. This has the effect of making the wall, floor

8.15
The wandering lines of light
in a first-floor gallery.

8.16
Unusual framing in a narrow window of unexpected depth. Like hope, light at the Jewish Museum is potentially perilous. Whereas conventional windows are always routes of escape from a building, in the Jewish Museum their shape and the aggressive detailing of the zinc facade makes them too dangerous for this purpose.

and ceiling surfaces equivalent. Like searchlights, these projections force the gaze in unexpected directions. It seems that one is being encouraged to experience the galleries as unwinding surfaces rather than potentially stable space. Walking through them is akin to walking through Libeskind's own drawings: in an encouragement of 'the lost art of straying', light wanders, the route wanders, space seems to continually unfold as one is led ever onwards by the meandering lines of light. In this situation, where light dissects and interrogates, windows have other purposes. Light is calligraphy. Windows are not only its alphabet,[22] but also its lexicon of views.

> 'Die Leere' (the Void) is a quality … It is not heated, it is not air-conditioned, furthermore it is not really a museum space. Yet 'Die Leere' is something else – it is the space of Berlin, because it refers to that which can never be exhibited when it comes to the Jewish Berlin history. Humanity reduced to ashes.[23]

The Void (Figs. 8.18, 8.19, 8.20, 8.21),[24] a set of discontinuous roof-lit empty spaces which cuts straight through the zigzagging line of the galleries from east to west and is invisible from the outside, composes 'a centre which is not' around which the museum is organized.[25] It is Libeskind's intention that the overwhelming emptiness of this set of spaces makes visible the invisible: the absence of the six million Jews murdered in the Holocaust. A series of 'bridges'[26] that cross the line of this Void therefore punctuate all journeys through the gallery spaces. Given gleaming black surfaces (in contrast to the white walls of the galleries and the naked concrete of the Void interior), it is through windows in these bridges that one can see into the Void.

Its light is very different to that of the horizontal galleries it interrupts.

8.17
Fragmentary views of the outside from the gallery interior. In contrast to the conventional window that provided a stable view of the ideal Renaissance city, Libeskind's window openings offer a deliberately fractured view over the messy contemporary city of Berlin.

Given its raw grey concrete surfaces, its vertical form and the fact that its only sources of daylight are narrow roof-lights above the side walls, light levels are not high, and the light is very diffuse, very 'flat'. One expects roof-lit atrium-type spaces to visually animate spatial sequences, and to open the rooms which surround them. This is anything but the case here. Views through a series of identical rectangular windows (in this case typical 'holes in the wall, there to look out of'[27]) aligned vertically one above the other, are of identical black holes or other people looking out into the lifeless greyness at the other end of the space. In a sense the Void that 'contains nothing',[28] the Void 'in which a particular piece of Berlin is obliterated',[29] constructs a tomb for light. The building is centred on darkness. The Void is darkness made visible, inverse light. It proposes an architecture of light that is counter-transcendent.

There is no doubt that the Jewish Museum is meant to be provocative. But what critique does it elaborate in light? What decisive blows does it strike? What questions about architecture and light does it raise?

Between the lines

I had always imagined the building as a sort of text, meant to be read.[30]

Maybe I think this way because I am an architect, but light becomes tangible only when it lands on something solid – a body or a building – when it crawls, darts, engraves its presence on a wall.[31]

It is hard to understate the importance of writing to Libeskind. In his work the acts of writing, drawing,[32] mapping and building are closely linked; and lines become an architectural metaphor of particular significance (lines that mesh,

8.18
The largest void interior, the
so-called 'Memory Void'.

lines that wander, lines that form characters, lines that write music or text). As Leung explains, 'A claim is made for the proximity of drawing and writing – and the interval between lines of geometry – both space and nothing – is associated with the disclosure and concealment of meaning'.[33] 'Between the lines',[34] his choice of title for the Jewish Museum project, is thus not unexpected, drawing attention to both the potential spatiality of writing (the imaginative inhabitation of a text described with such enthusiasm by Benjamin[35]), the writing that is music and the writing that is architecture, and more specifically to what either texts or buildings say by implication or omission, rather than what they say more directly. Encompassing a range between technical instrumentality and lyrical freedom, between lines that are edges or boundaries and lines that lie in, or move through, space (including our own trajectories), Libeskind's metaphor of the line provides access to the preconditions which underlie the fundamental metaphoricity of architecture. Where a line comes from, what lines stand for, where they lead, what character they have, and what may or may not lie between them, illuminate the intentions and achievements of this building.

Libeskind himself declares that rethinking the goals of post-Holocaust architecture is his primary ambition. This process, in which the erasure or negation of monumentality is a prominent theme, is achieved through a subversion of established architectural procedures. Such a set of priorities begs the question of how light, or people's experience and appreciation of it, might be undermined. If architecture is to open debate about what it is for, how it helps structure communication, or in other words if light is not to be forever stranded

8.19
Light through the eye of a
needle. The view from a
small internal window in a
bridge into the stair hall.

between the useful and the dramatic, we need to recover the order once disclosed through light.

Simplifying, traditional light symbolism may be summarized as follows.[36] Light can basically be divided into two, according to its opposites – matter and shadow. One has to do with the structure of reality, where matter is at the bottom of the hierarchy (the pre-eminent example being Dionysos Areopagita, whose Neo-Platonic light-ontology[37] was determinative for the Christian Middle Ages, as well as for the Renaissance and Baroque). The other kind of light has to do with understanding or morality, in which darkness signifies confusion or disorientation, intellectual or moral. What one sees in Plato's *Republic* (Books VI–VII,) is that this second, psychological, shadow-light dialectic strives to be united with the first, the structure of reality. This has comprised the basic drama of light symbolism: to reconcile the historical with the eternal, the human with the divine, the universal with the particular, giving a centred and oriented (from *oriens*, East, the direction of solar origins) world.

The premise of the Jewish Museum – its justification for a counter-transcendent light – is that this inherited set of understandings about light deserves to be challenged. There are two interrelated reasons for this. First of all, as someone who feels that the all-too-human inhumanity of the Holocaust has thrown doubt on the traditional sources of architectural order and on the reassurance it provides, it is necessary for Libeskind to propose a light that negates, at least to a degree, the idea of a centred orderable world.[38] Secondly, Libeskind believes that in the course of the Enlightenment traditional light symbolism has

been instrumentalized and made the means of control of a neat, clean architecture of 'goodness' that suppresses and ignores fundamental human conditions – that the world is disorder, strife and squalor at the same time as it is potentially order, harmony and purity: 'The museum … must give home to the ordered/disordered, chosen/unchosen, welcome/unwelcome, vocal/silent.'[39] The frightening homogeneity of 'daynight wintersummer warpeace',[40] and the 'deadly thinking of day in nighttime',[41] that this kind of 'technicised and flattened' thinking has generated demonstrates the bankruptcy of a cultural situation in which it is possible that 'traffic lights come to mean more than the light of the stars'.[42] On this basis, be believes that an unquestioning acceptance of orthodox light symbolism detaches us from the world rather than helps us make sense of it, encouraging us to become passive observers rather than active participants.[43] In Libeskind's view the thoughtless ease with which a light is now switched on is not unrelated to the ease with which the gas chambers were activated. In presenting the ideas that inform his project Libeskind suggests that 'the great figures of the drama of Berlin … who are traced into the lineaments of the museum … spiritually affirm the permanent tension which is polarised between the impossibility of the system and the impossibility of giving up the search for a higher order'.[44] It is precisely this poignant ambivalence about abandoning the search for meaning which his attitude to light seeks to mirror.

Light in question

At the Jewish Museum Libeskind proposes a light whose meaning is not certain. He does this in order to create conditions within which contemporary cultural and

8.21
Inverse light. A view
through a bridge window
into the void.

philosophical dilemmas become apparent, conditions which mean that visitors
are no longer able to take the current world for granted. He does this by pursuing four different lines of thinking about light: two vertical passages (the main
stair, the Void) and two horizontal passages (the gallery spaces, the basement
roads). From these separate passages two alternative narratives of light emerge.

First of all the building's two different vertical sequences in light
question whether a world that makes sense can be structured through light. At
the main stair one faces an explosion of light going up, unremitting darkness
going down. In this sequence, light and view are employed as sources of orientation. The traditional thematic of deep earth contrasted with sky/light is in play,
although, as already noted, the extent to which light is reliably transcendent is at
issue. In contrast, at the Void Libeskind foregrounds shadow and seeks to make
the malevolence of this shadow palpable by structuring a negative differentiation
of light. In this entirely introverted space there is no way out. The light cannot
be seen. Shadow overwhelms it. This inverse light denies orientation. The Void
is empty of light, a place where light dies. The Pantheon in Rome is perhaps
one of the clearest examples of a daylit, roof-lit building whose dependence on
traditional light symbolism allows it to structure space and time. It mediates
the distance and difference between the sky and the earth, the oculus and
the ground, what is transcendent and what is human, what is a source of light
and life, and what is subject to change and decay. Light dramatically brings the
Pantheon to life. Libeskind's proposes that his voids are 'dispersed traces sug-
gestive of past and future public use'.[45] As far as light is concerned, spaces any
less like the Pantheon are hard to imagine.

On the other hand, the building's two distinct horizontal passages argue the relation between light and movement, light and (dis)orientation. Both passages are to a degree disorienting. Both passages reject traditional apertures, and offer unexpected insights on the site, the building and the wider world. As Leung[46] underlines, the episodic character of the fragmentary wandering light of the galleries is the counterform to the insistent light and maze-like continuum of the underworld. The haphazard spatial rhythms created within the galleries (linear trajectories opened up by fractured light and fractured view) confer an oriented disorientation through light. In contrast, encounter with the extreme introversion of the basement seems to assert the significance of light's role as a vehicle of mediation (it demonstrates that sudden exposure to light or darkness is always destabilizing, that without light there is no hope).

The matrix of lines which we customarily wrestle into architecture with earnest deliberation seems here just as likely to dissolve and float away. Our capacity to earnestly produce catastrophe is exposed as part of our fundamental finitude. Libeskind's unsettling architecture throws into question what kind of rupture even 'ordinary' architecture represents. As Binet[47] has explored in her photographs, the windows of the Jewish Museum – that restate the building in miniature – also restate its visual premise: zigzagging lines that reframe the relationship between museum and city and rewrite spatial encounter by giving unanticipated thickness and weight to the division of light and shadow. In other words the windows are at one and the same time 'rupturous openings of light and disorienting fragments of the outside world',[48] their equivocation emphasizing that this building is an open proposition, and deeply vulnerable. We are led to acknowledge that every affirmation which would harness the sun, even a single line, is founded upon the subtle distinction between moral courage and blind arrogance.

> When I was seven years old, an aunt in Brazil sent me an extraordinary mounted butterfly, with phosphorescent wings of a deep indigo. It was one of the most beautiful things I had ever seen, and certainly one of the few objects of beauty we had in Lodz. In those wings that glowed with an almost radioactive light I could see everything I needed to know about Rio de Janeiro, about nature, cities, light, the afterlife, eternity.[49]

Notes

1 W. Benjamin, trans. E. Jephcott and K. Shorter, *One-Way Street*, Verso, 1979, p. 69.
2 D. Libeskind, *Breaking Ground*, John Murray, 2005, pp. 55–56.
3 The Berlin Museum occupies the 1735 Collegienhaus, by Philipp Gerlach. Originally this building contained judicial and administrative offices, but later became the Prussian Kammergericht or High Court. It was almost entirely destroyed in the war, only being rebuilt in the 1960s to rehouse the newly re-established Berlin Museum.
4 Libeskind, *Breaking Ground*, 2005, p. 82.
5 Ibid., p. 84.
6 Ibid.
7 Ibid.
8 Ibid.

9   H. Binet and R. Bunschoten, *A Passage through Silence and Light*, photographs by H. Binet, text by R. Bunschoten, Black Dog Publishing Ltd, 1997.

10 J. Derrida, 'White Mythology', in *New Literary History*, vol. 6,1974, trans F.C.T. Moore, p. 53. See also P. Ricoeur's response in *The Rule of Metaphor*, Routledge and Kegan Paul, London, trans. R. Czerny, K. McLaughlin and J. Costello SJ, 1978, p. 284ff.

11 Le Corbusier, *Une Petite Maison*, Éditions d'architecture, Artemis, Zurich, 1981, p. 24.

12 D. Libeskind, *Radix – Matrix*, Prestel-Verlag and D. Libeskind, 1997, p. 113.

13 D. Libeskind, 'Between the Lines', competition statement for a new extension to the Berlin Museum in *The Space of Encounter*, Thames and Hudson, 2001, p. 29. Arguably, these intentions have been less apparent to visitors than Libeskind had hoped, as a result of the fact that the current exhibition design, for which he was not responsible, is not always in sympathy with the building's unusual spatiality. That the topography of light discussed here was capable of drawing crowds even when the building was empty was reflected in visitor numbers of 350,000 prior to its official opening in the autumn of 2001.

14 According to Libeskind the spaces of the museum act in series or 'open narratives' (ibid.).

15 These axes symbolize the three realities in the history of German Jews. The Axis of Continuity represents the continuation of Berlin's history and is therefore the connecting route from which the other paths branch off.

16 Libeskind makes reference to the idea that in heavily bomb-damaged Berlin it was the streets that were unerasable, and that this was a significant insight as far as the design of the building was concerned. (Libeskind, *Radix – Matrix*, p. 113).

17 Despite wondering at first whether it wouldn't be appropriate for the space of the Holocaust Tower to be entirely dark (as he comments, the gas chambers were unlit), the introduction of a line of light was inspired by the story Libeskind quotes about the important source of hope such a line had represented to one holocaust survivor. See Note 2.

18 The third floor of the building, which has rather larger glazed openings than the lower floors, is occupied by offices. The ground floor includes the gallery spaces from which void 6, the 'Memory Void', may be entered.

19 Libeskind, 'Between the Lines', p. 29.

20 D. Libeskind, *Jewish Museum Berlin*, G + B International, 1999, p. 67. From the outset Libeskind's presentation of the project has focused on the idea that its architecture has been inscribed into, and indeed directly determined by, the geography of Berlin. First of all he explains that the shape of the building and the location of its windows represent a set of 'secretly woven' Berlin addresses. (By plotting a series of addresses of famous Berliners onto a map and drawing lines between them, he 'married' three Jews to three Gentiles he admired, and discovered that these lines formed a distorted Star of David over the sector of Berlin in which the site was located. The plan of the building was subsequently derived from this 'star'. In a similar process, he used the *Gedenkbuch*, the book which lists the names of all the German Jews murdered in the Holocaust, and a set of pre-war Berlin phonebooks, to locate the addresses of more anonymous Jewish inhabitants of the city, in order to compose a matrix of connections between them that would decide the facade design). See Libeskind, *Breaking Ground*, pp. 91–92.

21 In Libeskind's view metal is always associated with light (D. Libeskind, 'Three Lessons in Architecture', in *Countersign*, Architectural Monographs no. 16, Academy Group Ltd and D. Libeskind, 1991, pp. 37–61, p. 51). While his choice of zinc for the facade was prompted by Schinkel's suggestion that this material should be employed for all Berlin roofs, it seems that his intention was to create a 'visually denaturalised, luminous surface that creates tension between the hand and the eye' (Libeskind, 'Between the Lines' in *The Space of Encounter*, pp. 23–29, p. 29), or in other words what is made visible is made inaccessible to our body. The fact that this luminosity will slowly fade with time to give greater prominence to the hieroglyphic windows is apparently nevertheless not a problem: 'I appreciate that it's a modest material [zinc]; I appreciate that it slowly oxidises, and then sort of disappears. I'm not looking for a stainless steel that stays forever shiny. I want the buildings to blend

in to the city. I want to see how the windows, with their sharp angles and slashing effects, become even more emphatic as the building softens.' See Libeskind, *Breaking Ground*, pp. 217–218.

22 See Libeskind's drawing 'The Alphabet' in *Radix – Matrix* (p. 36) in which the Jewish Museum is rewritten as a series of lines of lines. Positive and negative lines and shapes rewrite the project in black and white (darkness and light) and are tabulated as lines of hieroglyphs entitled 'underground', 'internal', 'void', 'site', 'linear', 'window' and 'combination'.

23 Libeskind, 1999, p. 30.

24 Slightly confusingly the individual spaces out of which the Void is composed are entitled voids 1 to 6. The entrance stair is located within a tower entitled the 'Voided Void', while the Holocaust Tower is also sometimes referred to as the Holocaust Void. The Void space extends from the roof to the ground floor, from where it may be entered just once, at the east end of the easternmost void, void 6, though the exhibition halls of the basement also give access beneath voids 1 and 2 at the other end of the building.

25 Libeskind, 'Between the Lines' in *Radix – Matrix*, p. 34.

26 Libeskind relates the number of bridges crossing the void to the sixty sections into which Benjamin's 1928 'apocalyptic guidebook' to Berlin, *One-Way Street*, is divided.

27 Libeskind, *Jewish Museum Berlin*, p. 67.

28 Libeskind, *Breaking Ground*, p. 84.

29 Libeskind, *Radix – Matrix*, p. 115.

30 Libeskind, *Breaking Ground*, p. 94.

31 Ibid., p. 54.

32 As Vesely notes, Libeskind's drawings 'offer a unique insight into the constructive possibilities on the boundary of actual and imaginary space – in other words, an insight into the representative power of our imagination, challenged by the conceptual power of invention.' See D. Vesely, *Architecture in the Age of Divided Representation*, MIT Press, 2004, pp. 21–23, and D. Libeskind, 'Micromegas' (pp. 14–35) and 'Chamber Works' (pp. 109–119) in *Countersign*.

33 J. Leung, 'The Question of Emblematic Rupture. The Jewish Extension to the Berlin Museum by Daniel Libeskind', unpublished M.Phil. dissertation, University of Cambridge, 1996, p. 11.

34 'The world that revealed itself in the book and the book itself were never, at any price to be divided. So with each book its content, too, its world, was palpably there, at hand. But, equally, this content and world transfigured every part of the book … You did not read books through; you dwelt, abided between their lines, and reopening them after an interval, surprised yourself at the spot where you had halted' (W. Benjamin, 'A Berlin Chronicle', in *One-Way Street*, pp. 341–342).

35 See Note 19.

36 See further on these themes Vesely, *Architecture in the Age of Divided Representation*, p. 113ff., and Edgar de Bruyne, *Etudes d'esthetique medievale*, Livre IV, Lonrai, 1998, ch. 1.

37 See Pseudo-Dionysius, the Areopagite, 'The Mystical Theology' (pp. 133–142) and 'The Celestial Hierarchy' (pp. 143–192) in *Pseudo–Dionysius: The Complete Works*, Paulist Press, New Jersey, 1987.

38 'In the twilight zone where Order is eclipsed; where at the margins of experience, symbolic structures can no longer domesticate perception; where evaluations, opinions, and attitudes replace the certainty of shared conviction – order becomes an ironic sign inverting the relation between fiction and reality. Fictions of an ideal world with their pretended universality reduce the full implication of spatiality to a prior notion of a homogenous and empty datum ready for quantification' (Libeskind, *Radix – Matrix*, p. 153).

39 Libeskind, 'Between the Lines', p. 29.

40 Libeskind, 'Upside Down X', in *Countersign*, p. 9.

41 Ibid.

42 Libeskind, 'Symbol and Interpretation', in *Radix – Matrix*, pp. 152–154, p. 153.

43 According to Libeskind, 'The museum form itself must be rethought in order to transcend the

passive involvement of the viewer, actively confronting change.' See Libeskind, 'Between the Lines'.

44　Ibid.

45　Ibid.

46　Leung, 'The Question of Emblematic Rupture', p. 7.

47　See Binet and Bunschoten, *A Passage through Silence and Light*. See further on this theme L. Sandland, 'Architectural Space: Writing with Light', unpublished third-year dissertation, University of Cambridge, 2002.

48　Leung, 'The Question of Emblematic Rupture', p. 7.

49　Libeskind, *Breaking Ground*, p. 72.

Chapter 9

New light for old across London

Recent interventions at the Carmelite Priory, Kensington, by Niall McLaughlin, and at 1A John Campbell Road, Hackney, by Lisa Shell

The genius of the city – which I would distinguish from the genius of a discrete piece of architecture – lies in the tractability of its edges, in its permeability, in its support of accident. As a compound of territories and enclosures, a boundary making and measuring system, a labyrinth of spaces, the city relies on a certain illegibility, on the possibility that it can be read beyond the particulars of any single – or even complex of – containers. The places to describe are, of course, sometimes physical, sometimes conventional, sometimes imaginary and such zones depend as much on precedent and habit as they do on the instigations of construction. The nuances of such urban definition – of boundary making – are and must be rich, as rich as possible.[1]

It is often forgotten that as recently as 1840 Hackney was a small village to the north and Kensington a leafy suburb at the west end of London. The ordnance survey maps which chart the expansion of London – the swallowing up of market gardens and orchards for streets and factories, the introduction of railways and tramways, factories and service industries – give clues to a process in which the loose yet easily identifiable nuclei of former hamlets have been gradually lost in a sea of development. The result of this rapid urban growth was that the countryside that once surrounded London disappeared, and natural light, especially at street level, became an increasingly precious resource. As patterns of inhabitation and the understanding of locality were transformed, getting access to light became progressively more difficult and leaving room for it ever more important. That lives were restructured and new identities manufactured as old neighbourhoods changed beyond recognition, and new communities emerged,

9.1
The gradual densification
of the areas around Duke
Street, Kensington, and John
Campbell Road, Hackney,
over the last 150 years: Top:
1869. Middle: 1894. Bottom:
inter 1960. Kensington is
shown on the left, Hackney
on the right.

is not difficult to imagine. What the maps of this change also hint at is that the pattern of this expansion had to acknowledge growing concerns about how an individual property owner's ancient 'right to light' should be addressed through building regulations governing density of development. As the metropolis mushroomed to fill in the gaps between previously separate settlements, the issue of urban light came under the microscope as never before.

     Aside from the demands of a tighter and more compact urban fabric the Victorian drive to predict, measure and subdivide light had a second and equally important root cause. As London grew larger, its airborne pollution intensified. The smoke and fumes from new industrial processes – along with the open hearths of the now vast swathes of housing that were concentrated in the city – not only ensured that external surfaces were quickly blackened by soot, but that urban light levels were noticeably lower on an everyday basis.[2] In Victorian winters towards the end of the nineteenth century this situation deteriorated further when the dense fogs or 'London particulars' that the pollution brought on in cold weather made light conditions poorer still.

     As the city became more vast, alien and unknowable, it became more dark and disorienting, literally and metaphorically. Anxiety about its legibility and visibility mounted. While many were confident that scientific and industrial progress would allow the technological challenges of servicing such an immense

9.2
The Dome area at Sir John Soane's Museum, Lincoln's Inn Fields, London. © Soane Museum.

metropolis to be met without difficulty, some began to wonder whether the cost of progress – a labyrinthine crime-ridden and light-starved environment – was too high a price to pay.

For the Victorians urban light was no longer a given. It became obvious that the rules – scientific and pragmatic – governing its more effective exploitation had to be established if life in the city was to remain tolerable.[3] In this quest a more accurate description and prediction of the behaviour of light and its physiological impact (the theoretical work of Thomas Young [1773–1829] and James Clerk Maxwell [1831–1879]) was accompanied by technical innovations that amplified the amount of light available (larger window openings, windows with larger sheets of clearer glass and fewer mullions, light wells lined with washable ceramic tiles, lay-lights and pavement lights, prismatic glass to redirect light, glazed screens to enable light in subsidiary spaces to be borrowed from more generously lit major rooms). The drive to optimize light had a profound impact on how architectural designs were conceived and justified and revealed some of the inherent tensions of life in the new metropolis. A concern to meet expectations about certain aspects of architectural decorum – degrees of privacy and publicity in particular – while masking some of the means by which this was achieved, meant that the search for light alternately challenged and preserved architectural conventions. The right to invisibility in private (a secluded home or workplace) and anxiety about visibility in public (the navigability and transparency of public interiors) helped to decide what lighting strategies were pursued. And as the potential visual relationships in and between buildings were redefined with

9.3
Shell's 1989 project in
which a series of rooms
for listening to music were
perched on an enormous
retaining wall to a railway
line in Borough, London.

these issues in mind, the prudent exploitation of natural light via an appropriate intensity of development came to be understood as the valid index of political progress it still remains.

To what extent is London still a watchword for darkness? In the past century it has of course grown even larger, and parts of it have become even more densely occupied, but following the 1956 Clean Air Act cleaner buildings and brighter atmospheric conditions have improved lighting conditions within it enormously. Londoners may now spend more time indoors with the lights on more frequently than necessary, but they generally look out on a more light-filled urban environment than their grandparents did. The issues that architects now have to address when reworking its fabric to make the most of the light available are challenging, raising questions about how the renegotiation of boundaries and light redefines the city. In this chapter two recent rehabilitation projects of Victorian buildings, one in Hackney and one in Kensington, offer an opportunity to reflect on what urban light has to do with locality and locatedness, examining how the natural illumination of an interior can manifest urban ecology at the scale of rooms, buildings, the corner of a block. Stewart Brand's *How Buildings Learn: What Happens after They're Built* (1994)[4] exposes the fallacy of imagining that good architecture is necessarily something forever fixed once the last windows have been inserted and their paintwork allowed to dry. Building on several of Brand's insights, the discussion focuses on what changes to light have been sought in these projects, how light is being lived in them, what light and its manipulation have to do with orientation – within and towards – the ever-transforming city.

Embarked on during the 1990s, these two refurbishment projects, one by Niall McLaughlin and the other by Lisa Shell, have both involved the

9.4
Scott's church and Goldie's monastery define the leafy garden that lies to the north of Duke Street, Kensington. The location of the south facing windows of McLaughlin's chapel and sacristy are indicated on the ground floor of the monastery building in this sketch.

transformation of buildings whose own history is worth outlining. Indeed it is not possible to frame the evolution of light they represent unless the way in which their circumstances of light have changed over the last century and a half is sketched out.

Niall Mc Laughlin's 1992 interventions at the Carmelite Priory on Kensington Church Street have involved much secret stitching and mending but also the transformation of two neighbouring – but not quite adjacent – ground-floor rooms into a chapel and a sacristy respectively.[5] Located within a set of 1886 purpose-designed buildings (a long five-storey range constructed in stock brick with stone dressings) that the Gothic Revival firm of Goldie, Child and Goldie decided to dress in the Flamboyant style of sixteenth-century Northern France, the 'chapel' had already had a number of previous lives (common room, part of a temporary church, sacristy). The origins of the 'sacristy' space on the other hand are more recent. An ante-space that links the priory with its present church, this room was inserted by Sir Giles Gilbert Scott into the base of a light well between the two buildings when he completed work on his new 'freely interpreted Late Gothic' church in 1959. A replacement of Pugin's original 1866 'Early English' church, following its total destruction by an incendiary bomb in 1944, the clerestoried nave of Scott's building is considerably taller and longer than its predecessor. As a result the priory's ground-floor rooms now see considerably less of the eastern sky.

Lisa Shell's recent transformation (1999–2008) of a workshop/stable at the rear of a Victorian terrace in Hackney into her own dwelling is a project of comparable scale. Constructed in 1871, but first indicated on the ordnance survey map of 1894, this building underwent only minimal alterations in the first century or so of its existence. Its surroundings, however, are now very different – and more changes are planned – as adjacent buildings have multiplied or grown in size, and the configuration of the surrounding block has metamorphosed in response to the fluctuating fortunes of the local business community. The most

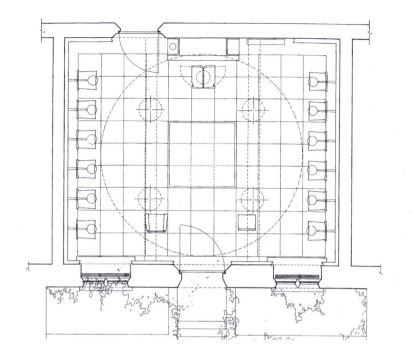

9.5
Plan of the new chapel at
the Carmelite Monastery
in Kensington.

significant of these changes has been the erection of a set of workshops at the centre of the block during the 1880s (later amalgamated into a furniture factory, 'The Stamford Works') and, in 1916, the replacement of three residential proper-ties on adjacent Kingsland High Street with a purpose-designed cinema. Divorced since the interwar years from the property to which it was once attached – it was in use as a market trader's workshop for approximately seventy years – the former workshop now offers a very particular niche in the local ecosystem. Just like the rooms in the priory already described this niche has gradually become more hedged about by building, more heavily concealed over time at the base of the urban labyrinth.

McLaughlin and Shell on light

> One of my revelatory moments on coming to London was going to John Soane's house on a spring day when there were rain showers and sunlight and wind and those spring clouds that come and go. You saw the building being animated in a rather overwhelming way by light and rain. The idea of architecture having an atmosphere or light having a thickness and visceral presence was something I learnt there.[6]

As these comments, and the following excerpt from his practice statement confirms, McLaughlin is ready to admit to a particular interest in light:

> The work shown here is less interested in the expression of techno-logy by bolts, junctions and gaskets, more in the overall presence

9.6
The tall chairs that line
the chapel's side walls.
The circular pattern of
light on the floor is from
one of four amber lamps
that represent the four
evangelists, Matthew,
Mark, Luke and John, whose
symbols are traditionally
located over the crossing in
church architecture.

of a space. In particular the way in which materials alter space by modulating light: combing it, diffusing it, storing it, reflecting it, dulling it or changing its speed.[7]

Trained at University College Dublin, but now based in London, he is conscious of the apparent divergence between the two major influences on his approach to design and to the role light plays within it. An Irish education (under the tuition of Sheila O'Donnell and John Tuomey, among others) that emphasized the influence of history and a concern for architectural precedent and reference, and from which he 'absorbed the canon of architecture as a pure discipline, a pure art',[8] has been subverted somewhat by the lessons of his own teaching at the Bartlett, a context in which innovation is encouraged and where they 'allow that architecture can fuse with other arts'.[9] He is now happy to have a foot in both camps it would seem, so that for him critically reviewing the past – and the design process – are equally important to design development. Thus while he acknowledges that a visit to the Soane Museum (Fig. 9.2) has been pivotal to the way he thinks about light, the development of experimental techniques to uncover the latent possibilities of design ideas with respect to light, or their previously hidden implications, is critical to his practice. Model photography and its manipulation is just one example of this. It is as if he has come to realize that with light he must be deeply responsible and blithely irresponsible at the same time. It should therefore come as no surprise that for McLaughlin light is typically an active and unpredictable protagonist, one that speaks of time and weather, referencing the stability of matter as it does so. Referring to his 2004 Peabody Housing project in Silvertown, London, he declares:

> When you try to photograph the building you get this sense of the
> fugitive properties of light: that it's time bound and undependable

9.7
View south towards the
garden from the chapel.

and it's always running away from you. It's like quicksilver. I find that
really interesting. There is so much else in architecture which has
to be fixed.[10]

In contrast, Shell's introduction to her practice[11] does not mention light as such.
She asserts rather that her architecture is 'process' (the piecemeal construction
of place) as much as it is 'sculpting of space'. While this may be explained by
the fact that the majority of her projects have involved refurbishment work, the
unwillingness she shares with McLaughlin to treat architecture as an object, a
completed or finishable thing, despite an engagement with the crafting of architectural elements, is significant. Shell sees herself as working from the interior
outwards, identifying and constructing the corners that will open possibilities
for inhabitation, sequencing and shaping interstitial darkness with respect to the
light outside. As she herself notes, garden themes are critical to this approach:

> I think my references are all very domestic. I was always excited
> by hidden, abandoned or very private parts of the city which had
> a domestic scale potential and garden nature … Pre-architecture,
> my favourite place was probably my dad's garage, its workbench,
> tools, and quiet … or the pet corner in the garden which was hid-
> den from the house and involved stacked hutches overlooking the
> vegetable patch.[12]

And in her work such themes are frequently intertwined with light. For Shell
light is not abstract. It is what nurtures plant growth, and is in turn filtered
and coloured by that growth. She does not compose with it. She plants it. In
refurbishment work she knows she cannot have any light she wants, but she is
also aware she does not want any old light. Immersed in inner-city gloom she

9.8
The tabernacle in the chapel:
the room writ small in gold.

redraws boundaries and re-navigates territories by breaking judicious openings to light and/or carefully remapping the interplay of light, space and inhabitation in accordance with her reading of the urban *terroir*. Although she does not say it, this process of rehabilitation can be seen as a kind of architectural light therapy – or alternatively, gardening for light.

Aspects of her training at the University of Cambridge and initial experiences in practice working for others have predisposed her to this way of looking at the city. A student project that prompted the making of a series of rooms for listening to music, perched high on a nineteenth century retaining wall in Borough (Fig. 9.3), was followed by the design of a garden in a an environmental research institute. Despite the rural gentility of the latter's Cambridge site, the group of buildings she proposed 'created private external spaces against quite uncompromising slabs of wall'.[13] The major insight of both these schemes was the idea that architecture should be able to respond to the local urban metabolism, that it can represent a kind of colonization process rather than wholesale change, and that this involves challenging assumptions about where people are prepared to live. Before final qualification as an architect, spells in practice in Dublin and London consolidated and extended this thinking in practical ways. As Shell herself explains, key aspects of life in O'Donnell and Tuomey's office in the early 1990s – 'the environment of the office (an old leaky school hall), Dublin social life, their project to refurbish their house'[14] – provided her with a refreshingly positive model of what an architect's life in the city might be. On the other hand, the high-end domestic projects she took on in London fostered a rediscovery of the elements that allow a building to be adaptive, 'the small bits that go into buildings, not indulged adequately throughout my education – ironmongery and fittings but not finishes',[15] while simultaneously teaching her to question 'how one should aim to live'.[16]

The refurbishment projects of McLaughlin and Shell considered here engage with the issue of what light, time and the city have to do with one another

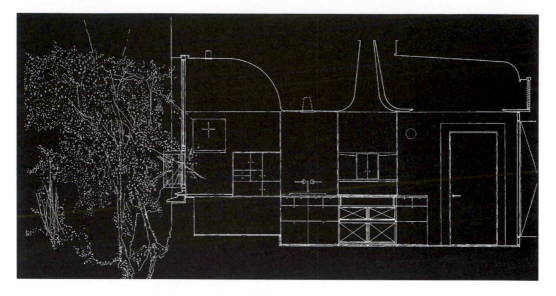

9.9
South–north section through
the sacristy. The original
horizontal window to this
space is shown to the right,
above some of the cupboards
that now line the room.

in diverse but comparable ways. From McLaughlin's perspective, reworking the light of a room is a chance to explore how, as a structuring of light, architecture is sculpting in time, whereas for Shell it is an opportunity to remould the city. As a result what is evanescent and what is fixed about the city – and the life it supports, both plant and human – remains an open question for both. In each of the projects analysed here how the process of exchanging new light for old is helping decide what degree of change – to the apertures, the building and the neighbourhood – is necessary or useful will be the issue on which the discussion focuses.

Rearranging Kensington: A chapel from a common room

Entered from a dimly lit corridor and looking out over a sunny and cloistered garden, the location of the new chapel at the Kensington Carmelite Priory gives its light an unexpected vibrancy. Unlike most sacred spaces this is a room whose contemplative mood does not depend on darkness (Figs. 9.5, 9.6, 9.7). On opening its heavy wooden door, a vision of the green field of the garden is framed by the lustrous honey-coloured panelling of a warm yet austerely furnished chamber. An effect reinforced by the decision to paint the upper walls and soffit a pale blue, the lower region of the room immerses its occupants in a glowing golden light. This is especially apparent on sunny days when ground reflected sunshine magnifies the contrast between the strongly lit floor and the more shadowy ceiling. Yet although the light may be bright the room does not lack gravity. Intimate and monumental at one and the same time, decisions about spatial order, colour and the fall of the light have been coordinated to ensure the chapel has a profound stillness. The basic principle of the transformation, as McLaughlin explains, was to make the room an end-point, a place without time, a staging of extra-ordinary tranquillity:

> It is the difference between getting there and being there. The chapel was all about being there. You are gathered around the still centre.

9.10
The view to the garden from
the sacristy.

> It is a contemplative place. There is nowhere else to go … All the
> furniture is centred, it's symmetrical, it's undemonstrative, it lacks
> any expressiveness.[17]

In his own words, McLaughlin's guiding principle with this chapel was to 'let the
light be what the light is'. Thinking about how the setting affects the light, rather
than doing anything to change the fall – or amount – of light entering the room
has been a critical decision. And so while blinds have been added, the generously scaled Victorian windows that McLaughlin considered the original room's
most valuable feature remain. In this institution, in a room for this purpose, in this
location, he chooses to qualify the existing light through a series of other less
obvious modifications that shape how the room is now experienced.

  Although it would have been possible for the chapel to have its altar
oriented towards the east, the arrangement McLaughlin has chosen represents
a break with convention. At the centre of the stone floor stands a square altar
between two lines of high-backed chairs along each side wall. In other words
an end-lit setting for worship has been created from an ordinary side-lit room.
Within this end-light simple furniture, simply arranged in a manner that takes its
cue from – and therefore strengthens – the room's basic symmetry, stages the
Last Supper.

  Other elements of the interior underpin the charged intimacy/monu-
mentality of the setting. Above each of the chairs for example, a tall conical glass
form containing a light fitting marks the place of each monk. Anthropomorphic
in character, these 'heads' both amplify the scale of the seats – and reinforce
the sense of enclosure generated by the head-height screen.[18] This means that
even when the room is empty twelve figures occupy the space. Further light

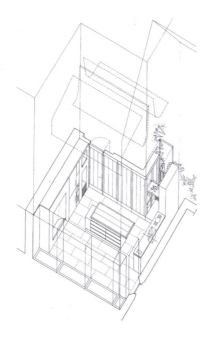

9.11
Axonometric of sacristy
looking towards Scott's
church indicating the
complex roof-light design
that creates the 'line of
light' across the centre of
the room.

fittings (circles of amber coloured hand blown glass) that hang from the ceiling over each corner of the altar throw swirling patterns of light onto the floor. Counter-intuitively, like the sunshine that enters through the windows, it is the dynamic play of this light across the floor surface that serves to reinforce the room's fundamental weight and tranquillity. Finally, opposite the windows, on the wall behind the altar, is a simple oak tabernacle. When open, its gleaming interior is the room writ small and entirely in gold (Fig. 9.8).

> For us it was almost a retinal thing where we were making everything gold so you could see the green through it, and we wanted that to give you a fizz. All the materials were gold so you saw the green through the gold.[19]

When asked about the aims behind his intervention, McLaughlin notes that 'There was a strategy to say that when you walk into the room you should sense the existing room, and then you should sense the things that have been changed, and all that that should be clear.'[20] In fact, the damage suffered by the existing fabric in the 1950s and 60s required him to get involved in a degree of trickery in reinstating certain features of the original room. As it turns out, what actually strikes one on entry now is the way the new stucco screen that defines and encloses the sacred space is viewed against the distant backdrop of a London street. While he suggests that the warm gold and simple form of the chapel are meant to contrast with the profusion and greenness of the garden outside (consciously mirroring the charged interplay of geometry and colour typical of many Renaissance paintings), the fact that the new arrangement brings the city – time-worn and grubby – into the equation is just as significant to the status and presence of the room. Typically made numinous through darkness, chapels

9.12
The west wall of the sacristy.

are not usually rooms with a view. In this case it places a still, intimate chamber, this 'common' room, away from, yet within, the tumultuous city, simultaneously establishing its fragile distance from everyday life and the idea that within its walls the mystery of the Eucharist is made real.

McLaughlin's description of the chapel as a symbol of paradise, the garden as a vision of paradise, underlines that their relationship had a special interest for him. In one sense, as just noted, the contrast between the architecture and its actual garden setting has been magnified by his intervention. Yet in another sense his qualification of the existing light implies that the interior might in fact be outside. As in Giorgione's 1505 painting *Madonna and Child Enthroned between St Francis and St Liberalis*, which inspired the introduction of the room's head-height horizon, beyond establishing a light-filled dining hall in the middle of the city the room also evokes a temporary encampment in an open landscape. For an order like the Carmelites whose members are expected not to form attachments to any particular location but to move around constantly from monastery to monastery, this would seem particularly apt.

Rearranging Kensington: A sacristy from an ante-room

Occupying the rift between the chancel of Scott's church and Goldie's priory, the location of McLaughlin's new sacristy may give it unusually poor access to skylight but it is not unexpected in relation to the overall plan of the monastery. Acting as a kind of workshop/storage space and dressing room for the priest, a sacristy is typically sited near the altar of a church. What is surprising about this sacristy, given its location, is that daylight predominates to make the space feel brighter, warmer and more animated than it has any right to (Figs. 9.9, 9.11).

There are not many rooms where the first thing one looks at is

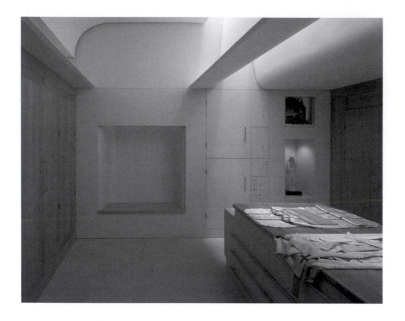

9.13
The east wall of the sacristy.
In its central location
immediately below the
'line of light' the vestment
counter receives the room's
highest levels of daylight.

the ceiling, yet here it is unavoidable. Above a closet lined with cupboards, alcoves, drawers and workbenches, its convoluted section emphasizes the fall of light from above, clouding the sense of spatial enclosure. Apart from this roof-light, the only other aperture is a small window that introduces an occasional 'wink of sunshine' and links one corner of the room more directly to the garden outside (Fig. 9.10).

> In the sacristy the light had been coming from the north – mostly anyway. The light coming down through that light well had got a bit mucky bouncing off all the brickwork. It was a bit dour that light. What we wanted to do was wrap it in white again just to calm it down and give it a stillness when it came into the room … Then, having established a dominant tone of still, white light, the light off the sky vault drops onto the vestment counter … it's the idea of the vestments being laid out and that on different days the colour in the room comes from the vestments. Also, the counter is the brightest surface in the room because it is the only one which is actually pointing at the sky vault.[21]

As these comments on the existing light confirm, in contrast to the chapel, wholesale change was McLaughlin's aim in the sacristy. The design process has been treated as an act of purification: the exchange of dirty urban gloom for clean white light. Stained by their descent through the city, the dregs of light from the sky are washed clean before being channelled into the room. As a result a mean and dimly lit cell with just one narrow and viewless clerestory becomes a dramatically top-lit chamber with its own spy-hole to a garden. What is worth emphasizing here is that for McLaughlin, as his choice of vocabulary reinforces, the primary aim when thinking about a design strategy is the appropriate tempo and colour of a place. To achieve the light he wants, he is acutely aware of the need to grasp the light that is already there and work with it, in order to decide how its urban trajectory and point of access will affect the final ambience of an interior.

In this intervention light comes first. It arranges space and places events, so that ultimately the room can speak of the religious calendar that colours its shadows. This can be put another way. A room in only occasional use as a place of preparation gets the light it deserves. Illumination is given to where it is most needed: onto the desk by the window where reading and writing is done, but also further back, onto the wardrobes, the sink area, and the vestment counter at the centre. In this respect light is thought of as the first – and final – enrobing of the room.

Finally, it is not irrelevant to this discussion of urban light and its architectural interpretation that McLaughlin's conception of the sacristy as an interstitial space which marks a frontier between different worlds is articulated through its division by light (Figs. 9.12, 9.13). Speaking about the organization of the room and its logic he notes:

> It was about the spiral, which always ran outside the room, and poin-
> ted to other places, so it was about transition. There was this theme
> of asymmetries and reversals, which comes from the idea of it being
> a place between two buildings.[22]

Speaking about the passage it negotiates, he adds:

> The order of the altar, which is the order of ritual and abstraction and
> ceremony, is completely different from the order of the humdrum,
> everyday world. You step through this room as a kind of pressure
> release valve in a way. Both physically in terms of the site and per-
> ceptually in terms of the two buildings, it becomes a liminal space.[23]

Within this dark gap, light signals a partition in the time and space of the city: the line of light in the ceiling establishes the boundary between the domestic space of the monks and the sacred space of the altar. A somewhat more emphatic marker than the votive statue which the sacristy also houses, this fissure must be crossed each time the priest enters and exits the church. It is thus light that centres – and divides – the room, to orchestrate not only the various activities that take place within its closely packed walls, but an important route across the space.

Light as figure and ground

> There is a tension in me, thinking about light, between the Soanean
> light, which is almost too much, it's almost overpowering, it's very
> theatrical, and the desire just to leave light alone and let it be an impli-
> cit presence in the space.[24]

Although they build on many of the same insights, McLaughlin's interventions at

the Carmelite Priory actually give light two different roles, as this more general insight confirms. Arguably, in the chapel light is primarily 'ground', but in the sacristy 'figure'. How thinking about light from these alternative perspectives has allowed him to re-understand the city is worth further consideration. The chapel seeks 'to raise the ordinary to sacred status' by 'letting the light be'. Its extraordinariness is dependent on the visibility, the co-presence of its ordinary walls, as much as its reworking of 'ordinary' side-light. Its locatedness (a remoteness from the everyday, a timeless presence) relies on its deliberate framing of the garden and the city beyond. In contrast the new light in the sacristy is intentionally dramatic. It is more demonstrative, more 'Soanean' and ensures that a chasm between buildings – and thus the deepest of roof-lights – is equally the light, the city, the room. A shadowy gap becomes an eye on a sequestered garden, the

9.15
North–south site section through John Campbell Road and the Shell House and its garden, indicating the high terrace to Kingsland Road that overshadows the site to the east.

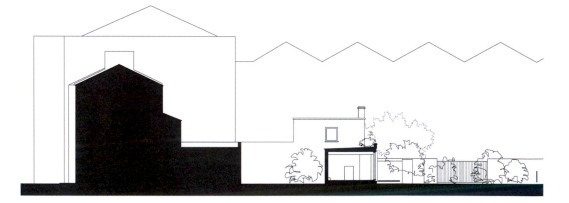

9.16
View through Shell House to
garden from entrance.

entry of light into it another act of clothing that transforms the chamber into a
critical boundary in the life of the institution, and by extension the city.

Remaking Hackney: A house from a stable

Hidden away at the bottom of a shadowy alley, fifteen metres or so behind the
street, 1A John Campbell Road is to all intents and purposes invisible to the city.
Nothing betrays its presence in the conjunction of anonymous walls and doors

9.17
Site plan, Shell House.

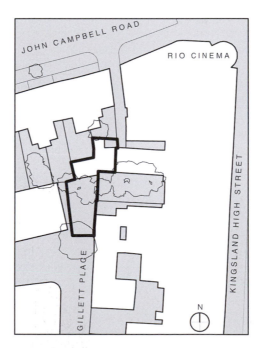

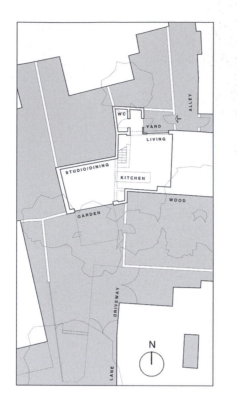

9.18
Ground plan, Shell House.

from which this abrupt cul-de-sac is composed. Here is the end of Hackney. On opening a solid timber door in the alley's side wall further progression is suddenly possible. At the side of a tiny courtyard a diagonal view across a dark interior reveals the green light of a garden beyond. Having been entirely lost, one is suddenly found. Leaving the noise and commotion of Kingsland High Street behind, light opens a route through a dark cave-like space towards a verdant inner world.

Behind the door is a large window beside a tiny entrance courtyard. This courtyard leads to another door. Inside, the L-shaped ground plan of the workshop/stable has been shrewdly reorganized by placing a stair at the centre, between the large north-facing window just described and its double, a second large window/door beside a leafy south-facing garden. Replacing an external stair that had previously occupied much of the entrance courtyard, this stair leads to the more private spaces above.

At ground level the two dark corners of the building accommodate 'fire' and 'water'. In the south-east corner is the original hearth, in the north-west a formerly external WC; between them is an island-kitchen workbench (the dwelling's visceral inner garden). Above this workbench, off the landing of the stair, is its more refined double: an open bathing/dressing space with a privileged view of the back gardens of the neighbouring terrace. An obliquely angled wall, the only new compartmentation of the whole building, divides this enlarged landing from a bedroom.

From the visitor's perspective the project can be summarized in a variety of ways: a house behind a door, a house between two windows, a house that is a stair, a stair that is a house. While Shell would not reject these formulations, she sees her work in a rather different way. In her view she has made a species of provisional dwelling, a set of spaces in flux, a house that doesn't stand still. After rummaging through this part of East London for several years she realized that this unlikely building only required relatively minimal excisions and insertions to change it into a dwelling (a roller shutter and stud wall have been removed, and one doorway partially in-filled to create a window, but not a single new opening has been necessary). Although it had only ever provided an intermediate environment previously, she found this aspect of the project particularly exciting, viewing the down-at-heel workshop, with its sloping floor and unfinished interior, along with the whole set of surrounding spaces entirely positively (the alley, the backs of the adjacent buildings, a cobbled yard it shares with neighbouring properties). Here was a stray piece of countryside, wild plant life colonizing the raw unkempt backland of the inner city to create a forgotten ruin, ripe for occupation. Tellingly, she herself chooses to encapsulate her project scheme as 'a cell above garden walls' (Fig. 9.19, 9.24).[25]

Shell's account of how she found the site and located where she was by walking through it is worth quoting in full, not only because it gives a strong sense of the physical character of this corner of Hackney and the kind of urban life it supported in the 1990s, but because it indicates what light – or rather lack of it – she initially encountered on the site. It also clarifies the importance of personal geography to the interpretation of a city neighbourhood. As will become clear, she initially encountered the building/site not from the north but the south, i.e. the inside, not the outside of the block:

> I actually saw the building two years before I bought it. It must have been in late 1996, early 1997. Donaldson's, the estate agents at Dalston Cross used to have a funny old notice-board on the street with a map of all the scraps of commercial in Hackney they had to sell. The site – 16 Gillett Place – showed up as $70\,m^2$ storage space with $80\,m^2$ of external yard.

9.19
A cell over garden walls.

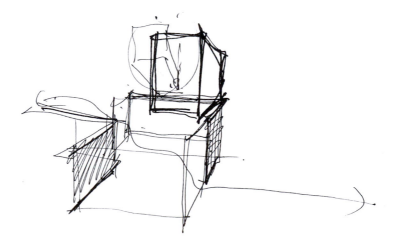

9.20
View to entrance courtyard
from kitchen, Shell House.

I came up Gillett Place, walked up the lane, saw the roller shutter, the road, the buildings on either side, and couldn't work out where the end of the site was, i.e. that even the road was part of the freehold ... At this point the car park was busy, people were transferring clothes from workshops to vans. This end of 'The Stamford Works' was filled with workshops for clothing manufacturers – and it held the Turkish Community Centre. It was bustling, with people, stacks of cotton reels and fabric.

Eighteen months later I saw that the same plot was for sale but now the building had planning permission for change of use. And so I had to go and see it again. I met Fred Sherrif (a local market trader), on Gillett Place. When he undid the padlock of the roller shutter all I could see were a few bags of onions and beetroot, cobwebs, cobbles, a cloud of steam. Then after a moment I could see that the space opened up diagonally, but I couldn't see through it. Though I was aware of the sun coming in from the back. It was morning, and there was just this little bit of light.

I was taken through the door to find the outside stair to the roof, and the gate. When I walked through the gate and up the alley to John Campbell Road it was such a surprise, but wonderful, to find that the building was on a street I knew.[26]

With its inner world of workshops and mews and outer world of terraced streets the corner of Hackney in which Shell's project is located is typical of the complex matrix of residential and commercial property to be found on either side of Kingsland High Street. A block structure originally developed for this neighbourhood by the Thyssen-Amherst Estate so that a set of predominantly residential streets could be connected in a more systematic way, its evolution has meant

9.21
The light in the market traders store at 1A John Campbell Road. Views looking north, 1997.

that the address, and thus the urban identity of the workshop/stable block has changed significantly over time.

As a small but oddly shaped volume with large openings to both north and south, it is not clear how the interior would have been organized initially when in use as a coach house/stable, only that it has approximately the same floor area as many London mews houses of this time. The hypothesis that the location of Gillett Place at the heart of the block was not a foregone conclusion in 1871 would explain the alternative openings to the north and south, the opening to the north allowing the stable block (like its neighbour at the back of Kingsland High Street) to open directly onto John Campbell Road, that to the south exploiting the building's potential location on Gillett Place. What is certain is that the ground floor would only have been daylit initially by way of its large stable doors. At the outset only the upper floor, where a groom would have slept, had glazed windows, along with a roof-light that Shell has since removed.

After World War I, when the building was in workshop mode, it was separated from the garden of 1 Campbell Road by a wall and given the address 16 Gillett Place. At some point during this period the large northern door opening was reconfigured to include an ordinary door and a high-level horizontal window, the southern door opening fitted with a roller shutter, and, as Shell's description

9.22
View to garden from kitchen,
Shell House, indicating
the light from above at the
centre of the house.

indicates, the poorly daylit workshop it became belonged to what was a messy workaday block interior.

It is these generous adaptable openings that have allowed the stable/ coach house to be transformed without difficulty, first into a workshop and subsequently into a dwelling. What is worth emphasizing about this change is that a large, rough, airy space has been reordered by Shell with respect to light and movement by reinterpreting the fundamental geography of this set of backland spaces in relation to the surrounding city. As Shell explains, her reconfiguration is:

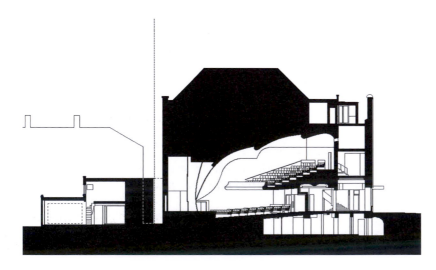

9.23
West–east stepped site
section illustrating the
relationship between Shell
House and the Rio Cinema
on Kingsland Road.

9.24
The window to the cell.

... the pairing of an internal and an external corner. These are the biggest elements. The space is always in flux. Defiantly not straight. You don't know which way to face ... I think of it as a square plan, one of whose quadrants (the north west) has been removed and given to the neighbour's garden ... The bedroom is the project's inner sanctum. The only room. I think of it as a cell above garden walls. The two windows downstairs are the through thing (for light and movement). Actually what we've got is an internal corner (where the hearth is) and an external corner (at the centre), and above them the cell without any openings.[27]

Equally her embrace of the interdependence of the building and its site is reflected in her characterization of the house as a 'pilot fish' to the 'whale' of the adjacent cinema.[28] Clarifying that this is another issue to do with diagonally related corners, her vision of the diminutive house keeping a weather eye open over the contested sea of a new development for the threatened leviathan reflects her sense of where the house belongs in the local neighbourhood (Figs. 9.22, 9.26). (The upshot of the serious dereliction from which the area suffered in the post-war years, Gillett Square, the new public space onto which the garden of 1A John Campbell Road now leads, remains incomplete as a self-sufficient public space. The first of London mayor Ken Livingstone's '100 new public spaces for London', it awaits an alternative solution following a contentious and unsuccessful proposal to replace the buildings which currently line its northern edge with a higher four-storey block that menaced the access to light and view of many houses on John Campbell Road).

9.25
View from garden towards
dining area beside living
room of Shell House.

Shell's assessment of the visual environment of the house illustrates once again how an exploration of boundaries – between interior and exterior, urbanity and wilderness, what is lost and what is found – is a nuanced interpretation of urban light. Asked to comment on what it was like to live here, her insights reveal how the passage she is creating in Hackney between street and garden is structured implicitly by its windows. As she notes, 'In winter, with the fall of the leaves, the south room seems at one with the garden when the low sun streams in. The two spaces are more separate in summer'.[29] Her comment that the unshuttered window at the heart of the plan has come to seem more pivotal to her dwelling during the time she has lived there is a final confirmation, if any were needed, of the fruits of an approach that aims to rediscover the city by adapting to its light:

> The sun is very striking when it comes through the window above the foot of the stairs in the summer, giving a last 6 pm pool of sunlight on the ground floor. In contrast the house has a very short day in winter. There is just a sense of glow, then you actually find the sunlight on the street.[30]

Gardening for light

> All truth is crooked, time itself is a circle.[31]

Alan Weisman's book *The World without Us*[32] begins its telling thought experiment by outlining in graphic detail the processes by which an abandoned and uncared-for building disintegrates as the forces of nature take their toll. For architects its account of the fundamental vulnerability of the human habitat is

9.26
The diagonal view towards
the light of the garden from
the first floor, Shell House.

especially unsettling. But as this study documents, artificial human habitats are always changing, even if the rules dictating their flowering or decline, their permanence or transience, are neither as clear or subject to the kinds of control we sometimes imagine.

This review of the evolution of two human habitats in relation to light has explored the process of small-scale change at the level of individual rooms by investigating the ecology of light in two corners of London. Each intervention has involved a significant change of use, but not a significant alteration to building form. In other words, despite their location at the base of the city, these projects have not significantly altered the local light environment for the surrounding buildings, i.e. they have not compromised others' access to light. In reworking old forms and old topographies to achieve these changes of use, integrated thinking about light and the city has nevertheless been critical. Arguably the new lease of life each intervention has achieved can be said to depend equally on the rethinking of spatial order in relation to available light and a reinterpretation of the local neighbourhood in relation to its potential for new occupation.

'Making do and mending' such work may be, but this is no small achievement in the contested urban environment. In the developed world rehabilitation work on buildings is still treated as something of secondary worth by most designers and commentators. This is a pity. It is frequently complex and time-consuming, but, as these projects show, when seen as an opportunity to rethink the city in relation to light, potentially highly therapeutic. Construing the inner city as a garden, or reinterpreting it in relation to garden themes, can make the pleasures and pressures of the light-starved urban condition more apparent, as it can help the city make sense once again.

Arguably this issue will be increasingly significant in the future. We are aiming to live sustainably, but the city can only change so fast. Being able to locate ourselves within it, to identify with it, to reinterpret its boundaries and territories will surely be just as important in the future as it has been in the past. In order to build the light we want, the light we depend on, the light we can afford, we surely require a deeper understanding of the processes of evolution already implemented. If light is time and time itself is a circle, the architecture of light must need to look backwards as it looks forwards. As this kind of work illuminates, knowing where you are is knowing the light around you, and the idea of the city as lost garden, lost fields, lost light, a provocative contribution to understanding both who we are and who we may need to be.

Notes

1   M. Sorkin, 'Container Riff', in the exhibition catalogue *Present and Futures. Architecture in Cities*, Centre of Contemporary Culture of Barcelona, 1996. Available online at http://www.publicspace.org/en/text-library/eng/a012-container-riff (accessed December 2010).

2   See P. Ackroyd, *London, The Biography*, Chatto and Windus, 2000, ch. 47, pp. 431–440, and P. Brimblecombe, *The Big Smoke*, Methuen, London and New York, 1987.

3   See O. Prizeman, 'Philanthropy and light: the formulation of transatlantic environmental standards for public interiors through Andrew Carnegie's library building programme 1889–1910', unpublished PhD thesis, University of Cambridge, 2010.

4   S. Brand, *How Buildings Learn: What Happens after They're Built*, Penguin, 1995.

5   For further discussion of McLaughlin's design approach see A. Macintosh, 'Evolving light: McLaughlin's Carmelite Monastery', unpublished diploma dissertation, University of Cambridge, 2005.

6   N. McLaughlin, personal interview with Andrew Mackintosh, December 2004.

7   McLaughlin's practice statement is available online at http://www.niallmclaughlin.com/Profile.html (accessed 26 November 2010).

8   N. McLaughlin as quoted by S. O'Toole, 'Trapping the Light Fantastic', in *The Sunday Times*, 13 February, 2005. Summary available online at http://ireland.archiseek.com/tesserae/000002.html (accessed 26 November 2010).

9   McLaughlin, as quoted by S. O'Toole.

10 McLaughlin, personal interview, December, 2004.

11 Shell's practice statement is available online at http://www.lisashellarchitects.co.uk/htdocs/practice/about.htm (accessed 26 November 2010).

12 L. Shell, personal interview, August 2008.

13 Ibid.

14 Ibid.

15 Ibid.

16 Ibid.

17 McLaughlin, personal interview. Often McLaughlin's ideas come from poetry. The origin of the idea that something expesssionless expresses God is a poem by Robert Lowell, 'The Quaker Graveyard at Nantucket', which in turn, refers to a verse of Isaiah (53:2): 'And he shall grow up as a tender plant before him, and as a root out of a thirsty ground: there is no beauty in him, nor comeliness: and we have seen him, and there was no sightliness, that we should be desirous of him.'

18 A painting by Michael Pacher, *Altarpiece of the Church Fathers* (c.1483), was McLaughlin's inspiration for the chairs. 'You get this nice tension in the painting between the monumentality of the figure and the humanity of the individual within it. It seemed to me to offer a clue to allowing the extended scale of the furniture to dignify the seated figure and also by increasing perception of their scale to make them seem closer to each other' (McLaughlin, personal interview).

19 McLaughlin, personal interview. Frequently inspired by poetry, McLaughlin notes that this particular visual sensation of seeing green through gold was inspired by the lovely opposition between the enduring and the ephemeral evoked in the first and third verses of W.B. Yeats's 'Sailing to Byzantium'.

20 McLaughlin, personal interview.

21 Ibid.

22 Ibid.

23 Ibid.

24 Ibid.

25 Shell, personal interview.

26 Ibid.

27 Ibid.

28 Ibid.

29 Ibid.

30 Ibid.

31 F. Nietzsche, *Thus Spoke Zarathustra, A Book for All and None*, (Webster's French Thesaurus Edition), ICON Group International Inc., San Diego, CA, p. 210.

32 A. Weisman, *The World without Us*, Virgin Books, 2007.

Chapter 10

The electricity of daylight?

Herzog and De Meuron's excavation of dusk at London's Bankside Power Station, 1998–2000

Thus they (white models) appear to comply with a view expressed by Le Corbusier who wrote in *Vers une architecture*, 'architecture is the scientific, correct and wonderful game of volumes assembled under light'. What however if the architecture is not a game at all, especially not a scientific and correct one, and if the light is often clouded over, diffuse, not so radiant as it is in the ideal southern landscape?[1]

As a matter of fact, the architectural plan and the architectural work interest us as tools for the perception of reality and confrontation with it.[2]

When the property developer Stuart Lipton first saw Herzog and De Meuron's competition drawings for Tate Modern he apparently asked if that was all there was.[3] He must have been bemused to discover it was the project's relative invisibility that had convinced the judges it should win. Since its completion in 2000,[4] this uncertainty about exactly what Herzog and De Meuron have done to the ex-power station at Bankside has been much discussed; the project's 'understatedness' its defining trait. Herzog and De Meuron have asserted that the building is one they had to accept, and yet paradoxically that their project represents its major transfiguration. Making the most of an opportunity to work in London, a milieu outside their normal field of reference, it is clear they came to see their task as a careful reworking of place. The architecture was interpreted as an unusual site within which to operate rather than a building to convert, and the outcome a 'work in progress' rather than a finished product. In catalysing their thinking about the transformation required,[5] this conversion process forced them to confront assumptions about not only what change would produce the 'hybrid' architecture they deemed appropriate, but the degree to which their hand in this change should be apparent. Just as importantly, it also forced them to think about light as a catalyst of change.

Past discussion of Herzog and De Meuron's work has concentrated on their conversion of matter into architecture, their disclosure of a 'poetry of materials' informed by a critical engagement with issues of observation and perception.[6] In pursuing such concerns the practice itself continues to place the greatest importance on the immediate obviousness of their architecture, a quality they describe as its 'self-evidence'. One consequence of this lasting emphasis on a clarity of making is that despite their interest in the environmental implications of their work, how Herzog and De Meuron's architecture is encountered, the memorable settings it creates, does not always seem to have prompted the appraisal it deserves.

The published analysis of Tate Modern is a case in point. Commentators are aware that in arriving at the final proposal lighting issues must have been decisive – 'change is from something impermeable to something accessible, light filled and almost delicate',[7] 'light enlivens the static mass',[8] 'light is a primary material'[9] – but the role that light, natural and artificial, plays in the overall *mise-en-scène* – and the overall thesis of the work – has yet to be fully assessed. Explaining why this architecture of light is central to the web of contradictions the conversion represents is one goal of this final chapter. By reviewing what its authors have said about light – and what they have left unsaid – it also aims to frame the significance of the uneasy gloom at the heart of the building by relating it to the wider thesis about the place of art in contemporary public life, that the project is seeking to construct.

Cutting into matter for light and passage

Architectural subterfuge has always been important to Bankside Power Station. This is a utilitarian steel-framed building dressed as a 'cathedral of power'; a building whose fabric promised permanence and weight but one which was fully operational for only twenty years.[10] Concerns over the external appearance of such a building type on this prominent riverside site in Central London led to the design of an imposing shell within which a series of gargantuan and elegantly lit pieces of machinery were housed. A series of tall 'cathedral' windows on the north, east and west facades and a roof-light running almost the entire length of the building provided daylight, but limited views, to the boiler house and turbine hall within. At the back a set of more prosaic horizontal windows brought light to the south-facing switch station.

Asserting 'Our strategy was to accept the physical power of Bankside's mountain-like brick building and even enhance it, rather than break it or try to diminish it',[11] Herzog and De Meuron have sought to frame Tate Modern as a passage of the everyday through art, a place where art can be encountered en route through the city so that its 'otherness' illuminates normality.[12] One commentator has deemed it a 'colonisation',[13] another a judicious dissection,[14] while the practice itself chooses to frame it an excavation – or a rather bolder reshaping than the former terminology would imply. It is true that outgrowths low down and high up have been cut away and a number of small-scale incisions now open an interior that was previously sealed at ground level. Yet the ground itself has been dug out with some ruthlessness to allow a huge new ramp to descend into the building from the west. At high level the reworking of the roofscape is hardly reticent either. A two-storey linear form, the so-called 'beam of light', now crowns Bankside's riverside facade. To complete the process, the interior has been gutted so that a working crane and a short section of floor are the principal traces of the building's previous existence.

Within this vast shell the organization of Tate Modern rewrites the basic dichotomy of the power station. A 'hollowed out' central space, the reshaped 'turbine hall', becomes the largest museum entrance in the world. Below the 'light beam' the former boiler house is packed with the rest of the new accommodation: galleries, bookshop, auditorium, cafés, education spaces and ancillary services. In the future a more demonstrative extension based on the building's 'hidden spaces' (three vast oil tanks and a switch station), also designed by Herzog and De Meuron, will break out of the building's southern flank on the opposite side of the turbine hall. While most of this excavation is certainly 'invisible', it is nonetheless critical to the practice's conception of the project as a new urban crossroads. It is clear that they hope that the new public space they have unearthed, a species of giant arcade, will become even more apparent on completion of phase two, when the north-south route it frames will finally extend into Southwark.

> We use light like a family, or a language, throughout the building. The light box on top and the glass boxes inside are mostly immaterialised; ideally they are only light. The boxes (in the turbine hall) are in front of the steel structure, physical, glowing. They *cut* through the steel, *cut away* the dominance of steel and the all-too- powerful verticality of the turbine hall. This was very important because you see the boxes mostly from an angle and you wouldn't see anything new if they didn't come to the front. It has to do with *perception* and orientation as you walk through the building. We reveal things that are already there, turn them into our own architecture, instead of always design-ing something ourselves.[15]

In their own introduction to this mountain-machine Herzog and De Meuron sum-marize the project as a series of juxtaposed elements and volumes, old and new, within a re-landscaped site. Taken together it is as if these components create a kind of beached ark (or container ship) for art. Framing their intentions under the following headings: the ramp, the platform, the turbine hall, 'hidden spaces' (as just described), the 'light beam', the chimney, the landscape, the concourses, the bay windows, the galleries, 'lighting' and the stairway,[16] it is only the quality of light in the 'cabin' galleries that is thought worthy of an explanation in this introduction,[17] despite the fact that Herzog's many other statements on the project reflect a consistent concern for how light affects visitors' impressions. The situation is further complicated by the fact that while the practice's work frequently demonstrates great sensitivity to natural light,[18] as for example at the 1998 Dominus Winery, the 2002 REHAB Basel, and the 2003 Laban Centre, their most explicit pronouncements on light at Tate Modern tend to focus on the building's artificially luminous volumes, as the quote above indicates, rather than its handling of daylight. Notwithstanding this difficulty, it is the purposes served

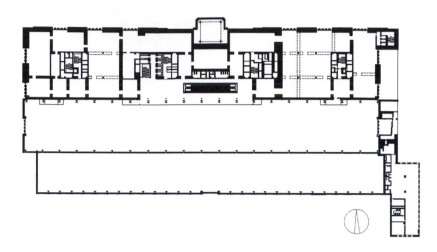

10.1
First-floor plan of Tate
Modern indicating the
arrangement of the gallery
spaces on the north side of
the building in the former
boiler house, after a drawing
by Herzog and De Meuron
Architects.

by the unspoken interdependence of daylight and artificial light at Tate Modern
that deserve closer interrogation. A consideration of the different elements of the
building in turn (as defined by its authors) will structure the analysis that follows
in order to reveal what kind of visual environment, and what kind of 'seeing',
this illumination supports.

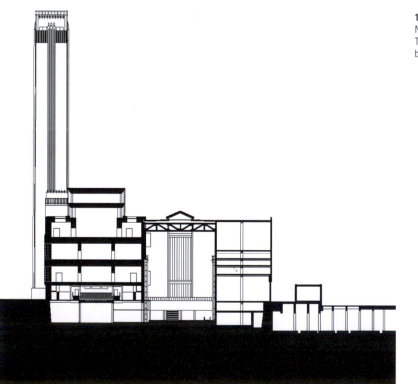

10.2
North–south section through
Tate Modern, after a drawing
by Herzog and De Meuron.

10.3
The daylight in the turbine hall prior to the power station's conversion. © Tate, London 2010.

The cloudy light of the galleries

Herzog and De Meuron's willingness to foreground the lighting of the galleries suggests this is a good place to begin an assessment of the building's argument in light. Divided into two suites to either side of the chimney, the galleries occupy three of the middle floors behind the river facade in what the architects stress is a non-hierarchical organization[19] (floor areas vary but most of the spaces in the lower two floors are of comparable height, as are the peripheral spaces on the upper floor [Fig. 10.5]). Distributed along the river facade the galleries on the two lower floors are in the obvious place to make the most of the north light the original windows introduce, and reflect Herzog's preference for conventionally side-lit rather than roof-lit space. In contrast, lying above the original windows and partially encased by the roof beam, the upper-floor galleries are either roof-lit or clerestory-lit and lack eye-level openings.

It is not the diaphanous whiteness of the lower-floor galleries that is in any way remarkable but the fact that their immaterial neutrality is thrown into relief by their location between a broken panorama over London (with all the lively intensity of the urban condition) and the much more sombre new turbine hall (with the sublime gravity of a cave). The experience of viewing art clearly demands visual focus but, according to Herzog and De Meuron, also deserves distraction. That Donald Judd is sometimes in London is good to know. Considered from this perspective, looking at the collection becomes an informal if visually demanding stroll past the art in the presence of a distant view. The mountainside supplies the path, the prospect and the light, the dark machine grounds and subverts the white otherworld of art.

10.4
New turbine hall at Tate
Modern from first-floor level
concourse looking east.

In this regard, it is not without interest that the architects describe their aim in the lower-gallery floors as 'artificial normality'. Like Hitchcock, they devise a *mise-en-scène* whose ordinariness is not what it seems. To disguise the newness and technical sophistication of the galleries, elements like industrial floor grills 'give the impression that the exhibition spaces have always been there, like the brick facades and the turbine hall'.[20] Walls which are lightweight and moveable have a depth which makes them appear solid, and all the technical equipment needed to transform the exhibition spaces is hidden away in the ceilings and walls. In this typically duplicitous contemporary architecture, austere to the eye but a complex mechanism nevertheless, the fact that the floor grounds the art is critical to Herzog and De Meuron. The counterpoint to machined normality is radical primitivism. Among the crowds of art-loving cognoscenti, the detached act of observation under shadowless museum light is brought down to earth by the raw physicality of untreated oak boards. As Herzog explains:

> The floor is the most outstanding element. The power station is a huge, almost brutal building. To have something that is so soft and sensual is not normal; it is abnormal. There is something archaic about it, when you place a Picasso in such a simple space with a wooden floor and a view of London.[21]

10.5
The cloudy light of the gallery spaces. These simple, calm, apparently unsophisticated and stable rooms constitute a neutral, evenly lit background for the wild and autonomous art and range from entirely artificially lit environments to spaces supplying long privileged views over London. © Tate, London 2009.

The solid light beam and the fractured concourse light

The 'light beam', the two-storey glazed volume on the roof, is thus far, Herzog and De Meuron's most obvious addition to Bankside power station (Figs. 10.6, 10.7, 10.8).[22] During the day its glassy delicacy contrasts with the dark bulk beneath (explaining perhaps why Herzog and De Meuron insisted the old brickwork did not need cleaning), while at night it becomes a glowing body of light. What seems worth underlining here is its place in the whole design strategy. From the inside it gives dramatic panoramas of the urban skyline. From the outside it acts as an urban beacon, broadcasting to London the building's status as a public arena by transforming its life into gigantic shadow theatre. Depending on the hour, it states light as theatre, as signal or as counterform to the turbine hall, this giant luminaire a recollection of the building's original function.

In a sense the concourses are the building's in-between territories, its 'open spaces' according to Herzog and De Meuron. Lying between turbine hall and the galleries, they not only give access to information desks and meeting places, but provide visual relief from the tiring process of viewing art (Figs. 10.9, 10.10, 10.12, 10.13). This is because they are rougher and darker than the galleries (the stair is black, the bathrooms are black, the columns are black), but just as importantly because they look out onto the dusky cave of the turbine hall. The concourses (dark topographies fractured by light) are set beside calm white gallery suites (rooms beside rooms) and remain half open to the long grey light of the turbine hall (the largest box in London). Here in this intermediate world, the building's old bones are no longer masked, ceilings recede to reveal veins and arteries, and the light fixtures construct interrupted lines of light. The unexpected visual effects this generates subtly throw the status of the museum into question. Is the glass box surrounding the first escalator art (echoing Dan Flavin), or life (the sharp transparency of shopping mall or train station)? What should the visitor expect beyond the mirror of ambiguous reflections presented by the thin

10.6
The 'light beam' above
Tate Modern from Foster
and Partners' 2000
Millennium Footbridge.

10.7
Reflection of St Paul's in
internal glazed wall of
'light beam'.

glazed screen which divides the more decorous cabins and deck spaces of this mighty ship from its yawning hold?

The gloom of the turbine hall

The turbine hall is a grey, rectangular and breathtakingly large space, so large that a small plane could be flown through it, so large that planning permission is required to build things inside it (Figs. 10.17, 10.18). Even when the sun is out its light is ashen, suppressed, predominantly diffuse. Although the outcome of an excavation process, why this interior is also an invention, beyond its incorporation of new elements, is worth exploring further. Natural light now enters from Scott's three original apertures (the tall cathedral windows at each end that face almost exactly east and west, and the long central roof-light[23]) but also from a line of glazed doors half-way down the ramp. Look closer and it becomes apparent that a row of floodlights recalling Scott's original fittings have been fixed to the south wall. More importantly, with its concrete floor, light grey walls (new to the north, old to the south) and dark grey steelwork, Herzog and De Meuron have given their new turbine hall additional weight and sobriety by the simple expedient of a monolithic appearance. In other words, the opaque sides of the box have been made to compose a symphony in grey that not only tempers the daylight but acts as a foil for the decidedly contemporary vocabulary of transparent glass walls and luminous bay windows of the north wall. Size is tempered by greyness. Greyness is contrasted with glitz. Whiteness is not everything. A major virtue of this greyness is that it helps to neutralize the sacred aspect of art, so that in this temporary exhibition hall, the pressured intimacy of a typical encounter with contemporary art is overwhelmed by the scalelessness and tough studio-in-warehouse feel of the space.

The impact of this light is determined in part by the turbine hall's almost complete interiority. At platform level this is relieved only by long

10.9
Concourse escalator at
ground-floor level.

tantalizing glimpses northwards to the green lawn and trembling birch trees of
the river bank (Fig. 10.11) (to the west only a momentary glimpse of the terrace
and a short stretch of the ramp is visible). In contrast, at floor level, which as
Herzog and De Meuron point out is below the water level of the Thames, London
is entirely out of sight and visitors finds themselves drowning in the subaqueous
light of an 'other' river.

    It seems worth noting here that close to the start of his memoir *A
Scientific Autobiography*,[24] Herzog and De Meuron's teacher, Aldo Rossi, plays

10.10
The broken artificial light of
an upper-level concourse.

10.11
Hall at ground-floor level in overcast conditions.

a game on the word 'tempo', which, together with several of the topics under review, recurs throughout the rest of the text. He is interested in its double reading, as weather/chronology, and in such phenomena as the fog inside the Galleria Vittorio Emanuele II in Milan, and in the nave of Alberti's church of Sant'Andrea in Mantua, which makes it a natural inhabitant of the Po Valley later on in these reflections. Beyond these more literal sources of inspiration for the innate fogginess of the turbine hall interior, perhaps it is also possible to see Rossi's anecdote about the room with the sheer drop of ten metres, as well as the authority of the corridor he describes in the 'villa' project, in addition to some of the comments regarding monuments and archaeology/re-use, as providing part of the climate of motivations for the turbine hall being regarded as a complement to the river/ city panorama (Figs. 10.19, 10.20, 10.21).

Interestingly, Herzog and De Meuron do not discuss the greyness of their largest box. What they have to say about the light of the turbine hall concerns the translucent/transparent bay windows, and their animating role:

> The bay windows, elongated bodies of light, afford an interior view of the museum and its exhibition activities. They are also architectural bodies that break up the mighty, vertical steel supports of the facade and generate an optical instability. Depending on lighting conditions, the brightly illuminated glass bodies may seem suspended in front of the facade, toning down the monumentality of the industrial architecture. The bay windows belong to the same family as the rooftop light beam.[25]

As in their discussion of the new roof element, what its authors decide to foreground instead is the light that acquires form, and its capacity to induce

ambiguity, defy gravity, draw the eye. Their comments support the idea that the building has no hierarchy. Nothing is higher and nothing is lower. Everything is equal in that everything can take form, even light, the antithesis of matter.

Inside light

> I believe that neither art nor architecture are here to entertain us but if you are interested it can be like a mountain. You know a mountain is boring but if you look at it in a special way it can be amazing for you. You can walk on it, you can discover the plants, the different shades, the different light.[26]

> Maybe it is a hybrid. It is a heterotopic place that, especially once the second stage is open, will have different sites that are expressing different ways of looking at the world.[27]

Two strands of thinking have dominated Herzog and De Meuron's approach to the transformation of Bankside. First, there is the idea that Tate Modern is a conceptual hybrid, an artificial mountain (or implicitly a stranded machine). Second, there is the idea that Tate Modern has no spatial hierarchy, i.e. that all its exhibition settings have equal status. While their work usually demonstrates such concerns, what matters here is how they influence their approach to light. As already noted, Herzog is eager to underline the way the 'bodies of light' (the rooftop 'light beam' and the turbine hall light boxes) qualify Scott's architecture and transform it into a new machine. He is less forthcoming about how natural light can enliven architectural experience or animate dark matter, but this nevertheless emerges in the landscape analogies he employs. Although it is not as easy to explain how light is implicated in his assertion that Tate Modern is a heterotopia, i.e. a non-hierarchical aggregate of places that constitutes a counter-site

10.13
View from the main stair towards the first-floor concourse and the turbine hall.

(in Foucault's own words, a 'simultaneously mythic and real contestation of the space in which we live'[28]), this is also worth doing.

The basic task of any art gallery is to provide a series of milieus for a kind of looking that is very demanding, and so the kind of contrasts in setting that foster visual concentration and its opposite ('looking at' and 'looking away') always deserve consideration. At Tate Modern it is as if this issue has been made central to the project. In essence the building establishes a number of discreet settings for art – and relief from art – that are orchestrated as a series of juxta-positions in light. Thus wherever possible long views – across London or into the turbine hall – animate strolls through austere galleries. Such differences are also important at a larger scale. Vertically the building is divided between a more gritty urban topography (the reworked ground of the turbine hall and the urban foyer it contains), the calm predominantly white world presented by the galleries, and the lantern to London of the rooftop 'light beam'. Horizontally it is split between

10.14
Busy Oxford Street in central
London is approximately the
height of the turbine hall at
Tate Modern.

the heavy grey turbine hall, the more chaotic and lively concourses, and the airy lightness of the galleries. In a strategy which depends on a complex interplay of natural and artificial light sources, it is these contrasts that order the spatial experience. The sunlight-shafted grey light of the turbine hall gives pause in the context of the steadier diffuse light of the north-facing galleries. The broken light of the concourses stands in contrast to both. The turbine hall is the 'light beam' drowned. Conversely the 'light beam' is the turbine hall lifted and glowing. The consequence for visitors is that views into the turbine hall's solemn greyness are contrasted with the breathtaking vision of St Paul's provided by the 'light beam'.

    What Herzog and De Meuron choose to say about the light of Tate Modern's is generally very measured, although some of their claims – particularly

10.15
Comparison of the volumes
of a series of urban interiors.
From left to right: St Paul's
Cathedral, London; the
Galleria Vittorio Emanuele II,
Milan; the train shed of
King's Cross Station, London;
Boullée's 1784 design for
the Bibliothèque Royale,
Paris; the new turbine hall,
Tate Modern.

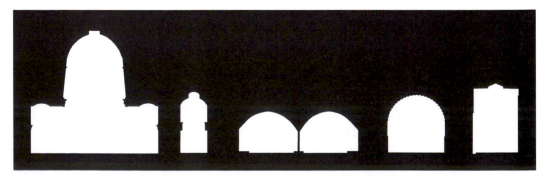

10.16
Ramped entrance into
turbine hall from basement
level in afternoon sunshine.

to do with the assignment of a mysterious 'body' to light have their roots in Romanticism. It is as if they want to remain balanced about the subject but – like many others – find this inherently difficult. In their own framing of the project the light for the galleries is described as neutral and resolutely conservative; it is only their 'bodies' of light that are presented as literally and figuratively electric. Conversely the powerful but reticent half-light of the turbine hall is something they barely touch on. This willingness to present light as something inherently exciting when given volume – the spark of anti-matter as it were – rather than to discuss the ambience it induces – the light we are within – is not unusual however, reflecting the absorption with visual spectacle that Romanticism introduced, and the pervasive commodification of light that electricity has promoted.

Cool it may be, but an overtly pragmatic statement of the practice's design philosophy clarifies this ambiguity somewhat, implying that as a matter of encounter, architecture and its light should be something worth interrogating, something that does not give everything away at once. As Herzog asserts, 'I always like things that don't bother me when I don't want them to. I like things which work, which are well done, which have shadow at the right moment, which are well lit, but where there is much more for those who want to discover it.'[29] According to this version of events, architecture is ultimately something one is surrounded by, not a distant vision, but rather the steady background, a topography or framework within which appearances 'have their place', and where a well-judged response to the interdependence of light and weight can contribute to the enigmatic quality of 'tetheredness' that Herzog and De Meuron are actively seeking.

However its authors have chosen to describe it, light at Tate Modern – electric and natural – is mercurial, sometimes figure and sometimes ground,

10.17
East end of turbine hall
from ground-floor bridge in
afternoon sunshine.

sometimes a presence but sometimes also a quality of place. The daylight is an aspect of the mountain landscape; the artificial light an element of the machine. One supports the other. To explain how this marriage of nature and artifice impacts on the public life the project sustains, it is worth returning at this point to how Herzog and De Meuron have reconfigured the Bankside building. Essentially their *parti* is to place within the shell of the power station a set of more or less conventional white exhibition spaces beside a vast and decidedly unconventional grey hall. In this arrangement the building's major new division is a mirror-window: the glazed wall between stacked-up galleries and hall that allows the latter to act as a reference point – and a reference light – on journeys to and from the art. What they have not done is to make Tate Modern 'easy'. What they have done is to accept and reinforce the shadowy gloom at the building's heart, a decision that is possibly the most audacious insight of this reticent, largely invisible, yet telling excavation of place.

10.18
The turbine hall from the
entrance ramp.

Exhuming light

The visual impact and ambiguous mood of the turbine hall – a consequence of its scalelessness, neutrality and predominant greyness – is hard to convey. Herzog and De Meuron themselves describe it as a covered street or arcade, citing the Galleria Vittorio Emmanuele II in Milan[30] as a precedent. In fact at 155 m long, 22 m wide and 35 m high, it is not as long but somewhat wider than this grandest of nineteenth-century shopping arcades, i.e. with a scale comparable to a major London thoroughfare but without the noise and multifarious activities of either. (Oxford Street has approximately these dimensions, for example [Fig. 10.14]) Other commentators interpret it differently. Slessor, for example, refers to it as a cathedral for an ascetic cult[31] (it is wider and longer but about the same height as the main nave of St Pauls, although without its carefully measured chiaroscuro[32]); Hart as a stage for art[33] (the proscenium to the main stage at Covent Garden is only 12.2 m wide by 14.8 m high); Marr as a vault;[34] and Curtis as a hangar for cultural and social functions.[35] Alternatively, in *Herzog and De Meuron: Natural History*, the Beaux-Arts precedent cited by Vogt,[36] Boullée's 1784 design for the Bibliothèque Royale in Paris underlines its monumental character. Quite

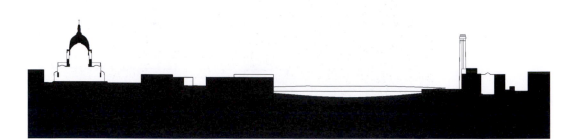

10.19
North–south site section of
Tate Modern, illustrating its
situation of light.

characteristically. Herzog has asserted they were not longing for monumental-ism,[37] and yet the decision to intensify the graininess of the industrial light by making the hall even higher and painting it grey has done nothing to mitigate its tomb-like character (Fig. 10.15).

The issue can be pursued by asking a different question. What kind of theatre of light does the new turbine hall evoke? As an inside/outside landscape of watching and waiting, a waiting room at the scale of the city, it surely has the toughness and soaring grandeur of the spaces in a metropolitan railway terminus. Comparable in height and volume to the concourse of New York's Grand Central Station; the turbine hall's central roof-light and axial entry route imply instead that it might actually be a converted train shed.[38] And yet although the dramatic mood of the turbine hall in late afternoon sunlight recalls momentarily Hal Morey's famous photographs of sunbeams in the New York building, the space does not thereby acquire Grand Central's status as a vital and celebratory platform for travel (Figs. 10.16, 10.17, 10.22). This is not a portal to the city for every-man, and the brief end of day projection of sunlight it stages is more brooding. It never has colour. Given the building's orientation and Britain's overcast skies, such interludes serve rather to underline the enigma of the hall's eternal fog.

Perhaps unexpectedly, it is the predominant greyness of the daylit turbine hall that makes it the most provocative space of Tate Modern and trans-forms it into an arena for art like no other in London. At once a strange terminus and a curious playground, it creates a twilight place – and public light – where the rules of the game are not obvious. The very antithesis of corporate pomp, this edgy half-light – the counter-light to the racy glitz of much of the recent architecture starting to surround it – is both menacing and thrilling, as much a portent of death as an uncertain darkness within which extra-ordinary things can happen.

Notes

1 J. Herzog, 'The Hidden Geometry of Nature', p. 208, in G. Mack, *Herzog and De Meuron 1978–1988. The Complete Works Vol. 1*, trans. B Almberg and K. Steiner, Birkhäuser Verlag, Basel, 1996.

2 Ibid., p. 209.

3 See T. Fretton, 'Into the void: Herzog and De Meuron's Tate Modern', in *Architecture Today*, no. 109, June, 2000, pp. 34–57, p. 35.

10.20
Counter-place. The grey
hold of Tate Modern. Right:
Ground-floor bridge. Below:
Entrance ramp and south
wall to turbine hall.

4   The competition for Tate Modern phase 1 took place between 1994–1996. The final design
    was constructed between 1998 and 2000. A major extension via a second building phase
    has been planned from the outset.

5   The importance the practice attaches to 'architecture's role in rendering the environment
    comprehensible' has been discussed by Wang. See W. Wang, 'Herzog and De Meuron:
    Interpreting the Place', in *Architecture Today*, no. 2, October, 1989, pp. 42–47, p. 47.

6   For comments by Herzog on the practice's rejection of a priori design thinking see
    R. Capezzuto, 'Herzog and De Meuron and Phenomenological Research. Jacques Herzog
    in conversation with Rita Capezzuto', in *Domus*, no. 823, February, 2000, pp. 6–10, p. 6.
    For further discussion of the practice's approach see W. Wang, *Herzog and De Meuron*,
    Birkhäuser Verlag, Basel, 1998; G. Mack, *Herzog and De Meuron, The Complete Works,
    Vols. 1 and 2* (1978–1988 and 1989–1991), Birkhäuser Verlag, Basel, 1996; P. Ursprung, ed.,

10.21
A machined river of fog. The
south wall to the turbine hall
in overcast conditions.

Herzog and De Meuron, Natural History, CCA and Lars Müller Publishers, 2002/2005; and also W. Curtis, 'The nature of artifice' (a conversation with J. Herzog, November 2001), in *Herzog and De Meuron 1998–2002* (*El Croquis*, nos 109–110, 2002), pp. 16–31; R. Moore, 'Beyond Architecture', in *Blueprint*, March, 1995, pp. 26–30; M. King, 'A conversation with Jacques Herzog and Pierre de Meuron on the Suburb, Self-Evidence, Tradition–Utopia', in *Forum*, 1988, 32nd year 01, pp. 34–39; Capezzuto, 'Herzog and De Meuron and Phenomenological Research', pp. 6–10.

7   D. Sudjic, 'Bankside Reborn', introduction to 'Tate Gallery: Selection of an Architect', *Blueprint*, no. 115, March supplement, 1995, pp. 1–22, p. 5.

8   C. Slessor, 'Art and Industry', in *Architectural Review*, August, 2000, pp. 44–49, p. 45.

9   See W. Curtis, 'Tate Gallery of Modern Art', in *Architectural Record*, no. 6, 2000, p. 242.

10   Sir Giles Gilbert Scott's power station was constructed in two phases between 1947 and l961, but energy production ended there in 1981. It still houses a switch station in 2010.

11   See Fretton, 'Into the void', p. 46.

12   See R. Moore and R. Ryan, *Building Tate Modern*, Tate Gallery Publishing Ltd, 2000, p. 54.

13   Slessor, 'Art and Industry', p. 47.

14   Fretton, 'Into the void', p. 34.

15   J. Herzog as quoted in N. Rappaport and S. Hart, 'Power Station', in *Architecture,* May, 2000, pp. 146–155, p. 153.

10.22
The subtle charge of
daylight. The turbine hall
roof-light through the
glazed screen.

16 See Herzog and De Meuron's own summary of the project in Fretton, 'Into the void',
    pp. 46–57.

17 Perhaps the focus on the light of the galleries – the light for viewing art – is driven by a
    pragmatic wish to demonstrate technical proficiency in exhibition lighting and its control, and
    yet these comments reinforce the idea that light is never a matter of technics alone. Herzog
    and De Meuron's text implies that the combination of natural and artificial light they employ
    is a competent means of displaying the permanent collection not only because it answers
    concerns about conservation, but because it ensures visitors in this large building have a
    sense of destination – as well as the stimulating variation in illumination that a daylit setting
    provides.

18 See R. Kudielka, 'Speculative Architecture: On the aesthetics of Herzog and de Meuron' in
    P. Ursprung, ed., *Herzog and De Meuron, Natural History, CCA and Lars Müller publishers*,
    2002/2005, pp 279–288, for a discussion of Herzog and De Meuron's careful handling of light
    phenomena.

19 See Moore and Ryan, *Building Tate Modern*, p. 39.

20 J. Herzog, in Fretton, 'Into the void', p. 54.

21 J. Herzog, as quoted in Rappaport and Hart, 'Power Station', p. 153.

22 As Herzog and De Meuron emphasize, the 'light beam' also structures the project visually. In
    their view it both counters the vertical thrust of the chimney and qualifies what they see as
    the existing facade's overbearing symmetry (the 'light beam' is deliberately not centred on
    the chimney, but is slightly shifted west). See Moore and Ryan, *Building Tate Modern*, p. 46.

23 To Herzog and De Meuron's dismay, it was felt that the original glazing to this roof-light, an
    elegant curving glass-block form was too expensive to repair. It was instead replaced with a
    very conventional and somewhat more transparent double-pitched roof-light. See D. Boudet,
    'Herzog & de Meuron, Tate Modern, Londres', in *AMC*, no. 108, June/July, 2000, pp. 56–69,
    p. 58.

24 A. Rossi, *A Scientific Autobiography*, MIT Press, 1974.

25 Herzog and De Meuron, as quoted in Fretton, 'Into the void', p. 48.

26 J. Herzog as quoted in Moore and Ryan, *Building Tate Modern*, pp. 52–53.

10.23
Light as ground for the dialogue between art and life. Between October 2003 and March 2004 the turbine hall staged a major public art installation like no other before it, whose staging of a 'last day' became the talk of London. Arguably, Olafur Eliasson's Unilever-funded *The Weather Project*, with its mono-frequency artificial sun and veils of actual mist, can be seen as a reaction to the provocative greyness of the turbine halls everyday light.

27 Ibid., p. 56.

28 M. Foucault, *Of Other Spaces, Heterotopias*, trans. J. Miskowiek, available online at http://foucault.info/documents/heteroTopia/foucault.heteroTopia.en.html (accessed 26 November 2010). Originally published as 'Des Espaces Autres', in *Architecture, Mouvement, Continuité*, no. 5, October, 1984, pp. 46–49.

29 J. Herzog, as quoted in Moore and Ryan, *Building Tate Modern*, p. 52.

30 The main arm of this complex cross-shaped set of passages is 196 m long by 14.5 m wide and 32 m high.

31 Slessor, 'Art and Industry', p. 49. With this analogy Slessor reflects the Romantic view of art as the secular-sacred.

32 The nave and side aisles of St Paul's are 28.8 m wide and 118 m long, while the nave itself is only 14.4 m wide.

33 Rappaport and Hart, 'Power Station', p. 147.

34 A. Marr, *Observer*, 9 April 2000, as quoted in *Tate Modern: The First Five Years*, Tate, 2005, p. 55.

35 W. Curtis, 'Tate Gallery of Modern Art', in *Architectural Record*, no. 6, 2000, p. 103ff., p. 107.

36 A.M. Vogt, 'Étienne-Louis Boullée Visits the Tate Modern', in Ursprung, ed., *Herzog and De Meuron*, pp. 173–178.

37 J. Herzog, as quoted in Moore and Ryan, *Building Tate Modern*, p. 53.

38 King's Cross Station's barrel vaults are approx 31.5 m wide, 21.6 m high, and 240 m long. The concourse of New York's Grand Central Station is 36 m wide, 112.5 m wide, and 37.5 m high, i.e. 150,000 cubic metres. The turbine hall at Tate Modern is 22 m wide and 35 m high, i.e. only about two-thirds as wide, but one and a half times as long, and about the same height, at 120,000 cubic metres.

Index

Note: page numbers in **bold** refer to illustrations.